FEEDING LONDON

In memory of Christine Robertson
and for Sheila and Victoria

First published 2003
by Historical Publications Ltd
32 Ellington Street, London N7 8PL
(Tel: 020 7607 1628)

© **Richard Tames 2003**

ISBN 0 948667 85 0
British Library Cataloguing-in-Publication Data
A catalogue record for this book is available from the British Library
Printed by Edelvives in Zaragoza, Spain

The Illustrations
The following were reproduced by kind permission.

London Borough of Camden: *14, 16, 36, 122*
London Borough of Enfield: *73*
Guildhall Library, London: *79*
International Distillers and Vintners: *66*
London Borough of Islington: *80*
Rowton Houses: *28*
J. Sainsbury plc: *71, 72*
Richard Tames: *1, 9, 29, 30, 31, 32, 33, 43, 47, 56, 60, 61, 76, 77, 83, 85, 86, 87, 89, 91, 95, 108, 121*
City of Westminster Archives: *81, 132*

FEEDING LONDON

A Taste of History

Richard Tames

HISTORICAL PUBLICATIONS

'In the Café Royal', by C.R.W. Nevinson (1889-1946). Best known for his work as an official war artist, Nevinson slyly conveys here the louche ambience of this Bohemian venue. The young man sports a newly-fashionable wrist-watch while the newspaper headline reminds the onlooker of the troubled world from which café society provided a welcome refuge.

Contents

Introduction

The unruly plebs of imperial Rome were allegedly pacified by the plentiful provision of bread and circuses. But, if the circuses have intrigued posterity more than the bread, it was breakdowns in the bread supply rather than gaps in the calendar of entertainments, that periodically threatened disorder. As with ancient Rome, so with her daughter city, London, destined to become the capital of "regions Caesar never knew". The building and peopling of London and its periodic devastation by fire, war, plague and planners, have been chronicled at length. But the routines and rhythms by which a vast metropolis has been sustained for twenty centuries are as worthy of investigation and record as more spectacular episodes of triumph and disaster. The daily urgency of feeding millions of mouths, of keeping the poor from riot and tempting the faded appetite of the invalid or the jaded palate of the epicure has given birth to a thousand fortunes and a hundred household names — Twining's and Sainsbury's, Peek Freans and Crosse and Blackwell, Tesco and the Ritz. It was the successful sale of his entire product range of seven lines to Fortnum & Mason that set Mr. H.J. Heinz on the highway to a global presence as he returned to Sharpsburg, Pennsylvania exultantly proclaiming that henceforth "our field is the world." It was a London publisher, George Smith, and his Jewish journalist friend, Ernest Hart, who turned Apollinaris into a global brand as 'Queen of Table Waters'.

The soup kitchen, the dining-club and the coffee-house all play their parts in this story. The Stock Exchange began in a London coffee-house and so did Lloyd's. Rock 'n' roll owes quite as much to the coffee-bars of Soho as to the subterranean clubs of Merseyside. The last of the traditional coffee-houses disappeared in Victoria's day. The annual whitebait dinners enjoyed by the ministers of her Cabinet went out of fashion even before her reign ended. But the Reform Club, where Alexis Soyer presided with justified pride over the capital's first scientifically-designed kitchens, is with us still, as is Mrs Beeton's celebrated volume of domestic wisdom, even if not one of her recipes survived a century of constant 'updating' of her original text. Fish and chips, another invention of Victorian London, has become an icon of national identity.

London's appetites and tastes have shaped both the nation and the wider world. As Britain's richest city and biggest port London has for most of its existence represented its greatest concentration of purchasing power and, as home to the court and to fashionable society, the most extensive arena for conspicuous consumption. The sheer scale of its gargantuan appetite has staggered foreign visitors for centuries. In 1562 the Venetian merchant Alessandro Magno observed incredulously that "it is almost impossible to believe that they could eat so much meat in one city alone." By then Londoners, even the poorer ones, had begun to shift their gastronomic focus from quantity to quality, leading the nation in the transition from brown bread to white and, in the following century, from pottage to pudding.

As that inquisitive and entrepreneurial Londoner, Daniel Defoe, repeatedly emphasised throughout his *Tour through the Whole Island of Great Britain*, London's historic destiny was to serve as the dynamo of the nation's entire economy. Its immense and endless demands even then, in the 1720s, had called into being regional specialisms, often hundreds of miles distant from the ultimate point of consumption – providing the capital's many markets with cheese from Cheshire, turkeys from Norfolk and salmon from Scotland, not to mention the fresh produce brought in daily from the market gardens of Ealing and Battersea, whose fertility was renewed in turn by the contents of the city's privies.

Over a century previously London's dramatically expanding market for spices had given birth to the mighty East India Company, Britain's first multinational corporation, as in later centuries the craving for coffee and cocoa, rice and pineapples, would create complex networks of plantation cultivation throughout the tropics. Global trading, centred on London, made such emphatically non-native products as tea and sugar essential elements of daily diet. The capital's voracious appetite for fish would sustain, sailing out of Barking, the world's largest commercial fishing fleet. Victorian technologies – canning, the steamship, railways and refrigeration – would bring grain and fruit and meat from the remote Australian outback and the far pampas of Argentina to the teeming wharves of Southwark. In London the same reign would witness the rise of the professional male chef and the evolution of the restaurant. These combined together to distance commercial catering from the domestic variety, just as the emergence of the gastronome and of magazine journalism brought a new self-consciousness to the matter and manner of eating itself. Consider, for example, the artfulness of Alexis Soyer's management, one might almost say manipulation, of a dinner party: "I do not have the dessert placed on the table until ten or twenty minutes after the cloth is removed; this gives an opportunity for ... guests to admire the beautiful Sèvres dessert plates, containing views of different French chateaux; this of course gives a subject for conversation to those who have visited them. In the dessert I generally introduce some new importation such as bananas, sugar cane, American lady apples, prickly pears etc. and these also give a subject for the gentlemen to talk about when the ladies have left, such as free trade, colonial policy etc."

London has thus not only decreed much of what its environs and its empire produced but also to a considerable extent, how it should be consumed. If the dominant cultural influence on the diet of medieval Britain was the church, it was to be succeeded by the London-based court, London-based commerce and a London-based publishing industry. Writing of Defoe's own time Professor E.A. Wrigley asserted that "one adult in six in England had had direct experience of London life ... this must have acted as a powerful solvent of the customs, prejudices and modes of action of the traditional, rural England. The leaven of change would have a much better chance of transforming the lump than in, say, France, even if living in Paris produced the same change of attitude and action as living in London, since there were proportionately four or five times fewer Frenchmen caught up in Parisian life than Englishmen in London life."

And as the world's leading port and the seat

of its greatest empire, London would reflect global influences even more than that of its own governing elite, in marked contrast to France – which explains why, at the beginning of the twenty-first century, there are currently over seventy different ethnic cuisines commercially available in what is still Europe's largest city. Comparison with France is almost unavoidable. The influence in culinary matters of England's nearest neighbour has for a thousand years been almost as continuous as it has been profound, while complicated by ambiguities of national sentiment. French cooking – and even more, French cooks – have been as much reviled as admired. The reaction of Robert Poole, visiting Paris in 1741, speaks for legions of his countrymen: "Would you have a carp stewed, they'll bring you a dish of carp smothered over with onions, wine, herbs etc., whereby it is become a perfect hodge-podge ... Hence then in regard to food in its proper taste it is far better dressed in the City of London than here." Revulsion in the face of continental sophistication has frequently been rationalised as a positive preference for plain fare based on the fruits of an excellent agriculture – note Poole's insistence on "food in its proper taste." As Gervase Markham counselled the ideal housewife in 1615: "let her diet be wholesome and cleanly prepared at due hours and cooked with care and diligence; let it be rather to satisfy nature than our affections

and apter to kill hunger than revive new appetites ... and let it be rather esteemed for the familar acquaintance she hath with it, than for the strangeness and rarity it bringeth from other countries."

Counsels of perfection, by definition, are at variance with actual behaviour, just as cookery books are a poor guide to what the mass of mankind was actually eating at the time of their publication. Their recipes certainly provide evidence of social aspiration and their assumptions about the availability of ingredients reflect changes in commerce and living-standards but what, and how often, was consumed, they cannot tell. Further distortions in our picture of the past arise from the fact that writers of letters and diaries, and indeed novels, were far more likely to record festive food associated with significant seasonal occasions, such as Christmas, or occasional celebrations, like weddings, rather than their everyday fare. Samuel Pepys was unusual in noting down not only the menus of his dinner parties but also the often rather eccentric snacks he ingested in the course of his long and crowded working days. The poor, of course, were also mostly the illiterate, so even less record survives of what they survived on, except through the distorting prism of the records of the workhouse, the prison and the social investigator. What follows, therefore, cannot pretend to any completeness – but it does not lack variety.

PART ONE

From Sausages to the Sixties

LONDINIUM

Roman London, Londinium, was the fifth largest city of the western Roman empire; its basilica, more than five hundred feet in length, was the largest north of the Alps, the adjacent forum four times the size of Trafalgar Square. Like other great cities Londinium depended for its food supply on what could be drawn from the immediate rural hinterland and what could be brought in overland or by water from more distant sources of supply. The city, like Rome itself, depended heavily on the riverine imports, rather than local produce brought by cart. To the north the whole area between the rivers Brent and Lea was covered by a heavy clay soil, deeply forested and undrained by streams and thus quite unsuited to the cultivation of grain. To the south the nearest cultivable land for such crops could be found on the chalk uplands, well beyond Croydon. The bulk of the most fundamental item of Roman diet therefore had to come from further away. Overland transport for such a relatively low value foodstuff would have been prohibitively expensive over any great distance – slaves didn't have to be paid but they did have to be fed and their labour utilised in a cost-effective manner. So most grain must have arrived by water, either downstream along the Thames from the rich farmlands of the south Midlands, or along the Lea from the Chilterns, or upstream from Kent, or even further afield. The most commonly cultivated grain crop was barley, used for both bread and brewing beer. Rye, oats and wheat were also grown. The Romans introduced a kind of flue or kiln which could be used for drying grain, thus enabling it to be stored for longer periods with less risk of spoilage, an important consideration for far-sighted authorities intent on accumulating stockpiles against years of dearth or distributing it onwards to supply military garrisons in inhospitable locations. Forts aimed to keep two years supply in reserve.

In the homes and commercial bakeries of Londinium most grain would have been turned into a variety of breads, the more expensive enriched with eggs, milk or butter or flavoured with honey or spices such as cumin or anise or topped with poppy seeds. Grains would also be eaten as a form of porridge, a staple of army diet, often thickened with beans. Hardened wheat was also turned into a sort of cornflour used for thickening sauces.

The forested areas around Londinium did, however, contribute to its food supply as an abundant source of acorns and beech mast

1. *The fishmonger in today's Leadenhall Market does business on the site of Londinium's forum, continuing a tradition of two millennia. Nearby a Japanese stand nowadays dispenses lunch-boxes of fresh sushi incorporating seafoods undreamed of by Roman consumers.*

and hence pannage for large herds of swine. Pig in its various forms was therefore the most common form of meat. The more affluent of the city's inhabitants could afford to consume it as a major source of protein; the poorer used it as a flavouring for stews and thick soups made mainly from vegetables. In the absence of cheap local supplies of olive oil, animal fat or butter would have been the most common substitutes for cooking purposes. A portion of lard formed part of every Roman soldier's daily rations. Pig's blood and fat would also have been mixed with grain and spices to make the sausages which served the army as iron rations on campaign. The fact that 'botulism' (food poisoning) is derived from the Latin for 'sausage' implies that smoking and seasoning were not always successful as preservative techniques. Horse-flesh, although not formally approved by the Romans for human consumption, may well have ended up in sausages, disguised by heavy seasoning.

Another useful product of the hinterland was honey, the main sweetener in Roman cooking. It was also useful as a preservative and medicine and therefore valuable enough to bear the costs of transportation by donkey or even on foot. The same would also apply to cheese, eggs, geese, chickens and the continental delicacies peculiar to the cultivated Roman palate, such as thrushes, snails and dormice. Rabbits, eaten new-born or even cut from the womb, were another Roman introduction, as were the peacock, pheasant and guinea-fowl. Eggs were produced and used in far greater quantities than in pre-Roman times. Not only were they eaten boiled or fried, they were also used extensively as a binding or thickening agent in making rissoles, stuffings and sauces and to make omelettes and custards.

The excellence of the Roman road network, which converged on London, made it possible to drive herds of sheep, goats and cattle over long distances, setting a precedent for the droving trade which would survive until the coming of the railways. Beef was the preferred meat of the rich and the army. Pork was the military's second preference, mutton a long way third, except among Syrian troops, for whom it represented a taste of their homeland. Sheep and goats were valued for their milk as well as for their flesh.

The river not only brought food to the city but was also a source of it. The Romans brought with them a gargantuan appetite for fish and improved techniques for obtaining it – barbed hooks, bronze tridents and lead net-sinkers. Sea-fish was valued more highly than river fish and Londinium's easy access to the sea made it unnecessary to construct ponds for fish farming. Other river products included ducks, cranes and eels. The Thames estuary was home to the most extensive oyster beds in the entire province of Britannia. Large finds of oyster shells at all kinds of Roman settlement, rich and poor, confirm that they were a great favourite with every class. Transported live in barrels of sea-water, oysters could be carried great distances, not only far inland but even to Rome itself, where oysters brought by sea from the Thames were considered a luxury – a dozen costing half the daily wage of a free labourer. In London itself the top grade of oysters seems to have come from the mouth of the river Colne. Pearls, though admittedly not of the highest quality, were an ancillary export.

Salt also came by river, most being drawn from extensive pans along the Essex coast. Some salt was also exported by sea all the way to Rome, its freightage cost amounting to less than a quarter of its selling price. Not only was salt essential for cooking purposes, it was also employed extensively in preserving fish and meat.

Cultivable land within a day's travel of Londinium would probably have been given over to the cultivation of perishables, such as fruit and vegetables. The Romans introduced new varieties of both. The apples they brought in were larger and sweeter than native types, stored well and could also be sliced and dried in rings. Cultivated sweet cherries, cucumbers, garden asparagus, marrows and cardoons were other innovations. New vegetables included cabbage, carrots, beet, turnips, parsnips, radishes, garden onions, shallots, leeks, lettuce and endive. The range of new herbs was equally extensive – borage, chervil, coriander, dill, fennel, mint, thyme, garlic, hyssop, parsley, rosemary, rue, sage, savory, sweet marjoram and white mustard. The British climate necessarily imposed limitations on what could be successfully transferred from the Mediterranean homeland of the Romans. And it took time for the local population to master new techniques of cultivation and food-processing. Liquamen, the all-purpose fish-sauce made from fermented fish-guts, sprats, anchovies etc., was brought all the way from Spain and southern France. Vineyards were successfully established in the south of England and so, in sheltered villa gardens, was the cultivation of almonds, apricots, figs and peaches. Roman vineyards not only produced wine but also vinegar, much used in cooking, in sauces and salad dressings. Diluted, vinegar was greatly favoured by the army as a refreshing drink when on the march. British wine was probably thin and sharp but there were well-practised techniques for doctoring it with honey and other additives. Local output of both wine and vinegar would, however, have fallen far short of Londinium's requirements and so imports remained essential, wine coming from Bordeaux and the Moselle region and vinegar from Spain and Gaul. The wealthier inhabitants of Londinium remained, moreover, permanently dependent on imports for their supplies of olive oil, raisins, pine-kernels, pepper, ginger, cinnamon and asafoetida. Apart from new foodstuffs the Romans were also responsible for introducing new methods of cooking and novel items of kitchen equipment – the pestle and mortar, frying-pans with collapsible handles so that they could be used inside an oven as well as over direct heat, portable ovens with double walls to conduct heat all round the food, and cheap, mass-produced, round-bellied iron cauldrons. The collapse of Roman rule in the early fifth century was followed by the gradual abandonment of Roman lifestyles and the disappearance of a degree of culinary sophistication which would not reappear for a thousand years.

LUNDENWIC
The early Anglo-Saxons kept clear of the eerie and deserted walled city of the Romans, establishing village settlements in what are now the inner suburbs, such as Fulham and Islington, or today's commuter areas, such as Ealing in the west or Barking in the east. Here Anglo-Saxon farmers produced barley, oats and rye to make bread, beer and porridges. Other major crops were peas, beans, cabbage, onions and root vegetables. Later a settlement and trading-place, known as Lundenwic, grew up to the west of decayed Londinium in the area of Charing Cross. Recent excavations have revealed a tangled network of narrow alleyways stretching inland as far as what is now Covent Garden. Pig-pens were much in evidence, the pig representing a useful means of recycling

household waste. Bacon was a favoured food and pig fat was used for cooking and as a dressing for vegetables. Outside London itself sheep were more numerous because, as well as meat, they supplied wool and milk to be turned into cheese and butter, which was used extensively both for cooking and as another dressing for vegetables. Both butter and cheese were routinely salted to preserve them.

Although salmon and eels were commonly eaten, fish was far less in demand than it had been among the Romans. The acceptance of Christianity, however, required the observance of meatless days when fish provided the main substitute for flesh. Fishing for herrings and mackerel with large drift nets developed to meet this demand. (So did the breeding of chickens and geese on a large scale as canon law decreed that only the flesh of quadrupeds was to be considered as meat.) Salted herring became the great standby for meatless Lent. Salted whale was regarded as a luxury. Shellfish initially lost, but then regained, their popularity. Christianity also discouraged the consumption of horsemeat, which had been regularly eaten in the newcomers' Germanic homelands. Eggs, eaten fried in lard or roasted in their shells in the embers of a fire, were brought into London by boat in quantity, paying a toll of five eggs per hamper according to a decree of Aethelred in 927.

The extinction of villa-centred agri-businesses within easy travelling distance of London saw formerly cultivated areas revert to woodland rich with game. 'Suburban' Anglo-Saxon farmers were keen hunters, eager to keep down predators which attacked crops and flocks, relishing the sport and prizing in particular the flesh of deer and boar. Falconry was introduced around the mid-ninth century and thus encouraged the consumption of herons, bitterns, cranes, curlews, pheasants, partridges and even larks. Vineyards initially disappeared but were reintroduced under the influence of the Roman church. By the time of Domesday there were nearly forty vineyards in southern England, established as far west as Gloucestershire and as far north as Norfolk. Many were attached to monasteries to provide wine for the mass. Unripened grapes were made into verjuice, a sharp vinegar for cooking and pickling. The poor made theirs from crab apples. As under the Romans demand for wine exceeded local supplies and imports came to London from the Rhineland and Rouen. Nevertheless ale, sometimes spiced or honeyed, was much the more common drink, with mead reserved for warriors and nobles. Non-alcoholic drinks were limited to milk, butter-milk, whey and water, the latter being even more risky than usual, as the relative concentration of population made pollution from human, animal or industrial wastes more likely. The disappearance of Roman lifestyles brought as an inevitable consequence the evaporation of demand for Roman luxuries such as olive oil and raisins. Such spices as were imported probably came at first as gifts for rulers or prelates, rather than in the course of regular trade. Spices were one of the few luxuries permitted to monks. By the end of the Anglo-Saxon period pepper at least was available in sufficient quantities for minor landowners to be able to afford it. Cooking likewise became simpler, though evidence for actual recipes is scanty, apart from 'leechdoms', which were collections of remedies, mainly herbal, rather than recipes. Bread was often cooked in a makeshift oven which was simply a cauldron turned upside down and packed round with peat or hot ashes, a procedure likely to cause frequent fires in the wooden huts which were the standard Anglo-Saxon home.

FASTING AND FEEDING – THE MIDDLE AGES

The daily texture of medieval life was dominated by two sovereign forces – Nature and the Catholic church. If the former determined how much there was to eat, the latter decreed to a considerable extent when, and sometimes how, it should be eaten. Where strict orthodoxy prevailed not only were Fridays and the whole of Lent (except Sundays) kept as meat-less 'fish days' but also Saturdays and Wednesdays as well. Add in major saints' days and a further three days at each of the Quarter Days and the result was that virtually half the days in the year were, in theory at least, days of fasting. Strict fasting meant eating only once in every twenty-four hours. The truly ascetic limited themselves to bread and water but most permitted themselves fish and vegetables. Wine and meat and animal products were forbidden, although eggs were eventually allowed as the church relaxed the rules. The economics of reality, of course, meant that the poor – i.e. the great majority – were unlikely to have been able to eat meat whenever they wanted anyway.

The wealthy could, however, eat well, even within the rules – princes of the church quite as much as courtiers and merchants. The ecclesiastical hierarchy was far less inclined to inveigh against gluttony than drunkenness, which was a vice the poor could indulge in, gluttony being beyond their means. The massive banquets of the rich, organised to mark seasonal festivals such as Christmas and Easter or major rites of passage such as the knighting or marriage of a son or the installation of bishop were intended to impress by their sheer scale. As Professor Stephen Mennell has argued:

> "the flocks of sheep, herds of cattle, gaggles of geese, shoals of fish and schools of porpoise mustered … bore only a remote and incidental relation to the nutritional requirements and capacities of the principal guests. Rather it was almost the other way round: the number of mouths would in a sense be determined by the quantity of food it was deemed necessary to distribute. For this reason there is little evidence that the quality of cooking played much part in the success of these occasions."

2. *The Bayeux 'tapestry' (actually embroidery) of c.1070-80 depicts the messing arrangements of England's Norman conquerors. Note the spit-roasted fowl and horn-blower summoning diners to the table.*

By the fourteenth century, however, there was an increasing emphasis on the aesthetic aspects of culinary excess. Richard II, whatever his other shortcomings as a monarch, was a connoisseur of the arts and extended his connoisseurship to the arts of living, being one of the first to utilise the fork, a novelty from Italy. The first major English culinary tome, *The Boke of Cury,* dates from his reign and was probably the work of a royal chef. London may have already become a great commercial centre but it was also a city with a huge religious presence. Whereas the average village might have a single parish priest – and count itself lucky to have one to itself – London by the twelfth century already boasted over a hundred parishes within and around its walls, many wealthy enough to support not only a vicar but also a team of minor clergy to assist or deputise for him. From the fourteenth century onwards, as the doctrine of purgatory assumed greater importance in church teaching, the larger parish churches added chantry chapels where masses were recited daily for wealthy patrons by priests paid for the purpose. In addition to the parish

and chantry priests there were also the staff of the great cathedral of St Paul's and of more than a dozen priories and monasteries, as well as those of the friaries associated with the Dominicans, Franciscans, Carmelites etc. and in addition the medical facilities run by religious personnel such as St Bartholomew's and St Thomas's, Bethlehem and Elsing Spital. Finally there were the London residences of the provincially based princes of the church, such as the Archbishop of Canterbury, the bishops of Durham and Ely, the abbots of Peterborough and St Albans and so on. All of which added up to a big demand for fish. Not that the monasteries, at least, were only consumers of provisions. The duty of Christian charity required that the broken meats and bread from their tables be redistributed to the poor, ensuring a gathering around the gates of each institution after every meal-time. Surviving accounts of the household of the bishop of Winchester record huge deliveries of produce and livestock from his estates at his Southwark residence, much larger certainly than even his well-staffed household could itself consume. Some may

3. Looking like a pioneer of today's famously foul-tempered celebrity chefs, this cook wields a ferocious-looking cleaver as a symbol of his authority. Marginal illustration from the Luttrell Psalter c.1340.

have been intended for sale in London's markets but some, at least, was distributed as charity.

The requirement to eat fish on so many days of the year condemned the poor, if they could afford it, to eat salted fish, though from the thirteenth century onwards it was possible to get smoked herrings as an alternative. The only other substitutes for the ubiquitous salted herring were eels and oysters, both of which were cheap. The rich could not only enjoy fresh fish but off-season luxuries such as pickled salmon all the way from Scotland or exotic varieties of sea-food including whale, porpoise and seal. Even when the rich, too, might have no alternative to salted fish they could turn to their cooks to have the taste disguised with sauces and spices or be transformed into a flavoursome filling for pies.

Despite the importance fish played in the medieval diet, London retained a massive appetite for meat, sufficient, indeed, to support a long-distance droving trade which brought fresh supplies to the capital on the hoof. Cattle were driven all the way from south Wales and even Scotland. Sheep, being smaller and less hardy, came from areas such as Somerset and Lincolnshire. Either way, they often arrived too tough and stringy for the market and had to be re-fattened, perhaps on the marshes stretching out from Barking to Dagenham and Rainham, before they could be sold on to the butchers and finally disposed of to the consumer in street markets such as Eastcheap.

Aristocrats could have game sent to their London houses from their estates, particularly in winter when it was less swift to spoil or when, like venison, it was improved by being kept back from the pot. Boar, often made into brawn, was especially prized. London was still so compact that even its less affluent citizens might hope for occasional game from the surrounding countryside. Henry I granted Londoners a day each year to hunt in Epping Forest. Henry III added another day at Easter. If few were likely to bag a deer, there was always the chance of a hare or, more highly rated, a squirrel.

Butcher's meat and game were varied with the consumption of almost everything that could fly. London's specialist Poulters had their own market at the eastern end of Cheapside; a short stretch of which is still known as Poultry. Their most expensive offering was swan, followed by crane, heron and bustard. Among smaller species blackbirds were rated ahead of larks. Pigeons, thrushes and gulls were also eaten. Finches could be bought roasted for literally ten a penny.

Pottage, a thick soup of almost stew-like consistency, was a universal dish for all classes. But whereas the pottage of the rich might teem with rare ingredients and aromatic spices, for the poorest pottage served as the major vehicle for the consumption of meat, usually in the form of by-products, such as the lungs, blood, lard or marrow. The often rank flavours such ingredients might produce were offset by liberal additions of onions, leeks or garlic. London's demand for that particular holy trinity was such that it proved necessary to import onions from the Netherlands and garlic from France and Spain. These were landed at a notoriously noisome wharf now commemorated in the name of a City church, St James Garlickhythe. Rice, usually from Spain, was another novel import favoured by the rich, who delighted in white dishes and white sauces. In this the royal household certainly set the style. In a single year, 1286, it consumed a staggering 28,500 pounds of almonds. A small proportion were eaten as a digestive snack after meals. Many more were used to decorate elaborate dishes, or as a thickening agent, or liquidised as a 'milk' or pounded with sugar to make 'marchpane'. London as a whole led the country in adopting a preference for white bread, a preference which over the centuries would be taken as a mark of national superiority. Originally there were separate guilds for bakers of white and brown bread, just as there were for sellers of fresh and

salt fish. In 1304 London had 32 bakers of brown bread as against 21 of white. By 1574 there were 36 bakers of brown bread but 62 of white. Bread was, of course, not only the great staple, given that potatoes were still unknown, but also much used in cooking both as a thickening or binding agent and as breadcrumbs to seal food for cooking.

The business of feeding London provided employment for much of its population. Apart from the unpaid labour of wives and daughters and the virtually unwaged efforts of household servants, the business of satisfying London's hunger provided occupations for street-sellers, stall-holders and a range of specialist dealers or producers. Analysis of the 1381 poll tax returns reveals that London's unruly southern suburb, Southwark, noted for its concentration of taverns catering to travellers, gave employment to no less than twenty-two brewers. Although there were only six local suppliers of bread there, plus four of meat, three each of fish and poultry and none of dairy produce, there were four pie-bakers, three each of dealers in fruit and spices and two in stockfish. This implies that, while there was clearly a thriving demand for 'treats', the bulk of locally consumed basic foodstuffs such as butter, cheese, eggs, milk and bacon were supplied by country people bringing in their produce from the surrounding area. In Southwark as a whole victualling seems to have accounted for a quarter of all local employment. London's position as England's premier port naturally made it the centre of the trade in sugar and spices. The Pepperers, later to become the Grocers, were already in existence by 1180. Wide profit margins ensured a destiny of affluence, though prices were much higher still in the provinces. Visitors coming up to London on business were invariably bidden to bring back spices which could otherwise only be purchased once a year at one of the great regional fairs, and then at something like three times the London price. For the very wealthy the most desired items were sugar and saffron, both of which came

4. This 15th-century depiction of a kitchen shows a male chef testing for flavour while his female assistant is relegated to humbler chores.

long disputed and whose consequences perplexed contemporaries. Doubtless the two phenomena were at least partially interlinked. Certainly the rich got richer and the poor poorer. Hens became a luxury too dear for the homes of the humble. The abolition of London's monasteries deprived beggars of a major source of sustenance. The affluent, too, were inconvenienced in at least one respect. In his *Description of England* (1577) William Harrison, himself a clergyman, observed that:

> "the stronger the wine is, the more it is desired, by means whereof, in old time, the best was called theologicum. because it was had from the clergy and religious men, unto whose houses many of the laity would often send for bottles filled with the same..."

The buoyant expansion of overseas trade with tropical countries enabled the affluent to buy such luxury ingredients as sugar, pepper, ginger or currants in larger quantities at lower prices. Harrison characterised sugar as "a device not common or greatly used in old time at the table but only in medicine". Less exotic but still novel importations included parmesan from Italy, cheeses from Holland and Normandy, oranges from Portugal and 'pickled cucumbers that come from beyond the sea'. The apricot was still a rarity and the melon and the raspberry, brought in from France, were novelties. Potatoes and tomatoes became known but took two centuries to gain acceptance. Their novelty gained them a quite spurious reputation as 'whetstones of venery' – i.e. aphrodisiacs. Harrison referred censoriously to "the potato and such venerous roots as are brought out of Spain, Portugal and the Indies to furnish up our banquets." Londoners' insistence on eating white bread necessitated the importation via coastal shipping of wheat from Norfolk, Lincolnshire and Yorkshire. The expansion of the population was inevitably matched, despite futile royal proclamations to the contrary, by an outward sprawl of new housing, much of it badly built. John Stow, whose *Survey of London* (1598) was the first chronicle of the capital's

from Spain and were incredibly expensive. The other Iberian luxury was citrus fruits. From the southern Mediterranean came prunes, dates, figs, raisins and walnuts. Wine, which had once come mainly from the Rhineland, was increasingly imported from the Bordeaux area, which was for centuries part of the patrimony of the English crown. Some wine, however, came from much farther away – Crete and the Canary Islands. Beer, made with hops, began to challenge traditional ale in London from the fifteenth century when it was introduced by Flemish brewers, but it was very slow to catch on anywhere else. As late as the 1540s royal physician Andrew Boorde counselled against it on the grounds that it made men bloated.

THE TUDORS

During the course of the sixteenth century London's population rose relentlessly, from fifty thousand to two hundred thousand. At the same time England experienced a prolonged surge of inflation, whose causes historians have

5. Detail from Joris Hoefnagel's celebrated painting of a Bermondsey wedding feast. It depicts a kitchen with a serving hatch in the centre, while in the building to the right a long table is laid. In front four female servants parade massive 'bride pies' supported by napkins slung around their necks.

past to be based on documentary sources and a first-hand knowledge of its topography, deplored the changes which had occurred in his own lifetime. As a boy he remembered picking berries from the hedges of what had become built-up Petticoat Lane and buying milk fresh from the cow in then rural Whitechapel.

Despite the break with Rome, the dissolution of religious houses and the introduction of a Protestant liturgy, Londoners were still obliged to observe 'fish days'. The main justification of this practice was now strategic rather theological. The large-scale consumption of fish supported an extensive fishing fleet, thereby sustaining a reserve of sailors who might be conscripted into the service of the state in time of war either as fighting men or, using their own ships, in the more humble roles of troop transports or provision carriers to fleets or garrisons; in the words of an authorised Homily

of 1562 "for the increase of fishermen, of whom do spring mariners to go upon the sea, to the furnishing of the Navy of the Realm ...".

Saturday was actually reintroduced as a fish day in 1548 and Wednesday added in 1563. At least there was plenty of variety for those who could afford it. Of domestic freshwater fish carp and pike were still regarded with favour, while increasing quantities of anchovies were being imported, though whale and porpoise were beginning to lose their appeal.

Meatless days, of course, also promoted the consumption of eggs and cheese. Elizabethan army rations provided for each man a daily allowance of eight ounces of cheese and four of butter. For Londoners the most common form of cheese was a sharp-flavoured type made in Essex and Suffolk from ewes milk. Formed into huge, hard blocks, it was also sold to ships' victuallers for consumption at sea – perhaps

6. Elizabeth I picnics while hunting. Woodcut from G Turberville's The Noble Art of Venerie, 1575.

because sailors were in no position to cavil at the qualities that had gained it notoriety in verse:

"Those that made me were uncivil,
They made me harder than the devil.
Knives can't cut me, fire won't light me,
Dogs bark at me but can't bite me."

By contrast Epping, also in Essex, was famed for the fine quality of its butter, so famed that inferior or tainted versions were often treated to be passed off as coming from Epping.

In the kitchens of the wealthy a new sophistication was increasingly in evidence. Whereas once a greasy boy had crouched by an open fire to turn the roast his place was increasingly taken by a dog working a turnspit mechanism. Alternative devices could be worked by the force of gravity-driven weights or even the hot air rising through a chimney to rotate a sort of weather-vane linked to the turnspit by a system of gears and chains. French fashion introduced cooks to the notions of fricasees, hashes, bisques, ragouts and the amulet' (omelette). (Harrison noted slightingly that in noble households the cooks were "for the most part musical-headed Frenchmen and strangers.") It was discovered that cooked meats and fish might be preserved under a layer of butter. An even more important discovery was that the whites of eggs, long regarded with suspicion, might, when beaten, be used as a raising agent in cooking to make macaroons or almond cakes using French or Italian recipes. At banquets it became customary, where the setting permitted, for the third and final course to be taken in a separate room or, better still, a rustic arbour set apart, where diners might consume a sort of indoor picnic of sweets, tarts, jellies, fools, syllabubs, junkets, biscuits, comfits and preserves. Some Tudor tart fillings might seem odd to a modern diner, among them pulped rosehips. petals of marigold, cowslip or primrose beaten with cream or curds or young peas flavoured with saffron, sugar, salt, verjuice and butter. Other bizarre treats included lettuce stalks, green walnuts and the roots of parsley or fennel candied in sugar syrup. The newly discovered virtues of the egg enabled it to be beaten with cream, sugar and rosewater to produce a 'dishful of snow' to be spooned over an apple or other fruit. Quinces were made into a stiff marmalade which could be moulded into fancy shapes and served sprinkled with sugar.

As a centrepiece banquet dish the boar, now virtually hunted to extinction, was losing favour as were the swan, heron, bustard and peacock, while rabbits were becoming more popular. In the country areas within reach of the capital wild birds such as wheatears and dotterels were snared as delicacies for London tables. England's expanding global commerce led to the introduction of the guinea-fowl from the slave coasts of west Africa and the turkey from America, probably via Spain, served either as a roast or made into a pie. The turkey had already become sufficiently common by the 1550s for its price to be regulated in London's markets.

The rapid advance of printing and the more hesitant advances of medical practice – scarcely yet deserving the name of medical science – combined to produce a novel genre of health handbooks, many which stressed the relationship between diet and wellbeing. Unlike abstruse treatises for the medical professional, these books were written in the vernacular and not necessarily by qualified physicians, to the ire of that increasingly well organised vocation. Andrew Boorde, for example, was an ex-monk, whose *Breviary of Health* enjoyed gratifyingly brisk sales. He recommended starting the day with an egg rare-roasted in the hot ashes of the kitchen fire (a tricky procedure to get just right) and eaten with a sprinkling of salt and sugar. Other physicians recommended bread spread with butter, fortified with herbs selected for their invigorating qualities. The medieval prejudice against uncooked fruit remained firm. Dr Thomas Cogan provided a 'scientific' explanation in warning that "all manner of fruit generally fill the blood with water, which boileth up in the body as new wine doth in the vessel, and so prepareth and causeth the blood to putrefy and consequently bringeth in sickness." This belief was so strong that in 1569, when pestilence broke out, the sale of fruit in the streets was banned.

THE STUART CENTURY

Seventeenth-century London continued to expand inexorably, despite the traumatic checks administered by terrifying outbreaks of plague in 1603, 1625 and, most famously, 1665. The latter carried off perhaps as many as 100,000 souls. A year later the core of the ancient city was devastated by the Great Fire which destroyed over 13,000 houses. Yet London still grew. In 1600, with a population of 200,000 it was already as large as the next ten English cities added together. By mid-century its population of 375,000 put it in the top league of European cities, surpassed only by Paris and perhaps Naples. By 1700 it was a fraction short of the half million mark, accounting for some ten per cent of the population of the entire country. Representing not only the largest concentration of consumers in northern Europe but also probably the richest, London's appetite for food continued to drive much of the nation's economy. Within the capital Clare Market *(see p.74)*, Covent Garden *(see p.78)* and Hungerford and Spitalfields markets were established to meet growing demand. Specialist food retailers appeared. Urban dairy herds were established. Some were sustained by the mash discharged from breweries; most were housed in cramped and insanitary conditions. Milk-maids proffering whey and buttermilk brought a bucolic touch to crowded city streets.

Changes in the countryside had their effect on the food habits of the capital. Advances in agriculture, many imitated from the best Dutch practice, led to the breeding of much improved livestock. Flesh from farm animals increasingly replaced the game much favoured in earlier centuries, though venison retained its popularity, especially in the form of spicy pasties. Hunting itself changed as the gun replaced the hawk. Hosts desirous of impressing guests with a boar would have to buy one imported from France. Better quality meat encouraged a trend towards simpler sauces, intended to enhance rather than disguise the flavour of what was being eaten. Better-fed cows improved their yields of milk to encourage the ever more lavish use of butter. Foreign visitors remarked with amazement on the routine manner in which meats and vegetables were served swimming in butter. Improved transport by road, river and coastal shipping also enhanced the capital's food supplies. Geese were marched down from Lincolnshire, turkeys from Norfolk and ducks from Berkshire. Cheeses were carried by water from Cheddar and Cheshire. The introduction of tanks in ships enabled the more expensive varieties of seafood, such as turbot and lobster, to be brought fresh to market.

The century's political turbulence, too, had its effects. The royalist chef Robert May

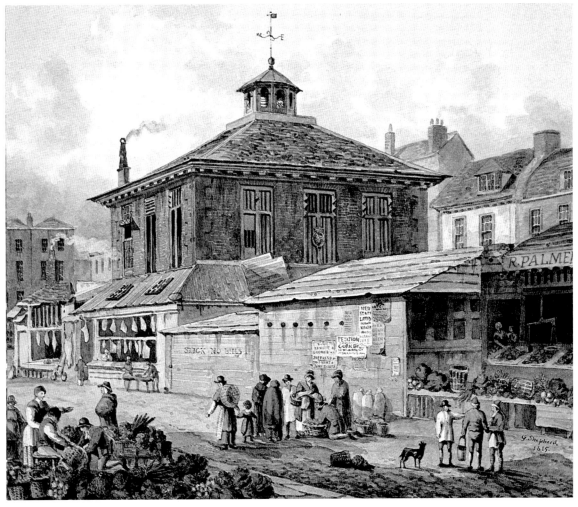

7. *Clare Market, drawn by Thomas H. Shepherd, in 1815. The posters feature the annual state lottery, the high price of bread, and the acting triumphs of Edmund Kean. The market was founded by the Earl of Clare in 1657.*

(see p. 52) looked back on the days before the civil wars as a lost golden age:

> "such noble houses were then kept ... then were those golden days wherein were practised the Triumphs and Trophies of Cookery; then was Hospitality esteemed, Neighbourhood preserved, the poor cherished and God honoured; then was Religion less talkt on and more practised ....".

Speaking of which ... fish days were abolished by Cromwell's Commonwealth regime as a Papist practice and proved impossible to reinstate subsequently. In consequence there was a fall in demand for salt fish and the coarser freshwater varieties, though as late as 1723 John Nott's recipe compilation still included eleven for tench, fourteen for carp and twenty-five for pike *(see p. 53)*. The distinction between meat and fish dishes became blurred as it became customary to add oysters or anchovies to enrich their flavour. French influences were strengthened thanks to the courtly entourage of Charles I's bride, Henriette Marie, by his son's lengthy period of exile in France and by the influx of Huguenot refugees

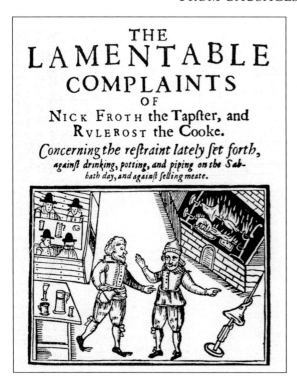

8. The Reign of Virtue – Strict Sabbatarianism enforced by Puritan regulations provoke a pamphlet protest.

from India. The pineapple and banana became known but remained exotic rarities thanks to transport difficulties. The Americas provided the kidney bean, ultimately from Peru, and the Jerusalem artichoke from Canada. Limes and grapefruits, transferred to the Caribbean by the Spanish, came to Britain from Jamaica, wrested from Spain in 1655. The development of sugar plantations boosted consumption from one pound per person per year to four. Surplus sugar in the form of molasses became known in England as treacle and was initially used in making gingerbread. English gardeners experimented with growing citrus fruits. Pepys recorded drinking fresh orange juice but remained wary of the experience:

> "I drank a glass, of a pint, I believe, at one draught, of the juice of oranges, of whose peel they make comfits; and here they drink the juice as wine, with sugar, and it is a very fine drink; but, it being new, I was doubtful whether it might not do me hurt."

(see p. 100). English cooks adopted the flour and butter roux as a thickener, mastered the mysteries of the meringue and the casserole, learned how to make lemonade and even experimented with snail dishes. Two important French cookery books became available in translation – *The Perfect School of Instruction for the Officers of the Mouth* (1682) and Massialot's *New Instructions for Confectioners* (1702).

The other main continental influence was Italy, from which came not only vermicelli and the Bologna (Polony) sausage but also cultivated rhubarb, celery, asparagus, cauliflowers and globe artichokes. Britain's expanding trade with the tropical world introduced sago, soy and ketchup from east Asia. Ketchup was originally a fish sauce but variant forms based on mushrooms and walnuts were soon developed. Piccalilli, coloured with turmeric, was imitated

Cooking and dining practices changed in several ways. The popularisation of the fork made it easier for the diner to deal with fish bones and for the cook to whisk egg whites. The introduction of coffee *(see p. 128)* and chocolate encouraged the wealthy to take them as early morning beverages, accompanied by a spiced bread or cake, thus displacing the traditional breakfast. Sausages began to be made in links. The general adoption of the pudding-cloth freed cooks from reliance on animal skins which were only plentiful at the time of the autumn

9. A blaze in a Pudding Lane baker's began the Great Fire of 1666. The offender made biscuits for the Navy.

10. *This late 17th-century depiction of a family meal shows the clergyman guest seated at the right hand of the paterfamilias on the side of the table furthest from the serving-door. Infants are seated on high chairs between adults. Service is provided by exclusively male staff.*

11. *Compared with its 15th-century predecessor (ill. 4) this 17th-century kitchen boasts a large open fire with multiple rotisseries plus a bread-oven (right) and a tiled stove (left).*

slaughtering. Puddings, available all year round, displaced the traditional thick pottage as the working man's staple fare. Its ubiquity by the end of the century inspired a positive paean from the French visitor Misson, for foreigners had no equivalent concoction to compare with it:

"The pudding is a dish very difficult to be described, because of the several sorts there are of it; flour, milk, eggs, butter, sugar, suet, marrow, raisins etc., are the most common ingredients ... They bake them in an oven, they boil them with meat, they make them fifty several ways: BLESSED BE HE THAT INVENTED PUDDING, for it is a manna that hits the palates of all sorts of people; a manna, better than that of the wilderness, because the people are never weary of it. Ah, what an excellent thing is an English pudding! To come in pudding time, is as much as to say, to come in the most lucky moment in the world."

THE GEORGIAN ERA

During the course of the eighteenth century London's population increased once more from 575,000 in 1700 to 900,000 in 1800. The pace of change was uneven, however, with virtual stagnation in the earlier decades, thanks at least in part to the hugely destructive effects of the 'gin mania' which prevailed until the 1750s when the combined effects of legislation and a fall-off in grain surpluses began to suppress excess consumption. Scarcely less addictive was the nation's growing obsession with tea. John Wesley, founder of Methodism, welcomed it as an accompaniment to sobriety. Dr Samuel Johnson feared that his own copious indulgence in tea might literally be the death of him. Eccentric philanthropist Jonas Hanway published a very intemperate *Essay on Tea* (1757) in which he argued that it very well might be. Johnson responded angrily in print – provoking an equally bellicose reply from Hanway – to which in turn Johnson, uniquely, riposted. A delicate luxury for the elite in the seventeenth century, tea became the national beverage in the eighteenth. Halved in price, it began to be taken in a new and very un-Chinese way – blended with milk, sweetened with sugar and drunk out of cups with handles. By the 1740s the comfortable middle classes had become accustomed to start their day with tea and "one or more slices of wheatbread, which they had first toasted at the fire, and when it was very hot, had spread butter on it." By 1800 even the poorest of the poor felt they could not live without their daily infusion of tea, even if it meant topping up and re-using leaves already several days old.

The increasing consumption of tea and the less rapidly expanding but still growing consumption of coffee and chocolate spelled out bad news for the manufacturers of pewter vessels; these conducted heat too well to be used comfortably for the consumption of hot drinks. The beneficiaries were the makers of porcelain who set up riverside factories at Chelsea, Vauxhall, Limehouse and Bow, the latter pretentiously appropriating the title of the New Canton Works, as though claiming some pseudo-authenticity for products clearly made in imitation of superior Chinese imports. Manufacturers of china likewise benefited from the banishment of pewter and wooden tablewares from even humble households. Wedgwood set up a London showroom in Greek Street, Soho to punt his wares.

Developments in the national and international economy continued to affect the capital's diet. The quality of livestock improved thanks to systematic cross-breeding with cattle imported from the Netherlands and even pigs from China. Improved milk yields encouraged a lavish use of cream in the kitchen in the preparation of dishes ranging from syllabubs to spinach. (Cows were still being kept and milked in London itself; a Board of Agriculture estimate of 1794 estimated that there were 8,500 of them.) A Swedish visitor, Per Kalm, observed in 1748 that "All English meat ... has a fatness and a delicious taste ... English men understand almost better than any other people the art of properly roasting a joint, which ... is not to be wondered at; because the art of cooking as practised by most Englishmen does not extend much beyond roast beef and plum pudding ... I do not believe that any Englishman who is his own master has ever eaten a dinner without meat" – an opinion firmly supported by James Boswell *(see p.113)*.

The thick, farinaceous pottage which remained a characteristic staple of the Celtic fringe, as of peasant households throughout most of Europe, became a thing of the past. Soups, based on a chicken or veal stock, became thinner and lighter – though there were strongly flavoured variants made of eels or oysters – and were increasingly served as an appetiser or even a light snack. Mr Horton, a confectioner, set up a soup room in Cornhill in imitation of Parisian establishments which promoted soup as a restorative – the original meaning of the word 'restaurant'. The sandwich was allegedly invented around 1760 so that the gambling-

Taking tea – an English institution

12. (Above). Painting by George Morland (1763-1804) of a group taking tea in a London tea garden. "If Morland had taken more tea himself he might not have died of drink at forty-one."

13. (Right) Dr Johnson taking tea with his friend Mrs Thrale in the Borough, c.1770-80. In such cultured households tea-time was the occasion for an intellectual conversazioni. In the 1840s the Duchess of Bedford pioneered the notion of tea as an intimate indoor picnic for ladies only, served in her boudoir. This change may have been prompted by the shift to serving the main meal of the day in the evening rather than mid-afternoon, creating a long gap between meals. By the 1880s prosperous working-class families used Sunday tea-times as an occasion for elaborate but informal entertainment of outsiders, allowing mothers to inspect prospective in-laws.

14. Selling asses' milk in Kentish Town c.1760. Valued for its restorative qualities, asses' milk was often prescribed for invalids.

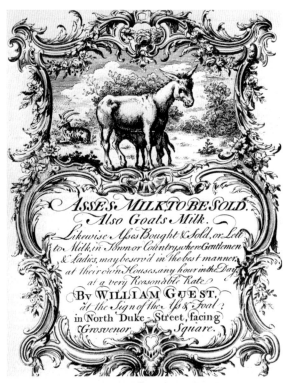

15. Trade card for William Guest of North Duke Street, Grosvenor Square, advertising asses' milk. The Royal Family still had an official purveyor of asses' milk in Victoria's reign.

mad John Montagu, fourth Earl of Sandwich, could take sustenance without dragging himself away from the gaming-table. Potatoes at last became accepted. A book published in 1744 under the engaging title of *Adam's Luxury and Eve's Cookery* gave recipes which used potato as a thickening agent in stuffings, sausages, puddings and fritters, as well as fried, boiled, roast or mashed. The tomato likewise began to lose its supposed air of mystery as a 'love apple' of aphrodisiac potential and was cautiously incorporated into soups and pickles. Rhubarb cultivation, encouraged by London's Royal Society of Arts, led to its wider use in fruit tarts.

The tables of the well-off impressed with quantity and variety rather than subtlety. The royal dinner served to George III and Queen Charlotte at Kensington Palace in 1780 was not, except perhaps in the number of dishes, much different from what might have graced the table of a well-beneficed country parson:

"Pottage vermicelly Pullets with Rice Pillaw Fillets of mutton and potatoes Cold chicken and sliced tongue Ham with pease and beans Small turbot and small lobster Quails Artychokes Cherry Tart Lambs Sweetbreads Ragou'd Omelettes en roulade".

Sophie de la Roche observed in the 1780s how big the dishes were on sale in the shops,

"because a quarter of a calf, half a lamb and monstrous pieces of other meats are dished up and everyone receives almost an entire fish. But since England knows nothing of separate cooking for the servants, who partake of all the courses sampled by the masters, the latter having first choice and the servants what remains — hence the large dishes and portions."

Ice-packed salmon was brought from

Scotland by sea. Salted haddock from Newcastle was valued for its keeping qualities. Stilton cheese began to be appreciated outside its own locality. Defoe, who dubbed it the English Parmesan, described Stilton being "brought to the table with the mites or maggots round it so thick that they bring a spoon with them for you to eat the mites with as you do the cheese." Ice-cream was a foreign novelty, for the making of which pewterers devised a special double-chambered device. An Irish guest of the brewer Henry Thrale recorded being offered ices made of grape, raspberry, pineapple and a fourth flavour he could not identify. Aspic jelly was introduced from France but far more significant innovations came in from far further away. The growth of Britain's empire in India spread a taste for curries, kedgeree and fiery mulligatawny (literally 'pepper water') soup (see p. 117). Commercially-produced curry-powder mixes were already on the shelves of London shops by the 1780s. The spread of plantation cultivation greatly reduced the price of nutmeg, cloves, allspice, vanilla and, above all, sugar, per capita consumption of which trebled in the course of the century to twelve pounds a year. From the West Indies turtles were brought live. Considered the greatest delicacy, the turtle swiftly became a featured dish in royal or City banquets. Its high price inspired the invention of a 'mock turtle' variant, made from a calve's head stewed in Madeira – an ingenious concoction which the *Larousse Gastronomique* concedes to be wholly English in origin. Not that this retrospective recognition need be taken to imply approval. Contemporary Frenchmen were not necessarily impressed with the original. Grimod de la Reyniere, observed sneeringly in 1806 that "a gourmet would scarcely hazard the Channel crossing to eat roast and grilled meats ... English cooking is limited to boiled chickens, of extreme insipidity and to what they call Plump Pudding ... a bizarre and indigestible mixture ... However, like every nation ... they have a few national dishes, of which they boast more out of patriotic spirit than conviction ... such as Turtle soup."

Both cooking and dining out bore the imprint of an increasingly commercialized society. Mrs Elizabeth Lazenby devised an anchovy essence which bore her name and her innkeeper brother, Peter Harvey, a sauce which bore his. Both soon became standard ingredients to be routinely specified in cookbook recipes. From 1742 onwards Keen's mustard factory (hence 'as keen as mustard') near St James Garlickhythe, offered jars of that ancient condiment ready prepared as a convenient powder. Cookery teachers set up to give courses of instruction, especially in the most prestigious of culinary arts, the making of confectionery. Edward Kidder (died 1739) published his *Receipts of Pastry and Cookery For the Use of his Scholars by Ed Kidder Who teacheth at his School On Mondays, Tuesdays and Wednesdays in the Afternoon, in St. Martin's Le Grand And on Thursdays, Fridays and Saturdays in the Afternoon at his School next to Furnivall's Inn in Holburn. And Ladies may be taught at their own houses.* (At another time he taught at "Queen Street near St. Thomas Apostle's"). Kidder's recipes were as much concerned with pies, pasties, pickles and potting as puddings and cakes and also included directions for making broths, meat balls, jellies and dozens of meat and fish dishes. Confectionery shops, such as Kelsey's in St James's Street, dazzled German visitor G C Lichtenberg with their brightly-lit windows festooned with sweets, pastries, jellies, fruits and cakes, their elegantly-appointed fittings and silk-clad staff. Tavern chefs capitalised on their celebrity, like today's TV chefs, to publish their own recipe books. John Townshend, author of *The Universal Cook; or lady's complete assistant* (1773), styled himself 'Late Master of the Greyhound Tavern, Greenwich and Cook to his Grace the Duke of Manchester'. Richard Briggs, compiler of *The English Art of Cookery* (1788) claimed to have been "many years Cook at the White Hart Tavern, Holborn: Temple Coffee-House and other Taverns in London."

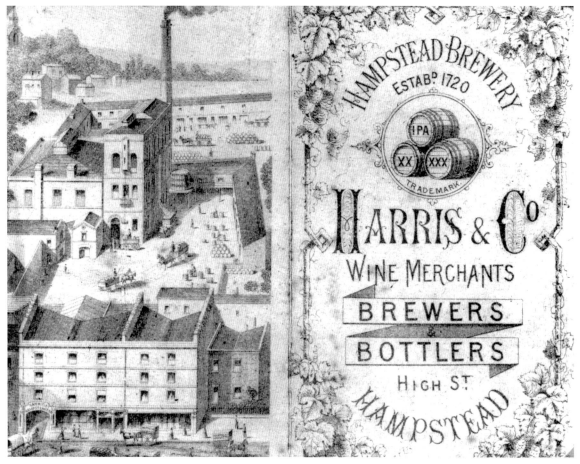

16. *At a time when distribution was cumbersome and expensive, local breweries flourished. The above illustration is of the Hampstead Brewery in Hampstead High Street, founded in 1720. The brewery did a good trade with the thousands of visitors to Hampstead Wells. Note the barrel designation IPA – India Pale Ale – the premium brew.*

John Farley was the principal cook at the London Tavern, Bishopsgate, which had an unrivalled reputation for its cooking, but *The London Art of Cookery* (1783) which appeared over his name was in fact ghosted (which may explain its competent organisation) by a hack, Richard Johnson, for a mere £21. Many of the recipes were lifted from Hannah Glasse *(see p. 53)* or the works of her Mancunian rival Elizabeth Raffald.

Such a concern for appearance over reality implied the emergence of a trend towards 'marketing' priorities which led from deception to outright dishonesty. As Smollett observed in *Humphrey Clinker:*

"The bread I eat in London is a deleterious paste, mixed up with chalk, alum and bone-ashes; insipid to the taste and destructive to the constitution. The good people are not ignorant of this adulteration; but they prefer it to wholesome bread, because it is whiter than the meal of corn. Thus they sacrifice their taste and their health, and the lives of their tender infants, to a most absurd gratification of a misjudging eye; and the miller or the baker, is obliged to poison them and their families, in order to live by his profession."

The commercial forces pressing for change should not obscure the continuities and conservatism represented by familial custom. The recipes passed on to Margaretta Acworth, wife of a government official, by her mother and added to by her, reveal the survival of such traditional techniques as the use of cock's combs in sauces and almonds in soups and as a thickening agent and such positively medieval notions as serving pigeons with their heads on and the inclusion of cinnamon, nutmeg and sugar in an artichoke pie.

THE RAILWAY REVOLUTION

London's population passed the million mark by 1811 and more than doubled again by mid-century. This continuing expansion would scarcely have been possible without the contribution made by railways in sustaining its food supplies. The capital's first railway, from London Bridge to Deptford and Greenwich, opened in 1836. Within fifteen years London was joined by rail to almost every major provincial city and trains were regularly scheduled to run at speeds of up to sixty miles per hour. As Charles Dodd pointed out in his pioneering study of *The Food of London* (1856), "double the speed and you increase four-fold the area of country from which provisions can be sent in a given time to London." And railways

did far more than double the speed of a creaking wagon or lumbering herd of livestock. The centuries-old droving trade was killed off in a couple of decades as beasts could now be loaded direct onto trucks and no longer needed to be refattened after the exertions of a long march. By the 1850s fish could be transported overnight – and nearly half of it already was – from the east coast ports, nullifying the locational advantage once enjoyed by Barking, which ceased to serve as London's doorstep fishing-port *(see p. 86)*. Salmon, packed in ice, could be brought all the way from Scotland year round. Milk was being carried by rail from the mid-1840s; a decade later the Eastern Counties Railway alone was delivering three-quarters of a million gallons a year. Prices as well as travel times were slashed. In 1846 St Thomas's Hospital ceased paying a local dairyman a shilling a gallon for milk and ordered instead from a farmer out at Romford who could supply the same amount for ninepence. Sainsbury's *(see p. 95)* from the very outset sold 'Railway Milk' despite the fact that there was a cow-keeper in Drury Lane where they opened their first branch. Cheap, fresh milk from country

17. One of the largest dairies in the inner London area was Laycock's, between Upper Street and Liverpool Road, Islington, which contained 500 cows. The premises could also house thousands of animals on their journey to Smithfield. Smocked yokels with pitchforks and yoked sellers with churns add a rural touch.

18. A banquet held at Farringdon Station in 1863 to celebrate the opening of the first Underground railway, the Metropolitan line. The occasion appears to have been exclusively male.

herds sounded the death-knell for the urban cow-keeper whose milch-cows were all too often kept in insanitary stalls in a mews or back-street. Medical Officers of Health were glad to see them go, although they could still be found even in up-market residential areas such as Bloomsbury as late as the 1880s. Other East Anglian delicacies freighted in to King's Cross included peas, celery and rhubarb. Not only did the railways offer fast and cheap transport, they were also virtually unaffected by all but the most severe weather, thus bringing a new reliability to delivery schedules. London's tentacles which, as Defoe had remarked over a century previously, already stretched out to Cheshire for cheese and salt, could now stretch onto the mainland of Europe. In 1854 British engineers laid a railway across Denmark to speed the importation of its agricultural produce via Lowestoft. From the 1870s railways began to penetrate the prairies of North America and the pampas of Argentina, linking their virgin soils with the teeming markets of Europe's great cities. Taken in conjunction with dramatic

improvements in shipping represented by cheap steel, the compound engine and refrigeration these improvements in communication radically altered the cost of freight and the international price structure of such basics as bread and meat. Terrible news for British landlords and farmers but a wonderful benefit to the urban working man and his family who no longer had to spend half his weekly income simply to stave off hunger. Farmers, especially those within easy reach of the London market, found salvation by switching to products in which they could remain competitive, such as high quality meat, or for which international supply was unfeasible – eggs, milk, temperate fruits and vegetables. In the Brentwood area, for example, the beleaguered Lord Petre shipped dozens of farmers down from Scotland on specially chartered trains, complete with their herds of prime livestock. Many of these newcomers scrapped the traditional Essex crops of wheat and barley in favour of potatoes.

The thrifty middle-classes were equally aware of how their living-costs had fallen as a

SO LIKELY!
SCENE—*Bar of a Railway Refreshment Room*
Barmaid: "Tea, Sir?"   *Mr. Boozy:* "Tea!!! Me!!!!"

19. Cartoon in Punch, *drawn by Phil May, depicting one of the new railway refreshment rooms. A toper indignantly rejects the offer of tea. The convivial May drew from the heart, dying of drink at 39.*

result of plummeting production costs and freight rates. Writing in 1888 Mrs J E Panton, the author of *From Kitchen to Garrett: Hints for Young Householders,* noted the change since the date of her marriage (1871):

"– everything is much cheaper ... than it used to be before New Zealand meat came to the front, and sugar, tea, cheese ... became lower than ever they had been before ... sugar was 6d a pound and now it is 2d; and instead of paying 1s 1d a pound for legs of mutton, I give 7½d for New Zealand meat which is good as the best English mutton that one can buy. Bread, too, is 5½d as against the 8d and 9d of seventeen years ago and fish and game are also infinitely less expensive, for in the season salmon is no longer a luxury while prime cod at 4d a pound can hardly be looked upon as ... sinful ..."

By 1899 premier chef Auguste Escoffier *(see p.70)* of the Carlton Hotel could have his supplies of lamb, poultry, *foie gras* and early vegetables, freighted over by cross-Channel rail from the famous market of Les Halles in Paris. Steamships had been integrated into the distribution system for over half a century by then. Oysters gathered off the Channel Islands were landed at Brighton within hours and then whisked up to Billingsgate by rail. Lobsters netted off the coasts of Ireland or Brittany were taken to Southampton and from thence to London not by rail, for they were easily damaged in transhipment, but by steamers carrying cargoes of up to twenty thousand.

THE ENTREPRENEURS

The second half of the nineteenth century witnessed a significant trend towards the systematic commercialisation of the catering business. Between 1866 and 1874 alone 116 companies involved in the hotel or restaurant branches of the trade were registered.

Frederick Gordon (1835-1908) brought to the restaurant trade what he had picked up from his father, a decorator, and what he had learned from his chosen profession, that of solicitor. He also had the advantage of being the brother-in-law of Horatio Davies, the owner of Pimms' chop-house at No.3 Poultry and subsequently a knight and Lord Mayor of London. Such connections gave Gordon useful insights into the catering needs of London's business community. His first venture was a restaurant housed in fifteenth-century Crosby Hall on Bishopsgate; unusually diners were served by waitresses rather than waiters. Leased and converted in 1868, it remained in business until 1907, after which the ancient mansion was disassembled and re-erected at Chelsea. The success of the Crosby Hall venture encouraged Gordon to launch a more ambitious project which added private banqueting-rooms to the usual public dining-room – the Holborn Restaurant *(see p. 158).*

Gordon progressed from restaurants to hotels, opening the luxurious Grand on Northumberland Avenue in 1881. This establishment introduced a novel practice to the trade, allowing non-residents to patronise the dining-room's *table d'hote* offering. In 1882

20. Frederick Gordon, 'the Napoleon of the hotel world'.

21. Crosby Hall in Bishopsgate, the home of one of Gordon's earliest restaurants. The old hall has since been re-erected in Chelsea.

Gordon bought grandiose Bentley Priory at Stanmore, home of railway engineer Sir John Kelk, and converted it into a rural retreat for the rich, complete with its own spur line to the station at Wealdstone. (In 1893, in collaboration with his friend Thomas Blackwell of Crosse & Blackwell *(see p. 89)*, he re-launched the golf course he had laid out for guests as the Stanmore Golf Club.) In 1883 Gordon then opened the First Avenue Hotel in High Holborn, and in 1885, the Metropole, also on Northumberland Avenue. He later acquired a third establishment in the same prestigious location, the Victoria, bought at the expense of its promoter, Jabez Balfour MP, whose long career as a swindler had finally landed him in prison. Gordon's hotel empire would eventually become the largest in the world, embracing the Grosvenor at Victoria station and hotels along the south coast and in Cannes and Monte Carlo.

Felix Spiers and Christopher Pond were two Englishmen who had learned their business in Australia and, as caterers to Melbourne Cricket Club, sponsored the first English cricket side to tour there in 1861-2. Returning to England, they put catering for railways at the core of their business. In 1874 they opened the Criterion at Piccadilly Circus. Built at a cost of £80,000 to the designs of Thomas Verity, this huge complex of rooms occupied the former site of the White Bear Inn and was extended in 1878 and again in 1885. In 1874 Spiers and Pond opened the Holborn Viaduct Hotel next to the station of that name. The firm also owned the Gaiety Restaurant in Aldwych but this proved too big to be economical on such an isolated site and closed in 1908. Spiers and Pond became

sufficiently well known to be referred to in satirical works by Kipling and W S Gilbert without further explanation.

Polydore de Keyser was a Belgian immigrant who began working in London as a waiter and ended up as a knight and the proprietor of a four-hundred room hotel. In 1887 he also became the first Roman Catholic since the Reformation to serve as Lord Mayor of London. Situated at the northern end of Blackfriars Bridge, on the site of Bridewell palace, de Keyser's Royal Hotel opened in 1874 and was much favoured by Continental businessmen visiting the capital. Impresario Richard D'Oyly Carte (1844-1901) was so impressed by the American hotels that he stayed in when touring with his Savoy Opera company that he determined to create one in London. The result was the Savoy (1889), its reputation for excellence secured by the perfectionist

22. The Holborn Viaduct Hotel, designed by E. Evans Cronk. From The Builder, *5 September 1874. Within five years it was recommended as one of the capital's top ten venues for "large dinners, when expense is no object and a good private room is a desideratum".*

23. *Sir Polydore de Keyser, proprietor of De Keyser's Royal Hotel at Blackfriars and caterer of Guildhall banquets. Rebuilt in 1873-4 with 400 rooms, his hotel was much favoured by foreigners but required that "every guest must be introduced personally or by letter."*

hotelier Cèsar Ritz and chef supreme Auguste Escoffier *(see p. 70).*

THE GREAT WAR

"The food question ultimately decided the issue of this war." Lloyd George's hyperbole was pardonable, given that the British government had given no serious consideration to food policy until the prospect of virtual famine suddenly manifested itself like some malevolent spectre. True, the government had appointed a Sugar Commission in light of the fact that peace-time Britain drew two-thirds of its supplies of that basic product from the Austro-Hungarian empire, now an enemy. A Royal Commission on Wheat was charged with building up a secret reserve against emergencies. Factories were also encouraged to set up canteens to provide their labour force with a hot meal, now perceived as invaluable, not only in maintaining morale, but keeping up output and protecting health – and thereby cutting both accidents and absenteeism. Licensing laws were amended to ensure that pubs closed after lunch, removing the temptation for workers on rapidly rising wages to stay there all afternoon. Later regulations would oblige pubs in many areas to close by nine in the evening and to forbid the buying of 'rounds', especially for soldiers. The capital's food-processing businesses also contributed directly to the war effort by victualling the hugely-expanded army with supplies of such staples as bacon and the ubiquitous plum and apple jam. Spratt's, an East End firm which claimed to be the world's largest manufacturers of dog biscuits, provided the hard tack 'iron rations' which the average Tommy thought appropriately so named. The sublime chef Auguste Escoffier, who had himself been an army cook and prisoner-of-war in the Franco-Prussian war, patriotically devised soup concentrates for the French army.

By June 1916 rising food prices were provoking civilian grumbling and accusations of profiteering. A Departmental Committee on Food Prices was established but as late as October 1916 the President of the Board of Trade assured the House of Commons that there was no need to appoint a Food Controller, still less establish a Ministry of Food. A month later. however, a Food Department was finally established within the Board of Trade and, following the replacement of Asquith's Liberal administration by the Lloyd George coalition in December 1916, was upgraded to a fully-fledged Ministry. In the same month a confidential report prepared by a Royal Society committee of physiologists warned the government that

> "in buying food the labouring population is buying energy – the power to do work ... If the rising prices curtail for any class of the community its accustomed supply of food, its output of work will, of necessity, be reduced. It is important to remember that a slight reduction of food below the necessary amount causes a large diminution in the working efficiency of the individual."

The first Food Controller to be appointed was Lord Devonport. It was to prove an unhappy choice. He had had great experience in the provisions trade but no knowledge of the science of nutrition. His preference for voluntary self-rationing proved self-defeating. In February 1917, in a misguided effort to conserve 'basics', he appealed to patriotic consumers to limit their weekly purchases per person to four pounds of bread, two and a half pounds of meat and three-quarters of a pound of sugar. Raising such allowances to ensure an adequate calorie intake, let alone other dietary requirements, would have required supplementing them with other foodstuffs which were fast becoming scarce – even if they could have been afforded. In April he appealed for a weekly 'meatless day'. Scientists pointed out that this would raise consumption of imported grain, increasing pressure on precious shipping-space. The success of the U-boat campaign was finally recognized as a major strategic threat as a stunned House of Commons was told that the loss of more than two million tons of shipping had brought the country to within a month of starvation. At the same time a Royal Commission on Industrial Unrest stressed the damaging effect on working-class morale of rising prices and food shortages. Belatedly Lord Devonport submitted to the War Cabinet a scheme for food rationing and then, in May 1917, submitted his resignation, ostensibly on grounds of ill-health brought on by overwork.

May 1917 also saw the issue of a Proclamation from Buckingham Palace calling on all patriotic Britons to cut back their bread consumption by a quarter and renounce the use of flour for any other purpose "being persuaded that the abstention from all unnecessary consumption of grain will furnish the surest and most effectual means of defeating the devices of Our enemies, and thereby of bringing the War to a speedy and successful termination...". Printed copies of the Royal Proclamation were distributed so that members of each household could by their signature "hereby pledge ourselves on our honour to respond to His Majesty's appeal." The same appeal was made from pulpits in churches and chapels throughout the land on successive Sundays throughout the month. George V also ordered that the flower-beds in front of Buckingham Palace be replanted with cabbages to encourage fellow-residents of the capital to enlarge its food supply through their own efforts. Those who wished to strengthen their resolve could buy, as a constant inspiration for their efforts, plates and butter dishes overprinted with a message from Prime Minister David Lloyd George:

> "I have no hesitation in saying that economy in the consumption and use of food in this country is a matter of the greatest possible importance to the Empire at the present time."

Devonport's successor, Lord Rhondda, swiftly surrounded himself with a first-rate administrative team. In the words of Lord Beveridge, who subsequently wrote the official history of wartime food policy, "The civilian population is catered for like an army; nothing is left to chance or private enterprise." Civilian rationing, starting with sugar, began on New Year's Day 1918 and guaranteed everyone eight ounces a week. In the same month London's public eating places such as hotels and restaurants – and for this purpose private clubs – were required to observe Tuesdays and Fridays as meatless days and forbidden to serve meat as part of a breakfast. Only children under ten were to be allowed to drink milk 'straight'; adults could only have it in tea, coffee, chocolate or cocoa. In February, London and the Home Counties led the way in having to accept rationing of meat (by value) and butter and margarine (five ounces). By April 1918 the scheme had been extended nationwide and in due course included jam (four ounces), tea (two ounces) and bacon (eight ounces – raised to sixteen after July).

Breaches of Rationing Orders were punished by the Enforcement Branch of the Local Authorities Division of the Ministry of Food. In August 1918 a West Ham retailer who had failed to detach the proper number of coupons for a purchase as a favour to a customer was fined twenty pounds. A Hendon offender who had obtained and used ration books unlawfully was sent to prison for three months.

The scientists were vindicated in their prediction that the people would accept severe restrictions on their diet providing they were confident that all classes were being treated alike and that they could get enough to stave off hunger, keep warm and do their daily work without undue fatigue – hence the imperative need not to ration bread or potatoes.

Compared with the pre-war quinquennium 1909-13 average consumption of butcher's meat and butter fell by almost half, sugar by a third and fresh milk by a quarter. Consumption of bacon and ham rose by a third, of potatoes by almost half, of margarine by double. The 'war bread' introduced in November 1916. with its later admixtures of barley, oats, rye, soya or potato flour, was universally disliked. The comfortable classes felt the shortages of butcher's meat and the substitution of margarine in place of butter more than did the poor.

In calorific terms the overall fall was neglible. The inhabitants of London never approached the deprivation which so demoralised the peoples of Berlin and Vienna. In the latter a post-war study-group of British scientists found abundant evidence of scurvy among infants, rickets among children and actual deaths from hunger oedema.

The families of the unskilled were, it was officially confirmed, slightly better fed than they had been on the eve of the war. School medical inspections revealed that in London "the percentage of children found in a poorly nourished condition is considerably less than half the percentage in 1913". The number of the capital's children whose abject poverty obliged them to rely on a daily school meal for their basic nutrition fell by three-quarters. (In Sheffield and Nottingham a half still did need it, in Birmingham and Liverpool scarcely any.) The singular improvement in the condition of children had little to do with food rationing, almost everything to do with the almost total disappearance of unemployment as five million men were extracted from the peace-time labour-force for military service.

Allowing for a rise in commodity prices from a base of 100 in July 1914 to 233 in November 1918 real wages still rose by twenty per cent in just four years. The most spectacular beneficiaries were married women who filled their husbands' absence in the workplace – and received additional income in the form of an 'overseas allowance'. Incomes more regular and often higher than they had ever received before enabled them to contemplate such indulgences as cigarettes, cosmetics, false teeth – and feeding their children adequately. The government could take the credit that there was food for them to buy.

THE KITCHEN FRONT

By the 1930s Britain had become once again heavily dependent on distant suppliers for many of its most basic foodstuffs. Just under four-fifths of the nation's wheat and flour came from Canada, Australia and Argentina. Argentina, Australia, New Zealand and Denmark between them supplied almost the same proportion of Britain's meat. Two-thirds of sugar supplies were drawn from Cuba, San Domingo, Australia and Mauritius. Even half the nation's fruit and vegetable consumption depended on imports.

With respect to food rationing the lessons of the First World War were learned – and not just by the authorities. In September 1938 George Beardmore, an insurance company clerk and commuter from Harrow, noted in the journal he had decided to keep

"as events crowd upon us. Today we spent 25/- on sugar, rice, flour, corned beef and Marmite which we have stored in the sideboard against the day when these things will be difficult or even impossible to obtain by reason of War."

As early as 1936 the government's Food (Defence Plans) Department had been set up and by 1937 it had organised the printing of ration books. Originating as a part of the Board of Trade what became the Ministry of Food came eventually under the Ministry of Agriculture. In Professor Jack Drummond (*see p. 197*) the government chose an expert adviser capable of setting its rationing system on a sound scientific basis. In Lord Woolton (1883-1964) it found a spokesman of genius to head the newly-established Ministry of Food, which would soon have fifty thousand civil servants in its employ. Woolton had been warden of a settlement in the slums of Liverpool and manager of a major Manchester department store. None doubted his administrative skills but it was as a radio broadcaster that he was to reveal an unexpected talent. He personally crafted his own carefully-polished scripts and skilfully enlisted the collaboration of Cockney comediennes 'Gert and Daisy' (Elsie and Doris Waters), 'radio doctor' Charles Hill and cookery expert Marguerite Patten to promote the dietary virtues of Dr Carrot and Potato Pete. A five minute *Kitchen Front* programme was broadcast daily at 8.15 am. A pre-war designer of department stores was seconded to plan kitchen layouts for converted premises such as church halls.

Even before rationing began shortages did. In October 1939 George Beardmore noted that chocolate bars were smaller, sausages and bread had gone up in price and "Lyle's Golden Syrup

unobtainable, presumably because it stores well." Rationing came into force on Monday 8 January 1940 but applied initially to only four commodities, of which the weekly ration per person was four ounces of ham or bacon and butter and twelve ounces of sugar. From March onwards meat was rationed by a price ceiling of 1s 10d per week for persons over six, half that for small children but there was no limit set on the amount of offal one could buy. Londoners – some Londoners – learned to appreciate what had become traditional Northern delicacies – pigs' trotters, cowheel and brains. Even the Ivy restaurant put tripe and onions on its menu – when it could get the onions. The fall of France in June 1940 cut off supplies of onions – normally imported from Brittany and the Channel Islands. Not until 1942 were domestic supplies able to make up the shortfall. Pickle manufacturers in the East End suffered from the curtailment of vegetables normally imported from the Netherlands. Vegetables as such were not restricted, although they were subject to a scheme of Controlled Distribution which rotated supplies around the country to ensure fair shares. The 'Dig for Victory' campaign was promoted in the capital with vigour and, as an example from the top, in the Royal Parks flower-beds were converted to the cultivation of cabbages and carrots. Even the grassed-over moat of the Tower of London sported lines of vegetables planted with fittingly military precision.

Flat-dwellers were disadvantaged by not having gardens but many acquired allotments or colonised patches of waste ground or bomb sites. Those who did have gardens were encouraged to erect Anderson shelters in them as a refuge during bombing raids. Inevitably this subtracted from the area available for cultivation – but not necessarily by much. The shelter was sunk into the ground and the spoil dug out then heaped over it as a further protective layer, ideal for growing vegetable marrows. Railway embankments supplied vegetables to the staff canteens of the London Passenger

Advice and Reassurance

FOOD FACTS

CALLING ALL MOTHERS

Don't worry because you can't give the children the foods you used to give them, foods such as fruit and meat. New potatoes, raw, shredded vegetables will give them sufficient Vitamin C, while for body-building you can't beat cheese. For the time being the cheese ration has been increased to oz. weekly. A meal of bread, margarine, cheese, milk, and a salad of raw, shredded vegetables is grand for children. This is, in fact, the Health Meal or Breakfast which greatly improved the health of the Norwegian school-children before the war. The Health Meal is ship-saving, fuel-saving, and easy to prepare.

Cheese Salad

Ingredients: 1 medium-sized cabbage, ¼ lb. cheese, nasturtium flowers. For the sauce: 1½ oz. flour, ½ pint milk, salt. *Method:* Shred the cabbage finely. Blend the flour with a little cold milk, put the rest of the milk on to boil. When boiling pour on to the blended flour, stirring well till smooth. Return to the pan and cook from 1 to 2 minutes. Add salt and grated cheese. Stir until cheese melts. Cool sauce, pour over the finely shredded cabbage, and serve decorated with nasturtium flowers.

are you a ship-saver?

RECIPE of the WEEK No 16

FARMHOUSE SCRAMBLE

Time: 15-20 minutes. **Quantity:** Four helpings. **Ingredients:** 2 lb. mixed, cooked vegetables, 4 oz. grated cheese, 3 oz. breadcrumbs, 2 eggs (2 level tablespoonfuls dried egg, 4 tablespoonfuls water), chopped parsley, pepper and salt. **Method:** Mix all the ingredients together. Melt a little dripping in a frying-pan. When it is hot put in the mixture and spread it over the pan. Put on a saucepan lid and cook for about 20 minutes, shaking occasionally until it is brown. Turn out on a hot dish and serve it with lettuce or shredded cabbage. This dish is just as successful when baked in an oven, but in this case add a little more liquid.

MAKE A 'POINT' OF IT — buy prunes this week, only 6 points a lb.

THE MINISTRY OF FOOD, LONDON, W.1   FOOD FACTS No. 197

While the government encouraged mothers to cook healthily within the constraints of the rationing system – and include nasturtium flowers – (illustration 24, left), Fry's Cocoa extolled the energy content of its product, compared to eggs (illustration 26, below).

More worrying to mothers was the fate of their children shipped off to parts of the country that were entirely unfamiliar to them. The picture of the school dinner for evacuated children (illustration 25 below), was no doubt taken to allay those fears.

Transport Board. In affluent Kensington two tennis clubs were turned into temporary allotments. In the leafy suburbs there was obviously even more scope. Hedgerows could be scoured for blackberries or elderberries. One way or another about half of all London families had access to a garden or an allotment.

Fruit was likewise unrationed but London was obviously disadvantaged compared to villages and small towns in rural areas. One London woman, hearing a rumour that a delivery of cooking apples had come to her local greengrocer, joined a queue at six am. Each person was allocated a single apple. Her turn came when the last had gone. Another woman fared better from her six am. stint on a Saturday, being offered the choice of three apples or a pound of rhubarb.

Fish also remained unrationed – if you could get it. The same applied to coffee, custard powder and pepper. From July tea was rationed to two ounces per week. Fats were next to be rationed – four ounces of margarine and two of cooking fat, with butter being cut from four ounces to two. In the summer of 1940 millions of chickens were killed to save on feeding-stuffs – inevitably creating a shortage of eggs. Chickens could be kept in a suburban garden and fed on kitchen scraps. The problem was that most kitchen scraps were recycled as far as possible for human consumption and poultry feed was hard to come by. Eggs could be eaten or bartered. Pre-war egg consumption averaged three per week – in wartime it was one per fortnight. Dried eggs from America took their place, one packet equal to a dozen eggs, every four weeks. Mixed with a little precious cheese or spread with dried mustard, they made a decent substitute for scrambled eggs. It was even possible to create 'hardboiled' eggs by spooning egg-powder mixture into greased egg-cups and steaming it until it set.

Keeping rabbits was also encouraged. Rabbits would eat greens inedible for humans, such as carrot tops, and transform them into two pounds of meat – and a pair of warm mittens. Policemen and firemen pooled potato peelings and other waste from their station kitchens to fatten up a pig. Wealthy Londoners with 'a place in the country' not only found it easier to keep fowl or livestock but also had a much better chance of acquiring game, which was not subject to rationing. The fact that the vast majority of London's children were evacuated to country areas meant that they certainly ate fresher and more varied food than the parents they left behind. Not that they necessarily appreciated this. Slum children reared on fish and chips, biscuits and bread and jam were often resistant to piles of vegetables and home-made soups. Even with the expansion of domestic food production imports remained essential. Much was canned, dehydrated or otherwise treated to economise on shipping space. Meat carcasses were boned and then compressed. Spam from America became a kitchen standby for the housewife, used to fill sandwiches or pies or fried in batter as a fritter. Restaurants offered it both hot *(Viennois)* and cold *(Haché a l'Americaine)*. It even appeared on the menu at the Ivy. Much food, of course, was lost at sea and more from enemy action. Council inspectors visited damaged food retailers and warehouses after bombing raids to supervise the removal of polluted goods. Tins might be needled with fine punctures of glass, leaving lethal slivers nestling unseen amid their contents. Heat from fires also affected canned goods as the inside lacquer permeated food with a metallic poison. Loose commodities like flour and sugar could be returned to mills for refining; remarkably even sugar filled with glass could be made fit for consumption. In Westminster alone some 462 tons of food were removed for examination by sanitary inspectors. Of this quantity 241 tons was passed as fit for sale and a further 86 tons approved for use as animal foodstuffs.

From March 1941 jam, marmalade and syrup were rationed, then honey, lemon curd and mincemeat. In May 1941 cheese was rationed at just an ounce per week, later two, so that

27. One of the least tantalising of still life pictures. Entitled 'Coupons Required', it was painted by Leonora K. Green in 1941. It depicts the weekly rations for two people. A companion picture of 1945, ironically entitled 'Lest We Forget', depicts an even less appetising prospect – meat and bacon replaced by Spam, sausages, kippers and dried egg-powder.

eight ounces to a pound could be made available to miners, farm labourers and others who carried a packed lunch with them where hot food was unavailable. A milk allocation scheme ensured regular supplies to children, adolescents and pregnant women. Pregnant and nursing women and children under five also qualified for a weekly dose of cod liver oil and an allocation of concentrated orange juice to guarantee their vitamin intake. Vegetarians could register for extra allocations of cheese, nuts and dried fruit in lieu of meat foregone. The bulk of the population were obliged to eat more vegetables than ever before just to fill themselves up. The

vegetarian cause achieved few converts.

Sausages were unrationed, although their contents were usually unknown – mostly bread, perhaps, but many suspected the inclusion of horse-meat. From November 1941 milk was also rationed – two to two and a half pints a week. It was supplemented by dried skimmed milk powder which went well enough in coffee and cocoa but was best used in cooking. Babies qualified for National Dried Milk, much creamier – adults hoped eternally to find supplies past their sell-by date.

Rationing acquired a new sophistication in December 1941 when the Ministry of Food introduced a new system of rationing by points, devised by the Board of Education's senior maths inspector, M P Roseveare. Consumers were allocated sixteen (later twenty) points per month as entitlements to purchase items of limited or erratic availability which could not be brought within the general rationing scheme – initially canned meat, fish and vegetables, later rice, canned fruit, condensed milk, breakfeat cereals, biscuits and oatflakes. By reintroducing an element of choice it enabled the housewife to exercise a degree of discrimination, to become a shopper rather than a mere collector of rations. The Ministry acquired an infinitely flexible instrument of manipulation – any product in temporary surplus had its points value lowered until stocks were cleared.

In April 1942 the Ministry of Food launched a new National Loaf made from wholemeal flour. Mills were under government control and ordered to include a certain portion of husk in the flour they produced. The British had prided themselves for two centuries on the purity of their white bread as against the rye and pumpernickel eaten by Continentals. Reactions to this 'dirty bread' were predictably hostile and even Lord Woolton referred to it in private as "nasty, dirty, dark, coarse, indigestible". The attempt to circulate a rumour that it had aphrodisiac virtues proved unconvincing. But the Ministry campaigned unrelentingly against waste, calculating that if the amount of bread wasted annually was actually consumed it would save the equivalent of thirty vessels' worth of shipping space. Leaflets were produced with recipe suggestions for using up stale bread: to make Apple Charlotte or Summer Pudding, or, as breadcrumbs, to bulk out scrambled eggs or Welsh Rarebit or to thicken vegetable soups.

Recruitment to the armed forces mopped up men who had formerly brought daily deliveries of milk and bread to the suburbs. Deliveries dropped to four, sometimes three a week. Few housewives had access to a car or, if they had,

could drive, or assuming that they had petrol to spare for shopping trips. Most had to carry home on foot what they could find for sale, and feel grateful. The ration book system effectively tied the housewife to a single butcher and a single grocer, so it clearly paid to be on good terms with them. Grocers might spare cheese rinds or scrapings from the bacon slicer which could be used for flavouring, butchers could provide bones to be boiled up for stock. There were alternatives. Communal dining economised on food, fuel and time. In May 1941 79,000,000 midday meals a week were being served on a communal basis; by December 1944 the figure was 170,000,000. Before the war only one child in 36 had their main meal of the day at school: by 1945 the figure was one in three. Factories employing over 250 people had by law to provide a canteen serving hot meals. Local authorities, supported by loans from central government, created a system of 'British Restaurants', largely manned by volunteers, which served bureaucrats but were open to the public and much patronised by office staff, workers in factories too small to have a canteen of their own, lorry drivers, refugees, servicemen on leave and the temporarily homeless. Some British Restaurants were actually located in town halls, others in schools or churches. London soon had over two hundred and they proved even more popular with the capital's inhabitants than they did in other parts of the country. Churchill, with characteristic flair, had himself coined their patriotic designation, rejecting with distaste the original bureaucratic term Community Feeding Centres – "Everybody associates the word 'restaurant' with a good meal and they may as well have the name if they cannot get any thing else." Names at least were not in short supply but were often misleading. A British Restaurant recipe for what was grandly titled Mock Turtle Soup *(see p. 27)* in fact relied for its main ingredients on left-over bones and vegetables, bacon rinds, gravy browning and herbs. Victory Pudding was an eggless sponge bulked out with grated potato, carrot and breadcrumbs. Another invaluable resource was the mobile kitchen, staffed by members of the Women's Voluntary Service, which took hot food to bomb-damaged areas to sustain both victims and members of the emergency services. London had over three hundred in operation, many sponsored by businessmen's clubs, trade unions and even clubs and societies in allied nations abroad.

J. Lyons and Co.'s chain of Corner Houses (see p. 91) and tea-shops proved a worthy exemplar of the bulldog spirit and many could match the Windmill Theatre's boast that "we never closed". The Oxford Street Corner House was out of action for three days in September 1940 because it had no water supply but even then managed to keep its 'Front Shop' trading. For 1/6d in 1942 a diner could choose from two starters, six main courses (fish, mince, curried vegetables or three kinds of salad) and four puddings plus coffee. Lyons' Brixton branch, able to open the morning after a raid because it had its own generators, was swamped with grateful customers and a 'Nippy' remembered that, because they were ordered to abandon their usual 'stations' to cope with the rush. "we couldn't recognise who we'd 'put down what for' so we just gave a bill for what we thought was OK ... our commission was the best we ever had."

Hotels and luxury restaurants were brought into line. From July 1940 onwards it was illegal to serve more than one more main course. The Blitz hit such elite establishments hard by making potential diners fearful of venturing out. It also changed attitudes to customers. A fireman recalled how, shortly after the outbreak of the war, he had been served most grudgingly in one West End establishment because he was still in uniform. When he returned, again in uniform, a year later and with his wife, the restaurant manager refused to present them with a bill — nothing was too good for a London fireman. From June 1942 there was a five shilling maximum on three-course restaurant meals. If bread was served it counted as a course. Luxury establishments were, however, allowed to make a 7s 6d cover charge. Many refused to accept bookings after 9.30, by which time the food had usually run out anyway, allowing some staff the chance to travel back to their homes while others slept over on the premises. The arrival of exuberant and well-paid Americans brought a welcome surge in business.

Resourceful chefs exploited the fact that such up-market delicacies as lobsters, shellfish, venison, hares and game birds — if they could be obtained — were not subject to rationing. In 1940 The Ivy was still full of "prosperous-looking people as usual, all eating a whacking good meal, meat, plovers and a delicious creamy pudding". In 1942 it was still able to offer smoked salmon, cold grouse and chocolate mousse but by 1944 it was down to oysters, elderly hens and Algerian wine. The eminent manager Mario Gallati confessed to shuddering at having to serve a mayonnaise concocted out of flour, mustard, powdered egg, vinegar and water. In her 1944 satire *Love on the Supertax* novelist Marghanita Laski lampooned the confections passed off at the fictional Mimosa restaurant in Mayfair — a 'Shellfish Cocktail', which was actually shredded cod disguised with a pink sauce made from the water a lobster had been boiled in and coloured with cochineal, a chicken main course which was actually rabbit and a 'chocolate' dessert made from custard powder and cocoa. Shortages of staff were as acute a problem as shortages of ingredients. Enemy aliens were rounded up on the outbreak of war, decimating the catering industry's labour force in particular. Hundreds of Soho Italians were long-term residents who had never bothered to take out naturalisation papers. Over seven hundred such aliens were herded onto the *Arandora Star* for deportation to detention camps in Canada. Four hours out of Liverpool she was torpedoed by a U-boat.

Special occasions required extraordinary expenditures of effort and ingenuity if the catering was in any way to resemble a pre-war occasion. In July 1940 the use of sugar to ice cakes was banned as wasteful. A parish clerk in suburban Pinner suggested that instead of regretting that they could not throw rice (also illegal) guests at a wedding should give the happy couple a packet of the precious commodity instead. Extra rations could, however, be applied for in the event of a wedding reception or a funeral, the number of guests being usually limited to forty, which provided a convenient excuse for trimming the list. Food parcels from abroad were another source of luxuries – a tin of ham or a packet of dried apricots – to be hoarded for Christmas or a birthday. The Ministry of Food's efforts must be judged a success, as must those of the Ministry of Agriculture. In 1939 Britain imported two-thirds of its food, in 1945 one-third. Six million additional acres of land were brought into cultivation. The number of allotments rose from 815,000 in 1939 to 1,400,000 in 1943. During World War One food prices rose by 130%, during World War Two by 20%. There was a black market but its operations were quite literally marginal, operating beyond the boundary of legality but on too small a scale to affect the overall effectiveness of the rationing system. There were moreover inspectors, working under cover, to keep the spivs' activities in check. Much food was bland and boring but the low-fat, high-fibre regime was good for the nation's health. The consumption of bread rose by 20%, of potatoes by 60%. Children and the poor especially benefited through guaranteed access to a minimum level of protein foods and vitamins. Average protein intake rose by 6%. The poorest were actually better fed than they had been in the depression years of the 1930s. In 1938 a third of the population had been discernibly undernourished, although it must be admitted that the incidence was far worse in the depressed industrial cities than in London. By 1941 this lowest third had been raised to the level of diet normal for a skilled workman in

employment. The incidence of deficiency diseases fell, as did infant mortality from 50 per 1,000 to 46.

Although German captives classified as hard-core Nazis were relocated to camps in the north and west many were initially held at football grounds or race courses around the capital and there were also camps at Stratford, Southgate, Kew, Tooting Bec and Harrow-on-the-Hill. Ironically German POWs were better fed than civilians, as they received the same rations as British servicemen – a weekly allowance of 42 ounces of meat, eight ounces of bacon, ten and a half ounces of margarine and five and a half pounds of bread. The Ministry of Food's official historian, R J Hammond, could record with justified satisfaction

> "the success of food rationing was something that the British people came to take for granted. Their satisfaction with control, generally speaking, varied directly with its completeness – it was the things amenable only partly, or not at all to rationing techniques, like fish, oranges or milk, that evoked complaint. They acknowledged the fairness of the system..."

In this they also acknowledged the example set by the Royal Family itself, if not always by top politicians. Mrs Eleanor Roosevelt never got over her visit to Buckinham Palace in October 1942 when she had been astonished to find herself eating grey-brown bread and spam off plates of solid gold.

THE AGE OF AUSTERITY
Throughout the Second World War rationing and the monotony of wartime diets had made food a common obsession and fantasising about post-war indulgences a popular pastime – in 1944, after five years of deprivation, the idea of having a fish course *and* a meat course *in a public place* could seem wildly outrageous. Victory, however, brought no bright gastronomic dawn. Self-indulgence had to be deferred. The return of servicemen from overseas increased the number of mouths to feed. At the same time most British Restaurants

closed down. In 1946, when British wheat was being sent to a starving Europe, bread, which had never been restricted throughout the war, became a rationed commodity. The extraction rate of flour was raised still further so that the already grey-brown bread became darker still. This lasted for two years. Bacon, egg and poultry rations were cut and dried egg became temporarily unavailable.

The reaction against continuing deprivation came not from frustrated foodies but from harassed housewives. In June 1945 vicar's wife Irene Lovelock formed the Anti-Queue Association in Croydon to protest at local shopkeepers acting like "domineering petty tyrants". On the other side of the metropolis Neasden rabbi's wife Alfreda Lansdau organised a similar movement. Uniting their efforts to establish the British Housewives League, together they won the backing of the London *Evening News* and the *Sunday Graphic.* In July 1946 the League forwarded to the Ministry of Food a petition against bread rationing which claimed to have 600,000 signatures.

The bizarrely severe late winter of 1947 was followed by a long hot summer, with inevitable damage to agricultural output. Weekly rations for adults hit their lowest point ever – 13 ounces of meat, one and a half of cheese, six of butter and margarine, one of cooking fat, eight of sugar, two pints of milk and a single egg. In 1948 there were destructive spring floods. Dr Magnus Pyke, then a scientific officer at the Ministry of Food, later a television personality, sent a report to the Cabinet warning that the wartime nutritional gains made by children were being lost. The visiting South African cricket team thoughtfully brought over gifts of tinned food.

By 1948 the limits of the long-suffering Londoners' powers of endurance was reached. An attempt to remedy protein shortages by importing eighteen million cans of tinned snoek, a virtually flavourless fish caught in South African waters, proved abortive. The very name

was off-putting and most of it ended up as cat-food. American visitors to post-war London found the food situation so depressing that many moved swiftly on to Paris where pre-war standards of gastronomy were swiftly restored. Londoners themselves were outraged by reports from British troops occupying defeated Austria that it was possible to buy as many bars of Cadbury's chocolate as one liked. Historian and gourmet Raymond Postgate *(see p. 199)* characterised London restaurant food as "sodden, sour, slimy, sloppy, stale or saccharined" – sometimes all six at once – and proposed founding a Society for the Prevention of Cruelty to Food. As far as he was concerned the only significant difference was between those restaurants that called themselves English and those that were foreign: "in the second case it would be dirtier but the food *might* have some taste."

As late as 1949 there were still London children who had never seen a banana or an orange. A brilliant Ealing Studios comedy *Passport to Pimlico* fantasised about a breakaway London borough which used its 'sovereignty' as an outpost of the former Duchy of Burgundy to institute a ration-free regime in defiance of the 'men from the Ministry'. When sweets were taken off the ration that year the shops were cleaned out in two days and rationing reinstated. *Punch* in 1949 noted the reappearance of the first Breton onion-seller much as though he were the first returning swallow, heralding a blazing summer of culinary excess. French cheeses also began to reappear in shops and on menus after an absence of a decade. In 1950, however, butchery students at Westminster Technical College were still learning their craft from drawings on a blackboard because they had so little opportunity to practise on real carcases. Rationing finally ended in 1954 when meat and sweets at last became available without limit.

28. Austerity at mealtimes was normal for residents of the Rowton Houses which housed itinerants and homeless men, respectably and economically. Of their kind Rowton Houses were regarded as a cut above the rest. A typical dining room is shown here in the 1950s.

THE 1950s

Hailed retrospectively by politicians as an 'age of affluence' because living standards rose 30% between 1955 and 1961, the 1950s saw memories of rationing fade. The British *felt* that they had endured, they had won and now they deserved to treat themselves. Raymond Postgate published the first *Good Food Guide* in 1951 to crusade against bad food. The accession of a young Queen inspired febrile hopes of a new Elizabethan age. The Gore Hotel at 189 Queen's Gate celebrated her coronation by opening an Elizabethan Room serving meals from the reign of the first Queen Elizabeth – boar, peacock and lamprey – in Elizabethan style, with wooden trenchers, pewter tableware, candlelight, troubadours etc. The 1951 Festival of Britain proclaimed the

benefits of new technologies which would transform daily life. Refrigerators, hitherto associated with frivolities like trifles and ice cream, were 'repositioned' in marketing terms to emphasise their value in maintaining food hygiene, diminishing waste (the spread of central heating nullified the effectiveness of the traditional larder) and saving the busy housewife time to devote to her family. Home-making represented a return to domestic normalcy rather than a mode of female self-denial. Joan Robins asserted in her briskly titled *Common Sense Cooking and Eating* (1953) that the evening meal remained "the main family event of the day and will be cherished and planned as such." This would have been especially true of the London region where commuting was the norm and it was not possible for most working adults to return home at mid-day for lunch, as more than half the working population still did as late as 1955. Rapidly changing consumption patterns revealed quite literally a hunger for what was tasty and convenient – sugar, sweets and processed convenience foods such as cake-mixes and sliced bread. In 1950 Sainsbury's opened Britain's first self-service store in London, and the first supermarket opened in Earl's Court in 1951.

London as the locus of women's magazine publishing and home of the BBC dominated the culinary aspirations of the nation. Television brought celebrity chefs – sensible Margeurite Patten, enthusiastic Philip Harben, pseudo-posh Fanny and Johnny Craddock and flamboyant Graham Kerr – into the living-room. London was also the home of increasingly influential cookery writers such as Elizabeth David and Constance Spry. The latter was initially far more influential but David's influence was to be seminal. *A Book of Mediterranean Food (1950)* was to be followed by *French Country Cooking (1951), Italian Food (1954)* and *Summer Cooking (1955).* Literary critic Auberon Waugh would hail her as the person who had done most to improve British life in the twentieth century. Journalist Katharine Whitehorn explained that Elizabeth David made cooking "seem colourful and fun and part of civilization."

The catering trade hesitantly began to follow Elizabeth David's lead. Mon Plaisir, opened in Monmouth Street in 1951, offered a bistro menu featuring French comfort food such as onion soup and cassoulet. In the suburbs growing affluence and the ever intensifying trend to white collar work encouraged aspirations to a mode of 'hostess cookery', which emphasised presentation and experimentation and the ability to make paté, canapes, vol-au-vents, souffles and flambé dishes. Fanny Craddock's 1950 publication was appropriately titled *The Ambitious Cook.* In servant-less semis the serving-hatch, the

electric plate-warmer and the hostess trolley became essential adjuncts to successful home entertaining. Meanwhile a new social being was seeking to escape the confining conventions of suburbia – the teenager. Teenagers' mounting earning-power in an era of labour shortage made them a rapidly expanding new market which encouraged the emergence of novel catering establishments, such as the coffee-bar and the Wimpy bar, serving a British version of the American hamburger. In 1953 Wimpies were first served at the Ideal Home Exhibition and at Wimbledon and by 1960 they were available at Buckingham Palace garden parties. In that same year Greater London had over five hundred coffee bars. One, the 2i's, in Soho, was to gain legendary status in the history of rock 'n' roll. Named for its first owners, the Irani brothers, it became a performance venue for the Beatles and visiting American icons such as Connie Francis and Little Richard as well as a launch-pad for the careers of Tommy Steele and Adam Faith, who, reincarnated as a successsful businesssman and actor, subsequently graduated to become a fixture in Fortnum & Mason's café.

THE 1960s

In 1972 food scientist and manic TV presenter Dr. Magnus Pyke published a book – *Technological Eating* – which revealed the extent to which modern methods of producing and processing foods were transforming the nation's food habits. Battery farming, for example, would increase the consumption of chicken per head twelve-fold in little more than a decade. Instant coffee, ideal for TV advert breaks, had become available in freeze-dried granules, which could be combined with "non-dairy creamer". Soft drinks became available in aluminium cans. For the benefit of a generation who vaguely remembered the labours of their mothers in baking cakes from the raw ingredients, cake mixes required the addition of eggs (which could actually have been substituted chemically to the mixture) in order to assuage their guilt at not 'really' cooking. Refrigeration strengthened its grip on the habits of hotelier and housewife. Spending on frozen foods, notably peas and fish fingers, rose from £7,500,000 in 1955 to £75,000,000 by 1963, although that still represented only 1.5% of total food expenditure. Purists like Elizabeth David deplored the loss of a sense of seasonality, "the pleasure of rediscovering each season's fruit and vegetables at the appropriate time is … quite blunted". The assumption that a refrigerator was part of every household's normal equipment led to changes in standard house design as provision for a larder simply disappeared. The visibility of technological changes caught the attention of commentators and perhaps distracted them from more profound social changes which were also changing the ways in which the British in general, and Londoners in particular, were eating. Longer commuting times and a growing trend to one-person households undermined the traditional 'full breakfast' just as more and more people became able to afford it. Compensatory mid-morning snacking was one result of this development. The trend to single person households became especially marked in larger cities, partly a result of increasing labour mobility, partly of the growth in student numbers, from 200,000 in 1961 to 390,000 in 1969. The consequent proliferation of 'bed-sit land' encouraged the emergence of 'take-away' outlets and cooking on gas-rings and miniature stoves, most notably the 'Baby Belling'. In 1961 Vesta Curries – 'just add water' – came on the market. In 1962 journalist Katharine Whitehorn published *Kitchen in a Corner* (later *Kitchen in a Bedsit*). Her approach was intensely practical.

"Cooking a decent meal in a bedsitter is not just a matter of finding something that can be cooked over a single gas ring. It is a problem of finding somewhere to put down the fork while you take off the lid and then finding somewhere else to put the lid".

But she was also piercingly philosophical:

"The principles of English cooking demand that a number of different foods should be cooked separately and served together. This is impossible on a gas ring … bedsitter people have far more natural kinship with nomads brewing up in the desert over a small fire of camel dung or impoverished Italian peasants eking out three shrimps and a lump of cheese with half a cartload of spaghetti."

In 1962 Len Deighton, a thriller writer and son of an hotel cook, published both *The Ipcress File* and *The Action Cookbook*. Between the two they hyped both snobbery and science in relation to cookery. Harry Palmer, Deighton's ex-criminal anti-hero, earns the disapproval of his secret service boss by paying over the odds for button mushrooms and insists on beginning his day with real coffee from freshly-ground beans. Deighton's cookbook, based on the strip cartoon instructions he published in the *Observer,* stressed system in the interests of simplicity, speed and certainty of outcome.

Those who had kitchens were less inclined to immure themselves in them and pass culinary wonders through a serving-hatch. Catching the spirit of Elizabeth David's Mediterranean message they increasingly made the kitchen rather than the dining-room the focus for family entertaining.

Despite its dominance in the cinema and popular music the tide of Americanisation was as yet only incipiently apparent in the culinary sphere. Londoners with transatlantic business contacts began to encounter the barbecue as an arena for male display. Television made more potential consumers aware of 'Cokes' and milk-shakes than could buy them. Not until 1972 would McDonald's open their first British branch, in Woolwich. More profound was the backwash of Empire. The aftermath of war, the continuing presence of POWs who had elected to settle in Britain, the continuing outflow of servicemen on National Service overseas and the influx of New Commonweath immigrants from Asia, Africa and the Caribbean all combined to

Ethnic eating – 2003

29. *Middle-Eastern falafels in Golborne Road, Notting Hill.*

30. *A Caribbean lunch club for senior citizens beneath Westway.*

31. *A great pun beneath Westway.*

32. *Turkish food in Upper Street, Islington, a thoroughfare of many cuisines.*

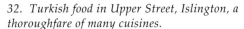

stimulate a growing demand for 'foreign' food. Whereas in 1950 Britain had only about a dozen Indian restaurants, by 1970 there were some two thousand. In 1964 London had the only Japanese restaurant in England and the only Thai restaurant in Europe. Eighth Army veterans brought back from the Italian campaign a taste for scampi. Former Italian POWs and postwar economic migrants opened trattoria *(see p. 112)* and delicatessen supplying what were then exotic rarities such as fresh pasta, garlic, olive oil and Parmesan cheese. The effect of foreign holidays should probably not be exaggerated. Although the number of British holidaymakers venturing abroad rose from 900,000 in 1950 to 2,000,000 by 1958 and most did go to Mediterranean countries where they could test the Elizabeth David doctrine for themselves, the majority went on package tours which attempted to insulate them from the unfamiliar. The publishing success of Elizabeth David's trail-blazing endeavours did encourage the publication of a broader range of cookery writing. In 1964 Scottish-American Lady Arabella Boxer struck an idiosyncratic note with *First Slice Your Cookbook.* Jane Grigson introduced the sceptical to *Charcuterie and French Pork Cookery* (1967) while those who shunned the pig in any form could find refuge and refreshment in Cairo-born Claudia Roden's A *Book of Middle Eastern Food* (1968). Prue Leith made her debut in the closing year of the decade with *Leith's All-Party Cook Book.* In 1960, aged twenty, she had started an outside catering service from her London bedsitter; by 1969 she had her own restaurant and by 1975 a cookery school as well. The advent of the *Sunday Times* colour supplement in 1962 created a vehicle for spreading an awareness of new food trends to readers who would not normally invest in substantial cookbooks.

Vegetarianism as yet made little headway with the general public, a fact conceded by the name chosen by the proprietors of a new (1961)

33. *English ethnic. Food to set you up for the day in Notting Hill.*

fifty-seater restaurant off 'swinging' Carnaby Street – Cranks. This venture would eventually become the first branch of Britain's only chain of vegetarian restaurants. In 1967 the Swiss-born Roux brothers opened Le Gavroche at 61 Lower Sloane Street. Michel had been a chef at the British embassy in Paris. Albert had previously worked as a chef at the French embassy in London. Tycoons were making their mark in the food sector. Tyro James Goldsmith founded Cavenham Foods in 1965 and would build it into Britain's third largest food empire. In 1968 Schweppes acquired Ty-Phoo Tea to add to a portfolio already containing Rose's Lime Juice, Apollinaris *(see p. 6)* and Dubonnet. In 1968 Brooke Bond merged with Liebig's Extract of Meat Co. Ltd to create the world's largest tea company, with 40,000 acres of plantations in Asia and Africa and 2,600,000 acres of ranches in Africa and South America. The merged company would in due course be absorbed into Unilever's empire. In 1969 Schweppes and Cadbury's also merged by a mutual exchange of shares.

PART TWO

Theory and Practice

BOOKS FOR COOKS

The London and royal printer Thomas Pynson published a *Boke of Cookery* as early as 1500 and his rival, Wynkyn de Worde the more famous *Boke of Kervynge* in 1508, thus establishing a genre which has been a mainstay of the publisher's backlist ever since, many volumes being reissued over the course of half a century or more. These pioneering titles were clearly aimed at the highest social echelons, as the introduction to the *Boke of Cookery* makes clear that it deals with "festes royalle" and is "a boke for a pryncis householde". The authors of many books remained anonymous, as in *A Proper Newe Booke of Cokerye* (?1545), *The Good Huswife's Handmaide* (?1588), *A Closet for Ladies and Gentlewomen* (1636), *The Widowe's Treasure* (1639) or *The Ladies Cabinet Opened* (1639).

Thomas Dawson's *The Good Huswife's Jewell* (1585) claimed to be based on the author's own practice. 'Imprinted at London for Edward White dwelling at the little North doore of Paules at the signe of the Gun', it was in its third edition by 1596. Its recipes included boiled larks, 'pigges feete and petitoes', 'fritters of Spinnedge', 'pigeons in black brothe', 'Mallard with Cabbadge', and 'Ducke with Turneps'. Dawson's recipe for a 'strong broth for sicke men' required a pound of almonds and the brains of a capon seasoned with cream, sugar and rose water.

Writing a cookery book did not apparently require that the author should himself be a cook. Sir Hugh Platt (1552-1608), son of a wealthy London brewer, dabbled in poetry before devoting himself to agriculture, notably experimenting with various types of manure in the gardens of his Bethnal Green house, Kirby Hall, where he also grew grapes. Platt's many other enthusiasms issued in volume form as *Delights for Ladies to Adorn their Persons, Tables, Closets and Distillatories, with Bewties, Banquets, Perfumes and Waters* (1602) which contained advice on cookery, distilling, housewifery and recipes for preserving fruits, making cosmetics and dyeing hair. These included directions 'To make an excellent Marchpane paste to print off in moulds for banqueting dishes' and 'To preserve Cowcumbers all the yeere'. Despite the fact that – or perhaps because? – Platt's recipes were written with the dry self-confidence of instructions for a chemical experiment, his book evidently met an eager readership, going through seven further editions after the author's death, the last published in 1656.

Like Mrs. Beeton *(see p. 63)*, Gervase Markham (?1568-1637), regarded culinary skills as the guarantor of domestic contentment. In *The English Huswife: Containing the Inward and Outward Virtues Which Ought to Be in a Complete Woman* (1625) he stated his case unequivocally:

"To speak then of the outward and active knowledges which belong to our English housewife I hold the first and most principal to be a perfect skill and knowledge in cookery, together with all the secrets belonging to the same, because it is a duty really belonging to the woman. And she that is utterly ignorant therein may not by the laws of strict justice challenge the freedom of marriage because she can indeed perform but half her vow, for she may love and obey, but she cannot serve and keep him with that true duty which is ever expected.

To proceed then to this knowledge of cookery you shall understand that the first step thereunto is to have knowledge of all sorts of herbs belonging to the kitchen, whether they be for the pot, for salads, for serving, or for any other seasoning or adorning, which skill of knowledge of the herbs, she must get by her own labour and experience, and not by my relation, which would be much too tedious. And for the use of them she shall see it in the composition of dishes and meats hereafter following. She shall also know the time of the year, month and moon in which all herbs are to be sown, and when they are in their best flourishing, that gathering all herbs in their height of goodness, she may have the prime use of the same."

Cookery, for Markham, was, if central, still only a part of a total curriculum of domestic accomplishment summarised in his book "Contayning the inward and outward vertues which ought to be in a compleat woman: As, her skill in Physicke, Cookery, Banquetting-Stuffe, Distillation, Perfume, Wool, Hemp, Flax, Dayries, Brewing, Baking and all other things belonging to an Household."

Markham, an ex-soldier, has a plausible claim to being London's first hack writer. (He claimed that *The English Huswife* was actually the work of a lady of rank, whose manuscript jottings he had merely organised. Interestingly his mode of arrangement was to organise chapters by method of preparation rather than categories of meat or fish as French authors did). Proficient in five foreign languages, Markham was a mediocre poet and dramatist, but fared better with his numerous practical handbooks on horsemanship, hunting and husbandry.

If Markham's main qualification for writing about cookery was his willingness to write about almost anything, the same accusation cannot be laid against John Murrell, author of *"A Delightfull Daily Exercise for Ladies and Gentlewomen, whereby is set foorth the secrete Misteries of the purest Preservings in Glasse and other Confrictionaries, as making of Breads, Pastes, Preserves, Suckets, Marmalates, Tart Stuffes, Rough Candies, with many other Things never before in print, whereto is added a Booke of cookery by John Murrell, professor thereof."* Published in 1625, this was evidently not Murrell's first publication although his previous works have not survived. In 1630 he published a further volume, *"A new Booke of Cookerie, with the newest art of Carving and Serving all set forth according to the now new English and French fashion".* Murrell's major work achieved its seventh edition in 1650. His recipes still include such medieval treats as boar and swan as well as baked curlews and blackbirds, salads of mallow or burdock roots, pasties filled with rabbit livers, sheeps' tongue pie, a vegetarian 'Fridayes Pye', baked tench 'with a pudding in her belly' and 'pancakes so crispe you may set them upright'. There was also a specific section on London Cookerie with formulae for capons with rice, oysters and pickled lemons or pippins, chickens with lettuce, rabbits with gooseberries or claret, duck with mussels and pigeons with capers or samphire. Murrell was obviously something of a celebrity chef because he took on paying pupils and used his books to advertise utensils and moulds of his own devising, on sale at his publisher's premises. *A True Gentlewoman's Delight Wherein Is Contained All Manner of Cookery* first appeared in 1653, bound up in a single volume with *A Choice Manual of Rare and Select Secrets in Physics and Surgery.* Over the course of the next fifty-five years *A True Gentlewoman's Delight* was to be reprinted twenty-one times. Both works have been attributed to Elizabeth de Grey, Countess of Kent (1581-1651), sometime employer of Robert May and owner of a house in Whitefriars. Elizabeth David questioned the Countess's authorship of the cookery section of the joint work, emphasising her eminence as a healer and the marked difference in style between the two parts.

Interest in French culinary techniques pre-dated the return of Charles II from exile in 1660. La Varenne's celebrated treatise of 1651 appeared in translation as *The French Cook* a bare two years later. In 1682 Charles II's master cook, Giles Rose, published a translation of Ribou's twenty-year-old *Perfect School of instructions for Officers of the Mouth*. Massialot's *Le Cuisinier roial et bourgeois* of 1691 was translated in 1702 with a slightly but significantly different title – *The Court and Country Cook*. Thirty years later Lord Chesterfield's French chef, Vincent La Chapelle, reversed the flow by publishing *The Modern Cook* in English *before* producing an expanded version in French.

Robert May, like John Murrell, was a professional. May's *The Accomplisht Cook, or the Art and Mastery of Cookery* (1660) summarised a lifetime's experience; one imagines few others would have been able to conjure up sixteen different ways of serving eels. His prescription for a spring salad combined spinach, sorrel, beets, currants and a sliced lemon, dressed with oil and red wine vinegar. Another mixes watercress and violets. May also included instructions for making egg shells full of scented water for ladies to throw at each other and pies filled with live frogs and birds. The son of a cook, May had also studied abroad and referred to Italian and Spanish cuisines appreciatively but was disparaging of the French, although he had lived in France and spoke French. This did not, however, prevent him from filching recipes from Varenne. Revised by the author in 1665, *The Accomplisht Cook* was reissued in 1685. Despite the fact that it was profusely illustrated with over two hundred 'Figures', May's book thereafter went out of print and thus achieved an active shelf-

life less than half as long as that of the posthumous publication attributed to his erstwhile employer, the Countess of Kent. May wrote as a professional chef for other professional chefs and his book thus differed markedly from the 'housewifely' compilations of Markham *et al.*, concentrating on cooking only and omitting medical remedies, cosmetic formulae and rules of etiquette and household

34. The frontispiece of this housewife's handbook of 1677 illustrates the allied arts of making preserves, medicines, cosmetics and meals.

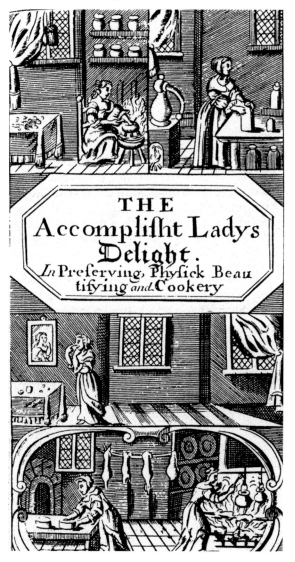

management, an 'omission' explicitly picked up by Robert Smith in his *Court Cookery* (1723).

> "I have not, indeed, filled my book with washes and beautifiers for ladies or making of ale for country squires, all of which is foreign to my purpose; and a person that's well acquainted with cookery cannot also be acquainted in clearing the skin ...".

Others in this genre include William Rabisha's *The Whole Body of Cookery Dissected* (1661), Patrick Lamb's *Royal Cookery; or, the Complete Court Cook* (1710). and Charles Carter's *The Complete Practical Cook* (1730). *The Closet of the Eminently Learned Sir Kenelme Digbie Kt., Opened* (1669), probably owes much of its compilation to George Hartman, Digby's assistant. The much-travelled Digby (1603-65), a member of Charles II's court circle, was a natural writer, qualified doctor, amateur scientist, soldier, privateer and bon viveur. Over a hundred of his recipes were actually for drinks, especially Meath (mead) and Metheglin, many credited to members of his wide circle of acquaintance, from the Countess of Dorset to 'the Muscovian Ambassador's Steward' to the king's own mead-maker. Digby's recipes for such 'English classics' as black pudding or pease pudding show that the gentry class who were his intended readers clearly enjoyed many of the same dishes, made from everyday ingredients, as their social inferiors did. The third edition of Digby's book was reprinted as an historical curiosity in 1910.

Ex-governess Mrs Hannah Woolley, a resident of Hackney, and then, as Mrs Challinor, of Westminster, wrote prolifically on domestic topics, including specialist works on *Choice experiments of Preserving and Candying* (1661) and *Receipts and rare Waters for Beautifying the Face and Body* (1672). Unusually for writers of cookery books, who frequently plundered their rivals' works without scruple or thanks, she was honest in acknowledging her debts to others, in particular Robert May. *The Gentlewoman's Companion; or A Guide to the Female Sex* (1672) combines advice on conduct with guidance on cookery and thus ranges from 'Rules to be observed in walking with persons of honour and how you ought to behave your self in congratulating and condoling them' to 'Quaint Directions for the Carving of all manner of Fowl', recipes for 'An Almond-Pudding in Guts' and 'Ox-cheeks baked in a Pie' and tips on 'Venison, how to recover when tainted' or 'How to cure the bloody Flux'.

The Cook's and Confectioner's Dictionary published by John Nott in 1723 was based on classic works such as those of May, Digby and the French master chefs. This process of reproduction would continue inexorably. Nott's recipe for apple Black Caps was copied in John Middleton's *Five Hundred New Recipes in Cookery* (1734), then appears in a slightly revised version in Hannah Glasse *(see below)*, from which it was lifted by John Farley *(see p. 160)* – or rather by his ghost. Nott's work, evidently the summation of a lifetime's professional experience, was reissued in two printings in 1724, three in 1726 and four in 1733.

HANNAH GLASSE – A GEORGIAN DELIA

Neither the date of her birth nor of her death *(?*1770) are known for certain. What can be said for certain is that Hannah Glasse's best-selling cookery book was first published in 1747 and, as it went through nine considerably enlarged editions by 1765, we may assume that it was not a posthumous publication. Modestly entitled *"The Art of Cookery Made Plain and Easy, which far Exceeds any Thing of the kind ever yet Published... By a Lady, London"* (two guarantees of quality?), it was self-published ('Printed for the Author') and offered for sale at "Mrs. Ashburn's, a China-Shop, the Corner of Fleet Ditch", which sounds rather less than appetising. The author's assumed anonymity was indirectly betrayed by the fact that the list of two hundred subscribers for the first edition included a Mrs Glasse of Carey Street (famed as the home of the insolvency courts) and a Mr Glasse, Attorney at Law, who clearly liked to live near his work. (Curiously, there appears in the list of bankrupts for May 1754, published in the *Gentleman's Magazine,* the name of 'Hannah Glass of St. Paul's, Co. Garden, Warehouse-keeper'.) Addressing her intended reader in a prefatory note Mrs Glasse explained the unusual mission she had imposed upon herself:

"I have attempted a branch of Cookery which Nobody has yet thought worth their while to write upon... If I have not wrote in the high polite Stile I hope I shall be forgiven, for my Intention is to instruct the lower Sort and therefore must treat them in their own way."

Mrs Glasse's intended contribution lay not so much in making cookery plain and easy but *in making the explanation of it so.*

"For Example, when I bid them lard a Fowl, if I should bid them lard with large Lardoons, they would not know what I meant. But when I say lard with little Pieces of Bacon they know what I mean ... the great Cooks have such a high way of expressing themselves that the poor Girls are at a loss to know what they mean."

Confident of her own powers of communication, she predicted that "every Servant who can but read will be capable of making a tollerable good Cook and those who have the least Notion of Cooking can't miss of being very good ones." As this quotation implies Mrs Glasse's intended market was to be the female one: "should I be so happy as to gain the good Opinion of my own Sex I desire no more, that will be a full Recompence for all my Trouble." The extravagance of French cooking came in for a severe kicking in the course of the subsequent text:

"if Gentlemen will have French Cooks, they must pay for French Tricks. A Frenchman, in his own Country, would dress a fine Dinner of twenty Dishes and all genteel and pretty, for the Expence he will put an English Lord to for dressing one Dish. But then there is the little petty Profit. I have heard of a Cook that used six Pounds of Butter to fry twelve eggs, when every Body knows, that understands Cooking, that Half a Pound is full enough ... But then it would

not be French. So much is the blind Folly of this Age, that they would rather be impos'd on by a French Booby, than give Encouragement to a good English Cook!"

Mrs Glasse's compilation contained the first known recipe for gooseberry fool and also included two recipes for home-made medicines, – one "A certain Cure for the Bite of a Mad Dog, attributed to Dr Mead" (the royal physician), the other a prophylactic to ward off plague "of very great service to those who go Abroad."

By the time the fourth edition appeared in 1751 the title page bore a facsimile signature in the name of H Glasse. On the fly-leaf opposite the title-page was an elaborate advertisement in copper-plate hand, announcing Hannah Glasse as 'Habit Maker to Her Royal Highness the Princess of Wales in Tavistock Street, Covent Garden'.

A subsequent work, tentatively dated by the British Museum at 1770, bore the authenticating sobriquet "By H. Glasse. Author of the "Art of Cookery" and was entitled *The Compleat Confectioner: or the Whole Art of Confectionery Made Plain and Easy &c &c.* Obtainable from the same China-Shop outlet, it was likewise addressed to a no-nonsense readership, having an introductory address 'To the Housekeepers of Great Britain and Ireland'.

Mrs Glasse's *'The Servants' Directory, or Housekeeper's Companion'* was published in 1770. Evidently capitalising on her fame, she had clearly reversed the pledge she had originally made in *The Art of Cookery* not to pontificate on "the Oeconomy" of the family because any sensible reader would already know best what needed to be done and rightly ignore any "Nonsense of that Kind". Hannah Glasse appears to have got right up the nose of the appropriately-named Ann Cook, a professional whose *Professed Cookery* (1754) is prefaced by a lengthy diatribe against her rival, stressing her technical errors and extravagances no less than the French she affected to despise. (Jennifer

Stead's painstaking study reveals that at least one in four of Glasse's recipes can be attributed to other writers).

Hannah Glasse's reputation also outlasted her long enough to become a subject for satire. In 1800 Elizabeth Cobbold, writing under the pseudonym of Carolina Petty Pasty, prefaced her poetical skit 'The Mince Pye' with a portrait of Mrs Glasse. Already well-established on the other side of the Atlantic, *The Art of Cookery* appeared in an American edition in 1805.

MASTER AND PUPIL

Marie-Antoine ('Antonin') Careme (1784-1833) reinvented French cookery as the standard by which other European cuisines measured themselves. As chef to Talleyrand at the Congress of Vienna, which met for months to settle the map of Europe after the defeat of Napoleon, Careme himself became a figure of continental repute. The self-taught son of a Parisian labourer, he had allegedly been turned out onto the streets at nine and served his apprenticeship in a working-man's restaurant before being spotted by the confectioner Bailly, who encouraged him not only to cook but to read and to draw. A frustrated architect, Careme came to specialise in confecting massive table-pieces of staggering complexity representing ruins, temples or fortresses in sugar, marzipan and lard: hundreds of his designs were reproduced in his books *Le Patissier Royal* and *Le Patissier Pittoresque*. Careme also excelled in the preparation of cold buffets, using aspic to seal in the flavour of pre-cooked dishes. After two years with Bailly, Careme was taken on by Talleyrand, initially as his pastry-cook. In 1804 his new employer set him a professional challenge – to devise menus for an entire year, using only seasonal produce, and without repetition. After twelve years Careme finally outclassed his mentor, Talleyrand's chef de cuisine, Bourcher.

After the Congress of Vienna Careme came to London in the service of the Prince of Wales *(see p. 174)*. His stay lasted only two years. The other kitchen staff resented his star status and the climate depressed him. After a similarly abortive foray to work for the Tsar of Russia, he returned to Paris in the service of the British ambassador. Perhaps, as a Frenchman, he particularly appreciated the acknowledgment by his country's former enemy that in one field, at least, France remained invincible. Careme's recipe for Lady Morgan English fish soup certainly assumed that the pockets of the English milord were bottomless (though, admittedly, it was first prepared in the house of Baron de Rothschild) – the twenty-five ingredients included twenty-four each of crayfish tails, shrimp and oysters, plus a bottle of champagne and a *pound* of truffles. Lady Morgan's own tribute to Careme's creative expertise is notable for its listing of the absence of what were evidently familiar features of contemporary English cooking: "no high-spiced sauces, no dark brown gravies, no flavour of cayenne and allspice, no tincture of catsup and walnut pickle . ...."

The basis of Careme's cuisine was a trio of sauces – espagnole, veloute and béchamel – which could be elaborated into a hundred more variant forms. Elaborate preparation was a marked feature of almost every recipe, involving labour-intensive sieving, straining, concentrating or reducing. Careme's last major publication was a massive three-volume survey of *L'Art de la Cuisine Française au Dix-Neuvième Siècle* which became a canonical text and also confirmed the notion that a great chef should summarise his experience and achievements in a synoptic review of his craft.

Born in London of Italian descent, Charles Elme Francatelli (1805-76) was educated in France and studied under Careme. After serving as chef in a succession of aristocratic English households Francatelli found a larger forum for his talents at Crockford's, the exclusive gambling club, where he succeeded Ude *(see p. 58)*. From there he moved on to serve the royal household itself before taking over the Coventry House Club, then working for seven years as

35. The old Freemasons' Tavern in Great Queen Street. Drawing by J. Nixon, 1811. At this time it was favoured as a venue by the Canada Club – see p. 137.

chef to the Reform Club in succession to Soyer *(see p. 59)*. From there he went on to manage the St James's Hotel in Berkeley Street, Piccadilly and finally the Freemasons' Tavern. Running parallel with his managerial career, Francatelli developed an equally successful public profile as an author. His *The Modern Cook*, first published in 1845, ran to twelve editions. In 1852 came a *Plain Cookery Book for the Working Classes*, which included recipes for such humble and 'classically English' dishes as Pigs Trotters and Plum Duff. This was followed in 1861 with *The Cook's Guide and Butler's Assistant*. Like his contemporary, Alexis Soyer, Francatelli had not allowed his association with the rich and powerful to blunt his social conscience, and, like all good kitchen managers, he deplored waste, remarking that he could easily feed a thousand families a day on the food thrown away in London. Being familiar with French lifestyles Francatelli knew how important haricot beans were as a staple of French peasant diet and wished that some way might be found to popularise them amongst the British proletariat. Francatelli's own special field of expertise was celebrated in 1862 with the publication of his *Royal English and Foreign Confectionery Book*. Francatelli was sufficiently famed in his day for his endorsement of Liebig's Extract of Meat still to be featured prominently in the company's advertising twenty years after his death. He was also included in the first edition of the *Dictionary of National Biography* and the 1911 edition of the *Encyclopaedia Britannica*. A brief trawl through the Internet reveals that in 2003 Francatelli's *Modern Cookery* recipes were still being used in New York's Institute of Culinary Education, in the Servants' Hall Restaurant at Lanhydrock House, Cornwall (where it was referred to on the menu as their 'culinary Bible') and in Westfield, Ontario ('The Village where time stands still'). The promotional campaign to revive sales of Welsh meat in the aftermath of the 2001 foot and mouth debacle was likewise pleased to invoke Francatelli's memory – by quoting his endorsement "Welsh Lamb from the rolling hills of Wales must surely be the best in the World and an unique delicacy."

THE COOK'S ORACLE

While the names of Grimod de la Revniere and Brillat-Savarin are still honoured as founding fathers of gourmet writing, their English contemporary, William Kitchiner (?1775-1827) is all but forgotten, despite the fact that he not only enjoyed and wrote about food, but also frequently prepared it himself and was responsible for such bizarre-sounding delicacies as spatchcocked eels and wow-wow sauce and a recipe for 'Tomata Catsup'. Kitchiner would nowadays be classified as a lifestyle guru, being the author of handbooks on keeping household accounts and managing a horse and carriage and such works as *The Art of Invigorating and Prolonging Life by Food Clothes, Air, Exercise, Wine, Sleep etc., Peptic Precepts to prevent and relieve Indigestion* and *The Pleasure of Making a Will*. He was also an expert on optics. published a collection of patriotic songs and invented a stove with rotary hotplates for use at sea. Kitchiner styled himself 'Dr' but there is no conclusive proof of a medical qualification from the University of Glasgow, which he claimed as his *alma mater*. A Scottish degree, in any case, did not at that time qualify him to practise in England. Fortunately he inherited a fortune of over £60,000 from his father, a coal-porter who had become a wealthy coal-merchant. Thus free to indulge the interests of a dilettante, Kitchiner experimented and entertained at his home, 43 Warren Street, off Fitzroy Square. Aided by Henry Osborne, personal chef to the President of the Royal Society, Sir Joseph Banks, Kitchiner not only prepared many dishes himself but also did his own shopping and even the washing up.

Kitchiner regularly organised celebrated

36. *William Kitchiner. The use of a stuffed tiger as a hat-stand does hint at a certain cultivated eccentricity.*

Wednesday evening *conversazioni* for a select circle of friends, known as the Committee of Taste. A stickler, not to say fanatic, for regularity and punctuality – all meals in his house were served to the sound of a clock striking the hour or half-hour – Kitchiner expected acceptance of his printed invitations within twenty-four hours. Failure to reply in writing within the time limit was deemed a refusal. Lateness was regarded as unforgivable and punished accordingly – "The Specimens will be placed upon the table at Half past Five o'clock precisely, when the Business of the day will immediately commence"; at which time the street door was locked. (The Committee's official motto was BETTER NEVER THAN LATE). This implacable rule was decreed in deference to the fact that the "perfection of several of the Preparations is so exquisitely evanescent, that the delay of One Minute after their arrival at the Meridian of Concoction, will render them no longer worthy of Men of Taste." Kitchiner was likewise insistent that coffee should only be made from beans which had just been roasted and ground. Guests were expected to depart either when a further supper was served at half past nine or on the stroke of eleven.

Apart from the eminent Banks, the 'Men of Taste' routinely included Dr John Haslam, a specialist in mental illness, the poets Samuel Rogers *(see p. 164)* and Hans Busk, actors Charles Mathews and Charles Kemble, dramatists George Colman and Charles Dibdin, the celebrated tenor John Braham, the humorous writers Theodore Hook, William Jerdan and Thomas Hood and the architects Sir John Soane and Philip Hardwick. The guest list on any one occasion was normally limited to six or eight. More rarely Kitchiner issued invitations to lunch or informal suppers. The Prince of Wales *(see p. 174)* certainly accepted one of these on more than one occasion.

Recipes tested before the Committee of Taste, over six hundred of them, were published by Kitchiner as *Apicius Redivivus or The Cook's Oracle* in 1817. This work was prefaced with the usual immodest self-congratulation customary among authors of cookery books: "This is the only English Cookery Book which has been written from the real experiments of a housekeeper for the benefit of housekeepers, which the reader will soon perceive by the minute attention that has been employed to elucidate and improve the ART OF PLAIN COOKERY." Kitchiner also claimed to be the first to include precise weights and measures with his recipes.

Contemporaries hailed *The Cook's Oracle* as a masterpiece and it remained in favour for decades afterwards. The book reached its seventh edition in 1840. The 1868 edition of *Enquire Within upon Everything* quoted Dr Kitchiner's Rules for Marketing at length. They can, however, be summarised briefly – don't be a cheapskate. Deal with respectable tradesmen, pay cash and don't waste time looking for false bargains which will invariably be sub-standard fare: "All the skill of the most accomplished

cook will avail nothing unless she is furnished with prime provisions." He did, however, favour taking advantage of natural opportunities for bargaining: "butchers on a Saturday night in summer will sell upon almost any terms, as the meat, although perfectly good and fit for eating on Sunday would not resist the assault of Captain Green until Monday. Upon these occasions, a fine joint of veal or lamb may often be purchased for 3d or 4d a pound."

Ironically in view of his obsesssion with early rising, healthy eating and a strictly ordered regimen, Kitchiner died at fifty-two, *apparently* of a heart attack, the day before he was due to sign a new will disinheriting his illegitimate, wastrel son.

A Philosopher in the Kitchen

If he were remembered for nothing else Louis Eustache Ude should at least be credited with introducing the term soufflé and the rum baba to English. A refugee from the revolution in France, Ude was much given to the sort of philosophical reflection and bold generalisation characteristic of the French intellectual tradition, much of which boils down to stating a platitude with attitude – as in Ude's observation that "there are cooks and cooks, as there are painters and painters. The difficulty lies in finding the perfect one." Quite. As arrogant and temperamental as any modern celebrity chef, Ude certainly took an exalted view of his craft:

"What science demands more study than Cookery? You have not only, as in other arts, to satisfy the general eye, but also the individual taste of the person who employs you; you have to attend to economy, which every one demands; to suit the taste of different persons at the same table; to surmount the difficulty of procuring things which are necessary to your work; to undergo the want of unanimity among the servants of the house; and the mortification of seeing unlimited confidence sometimes reposed in persons who are unqualified to give orders in the kitchen ... and giving themselves airs which are almost out of reason and which frequently discourage the Cook."

Having quit the royal kitchens of the late King Louis XVI, where he had been head chef, Ude found employment first with Princess Letizia Bonaparte and then with the Duke of Sefton, whom he served for over twenty years. He then became steward to the United Service Club in London and worked for the Duke of York. In 1828 Ude was appointed chef at Crockford's, London's most fashionable and exclusive gambling club, at the astonishing salary of a thousand guineas a year. On the whole he thought the English unappreciative of culinary excellence, a national failing he blamed on the fact that they were not introduced to their parents' table till their palates had been completely benumbed by the strict diet observed in the nursery and boarding-schools. Ude's gastronomic philosophy permeates his book *The French Cook: or, The Art of Cookery developed in all its various branches* (1813) with counsels of perfection. The ideal cook will be as industrious as intelligent, an efficient manager of time and staff, sober and devoted to the mastery of his craft. balancing creativity with economy, pleasing the eye as well as the palate and always remembering that the satisfaction of the diner must take precedence over the *amour propre* of the chef. *The French Cook* went through eight editions by 1827.

COOK WITH A CONSCIENCE

Florence Nightingale is naturally the central and dominating figure in the National Portrait Gallery painting which shows her attending sick and wounded soldiers from the fighting front in the Crimean War (1854-6). The artist placed himself, discreetly sketching, in a window behind her, screened by bars. At the far left of the picture, clutching an umbrella, beneath a broad-brimmed hat and dressed in unmistakably civilian attire, stands a portly but equally self-effacing figure. Ironically it is only thus, as a marginal figure depicted in the

37. *Alexis Benoit Soyer, sketched by his English wife. A Memoir of his remarkable life appeared within months of his death.*

unlikely setting of a casualty clearing station, that the national pantheon of the great and the good records the existence of Britain's first celebrity chef.

Alexis Soyer (1809-58) was born, the youngest son of a small shopkeeper, in Meaux-en-Brie on the Maine. That the name of his birthplace should combine the celebrated names of both a mustard and a cheese was fortuitously prophetic. Apprenticed cook at twelve, Soyer served a five-year training before being taken on in the restaurant of M. Douix on the Boulevard des Italiens, where he stayed for three years, quickly becoming head chef over a staff of twelve. In 1830 he became second cook to Prince Polignac at the French foreign office but the outbreak of revolution in July of that year brought down the government and with it ended his employment. Fleeing France, Soyer joined his brother Philippe in the kitchen of the Duke of Cambridge in London. He was soon cook to the Duke of Sutherland, from whose employ he passed to the Marquis of Waterford and the Marquis of Ailsa before being appointed chef at the Reform Club in 1837. In the same year he married a precociously talented young British painter, Elizabeth Jones.

At that time the Reform Club was housed in temporary premises at 104 Pall Mall and then removed to Gwydyr House (now the Welsh Office) on Whitehall. Notwithstanding these disruptions Soyer, on the occasion of Queen Victoria's coronation in June 1838, rose triumphantly to the challenge of preparing a breakfast for two thousand people. When the Reform Club finally moved into its permanent Pall Mall premises in 1841 Soyer installed gas-ovens which were to become one of the capital's more offbeat visitor attractions. The scepticism and snobbery of professional colleagues blocked the general adoption of gas in cooking for another thirty years but Soyer was unshaken in his belief that this technological advance represented "the greatest comfort ever introduced into any culinary arrangement". Soyer's individualism as a professional was similarly exhibited in his dress. Eschewing the white double-breasted jacket and stiff, pleated toque decreed by Careme *(see p. 55)*, Soyer dressed in a style he called "a la zoug-zoug" and had his work attire tailor-made with such 'impractical' features as large lapels and cuffs. Initially adopting a chef's hat made of red velvet, he later opted for a black skull cap with a tassel. Soyer's personal life was blighted in 1842 when his pregnant wife, Elizabeth, was so distressed by a terrible thunderstorm that she miscarried and died at the age of twenty-nine. The grieving husband erected an extravagant monument to her memory at Kensal Green cemetery.

In 1846, the year in which he produced a notable banquet for the visiting Egyptian

38. The kitchen at the Reform Club, from a drawing by G B Moore, published in London Interiors, *c.1860. The central figure is probably Alexis Soyer. Note the prevalence of female staff.*

viceroy, Ibrahim Pasha, Soyer published his *Gastronomic Regenerator, a simplified and new system of Cookery,* which sold two thousand copies, despite being priced at a guinea. This contains a recipe for what some three decades later would be known as Cumberland Sauce – a compound of port, redcurrant jelly, oranges and mustard to go with boar's head; this sauce, despite its name, Soyer himself referred to as German in origin. The book also contains the first mention in English of a flan in the sense of an open tart. As well as recipes, the *Gastronomic Regenerator* also contained plans and drawings for model kitchens, from those of the Reform Club to examples for a humble cottage.

In 1847 Soyer joined the campaign to relieve the appalling sufferings of the victims of famine in Ireland. Not content with writing letters to the press, in April 1847 he accepted a commission from the government to go to Ireland where, on the Royal Barracks Esplanade in Dublin, he organised emergency kitchens to dispense rations of soup and meat at half the usual cost. He also published a sixpenny book *Soyer's Charitable Cookery or the Poor Man's Regenerator.* Aware that there was hunger enough in London as well, in 1848 Soyer exhibited a hundred and forty of his late wife's works as *Soyer's Philanthropic Gallery,* to raise funds for the Spitalfields soup kitchen *(see p. 187).* He also greatly boosted his own fortunes with the invention of a 'magic' spirit stove small enough to enable dishes to be cooked at the table. With his usual flair for publicity he gave daily demonstrations of its use before admiring audiences at his office at 15 Charing Cross. *The Observer* paid fulsome tribute to Soyer's eminence:

> "At present we do not know of any person who administers more assiduously and effectively to our corporeal wants – at least the most craving of them – than the renowned Soyer ... Now that he has abandoned the service of the Reform Club we see him erecting soup kitchens for a famishing nation; inventing a 'magic stove' for the benefit of the affluent classes; distilling a cooling water to 'quench the spark in the throat' and compounding a sauce which undoubtedly will prove 'a relish' to the most used-up of palates. M. Soyer is an artist as profound as he is versatile"

In 1849 Soyer published *The Modern Houswife: Comprising Nearly 1,000 Receipts for the economic and judicious preparation of every meal of the day, with those of the Nursery and Sick-room.* The book went to a second edition within a fortnight.

By May 1850 Soyer was ready to embrace his most ambitious project to date. Preparations were already well advanced for the realisation of Prince Albert's visionary enterprise, The Great Exhibition of the Arts and Industry of All Nations, scheduled to be held in Hyde Park in the summer of 1851. Inspired by the seductively glittering prospect of opening a top-line restaurant to cater for the anticipated millions of visitors, Soyer took over Gore House, former home of the disgraced society hostess, Marguerite, Countess of Blessington, who had fled to France to escape her debts. Not only did Gore House stand almost opposite the exhibition site but its grounds also afforded sufficient space for the erection of a 'Baronial Banqueting House' and a 'Pavilion of All Nations' four hundred feet long. Soyer's ecumenical palate allegedly drew the line at New Zealand, as he allegedly joked at the impropriety of preparing "baked young woman for two or boiled missionary". The opening of *Soyer's Gastronomic Symposium of All Nations* was a huge success, thanks largely to the press coverage vigorously orchestrated by tyro journalist George Augustus Sala *(see p. 65),* an enthusiastic backer of the project. Soyer's daring essay into mass-catering brought in £21,000 – but cost £28,000.

Soyer recovered his fortunes by once more taking up his pen to compile a monumental *History of Food in all Ages* (1853), whose three thousand references reveal the scope of his learning, as well as another popular work *A*

39. An East End soup kitchen for children.

40. Gore House in Kensington, scene of Soyer's most extravagant investment in 1851.
Watercolour by Thomas H. Shepherd, c.1850.

Shilling Cookery Book for the People (1855), which sold a quarter of a million copies by 1867. In its intentions *The Shilling Cookery* was more an act of philanthropy than a money-making venture as Soyer agreed to a payment of just £50 for the first edition of ten thousand copies and pledged not to attach his name to any other publication at a similar or lower price. Within four months sales had reached 110,000.

Like most of his adopted countrymen Soyer was both moved and angered by reports of the needless suffering of British soldiers in the Crimea. In February 1855 he volunteered his services to the government in support of Florence Nightingale's efforts to aid the wounded, diseased and dying. Visiting the theatre of operations at his own expense, Soyer reorganised the diets and victualling of the hospitals at Scutari, Constantinople and Balaklava and additionally took on the cooking for an entire division of the army in the field. The 'cooking wagon' he devised was soon adopted by the army as its official field stove and in its essentials remained in use until the Second World War. Soyer did not return to London until 1857 when he published a handbook entitled *Soyer's Culinary Campaign, with the plain Art of Cookery for Military and Civil Institutions.* Perhaps realising that the manly palate relished a challenge, or perhaps suspecting that insipid or sub-standard ingredients might need muscular assistance, Soyer included in this volume a recipe for an aptly named 'Universal Devil's mixture', which compounded horseradish with pepper, cayenne, mustard and chillis. In March of the following year he lectured at the United Services' Institute on cooking for the army and navy.

Continuing his commitment to the public sector, Soyer next reformed the dietary arrangements of the government emigration commissioners and of the army's hospitals. He also designed and supervised the construction of a model kitchen at London's Wellington Barracks. Weakened by a bout of 'Crimean fever' and a riding accident and exhausted by his self-imposed labours, Soyer died at his home, 15 Marlborough Hill, St John's Wood, before the age of fifty, leaving a personal estate of less than fifteen hundred pounds. Thackeray almost certainly took him as the model for M. Mirobolant in his *History of Pendennnis. Instructions for Military Hospitals: the Receipts by A. Soyer* appeared posthumously in 1860. Florence Nightingale wrote in admiring tribute "His death is a great disaster. Others have studied cooking for the purpose of gormandising, some for show but none but he for the purpose of cooking large quantities of food in the most nutritious manner for great numbers of men. He has no successor."

MRS BEETON'S COOKERY BOOK

The very name of Mrs Beeton has become synonymous with 'cookery book', and conjures the image of a middle-aged matron of awesome domestic experience and imposing mien. In fact she died at the age of twenty-nine, a victim of childbed fever, eight days after the birth of her fourth child. Isabella Beeton (1836-65) (née Dorling) was born in Milk Street, off Cheapside. Thanks to the remarriage of her widowed mother she grew up as the eldest of a family of twenty-one children, which certainly enabled her to hone domestic skills from extreme youth. She did, nevertheless, have some formal education, first at a school in Islington, then in Heidelberg, where she showed a talent for music and a gift for languages. Her only formal training in domestic skills, however, consisted of pastry-making lessons from a local confectioner in Epsom where she grew up. Isabella married Samuel Orchert Beeton, an ambitious publisher of magazines and monthly part-works, when she was just twenty-one and immediately began to edit or write contributions to his *Englishwoman's Domestic Magazine.* What was to become her classic *Book of Household Management* first appeared as monthly supplements to sustain the sales of this publication in an expanding but fiercely

41. Household Goddess – Isabella Beeton, doyenne of domesticity, who died aged just 29.

As its title implies Isabella's enterprise was far more than a compilation of recipes and menus, supplying as it did advice and information on the origins, costs and seasonality of foods and the management of servants and household budgets and even including chapters on sanitary, medical and legal matters, "with a history of the Origin, Properties and Uses of All things Connected with Home Life and Comfort". Readers would learn not only how to stew endive and 'ragout a duck whole' or come to esteem the under-appreciated haricot bean as it was in Catholic countries, but also become aware of the migratory patterns of the salmon, the intellectual capacity of the domestic pig, the cultivation of almonds and the place of the sheep in poetic imagery.

Although Mrs Beeton's recipes were usually cast for a family of six, she also envisaged situations in which a hostess might cater for up to sixty. The prescription for a picnic for forty includes nine joints or cuts of meat, six each of fowls and lobsters, four pies, fifteen lettuce, six cucumbers, four dozen cheesecakes and two dozen fruit turnovers, a cold Christmas pudding and two each of plum cakes, pound cakes and sponge cakes, not to mention quantities of bread, rolls, biscuits, butter, cheese, condiments, fresh fruit and stewed fruit. To sluice this down she specified two dozen bottles each of ale, ginger beer, lemonade, soda water plus half a dozen bottles each of sherry and claret and "champagne at discretion and any other light wine and brandy." This formidable list closes with the curt reminder to "take three corkscrews". Inviting readers to send in their favourite recipes, Isabella found most of them totally unsatisfactory and turned instead to Eliza Acton's classic cookery book, and other commercially successful contemporary works. No credit was given to the originators of the recipes she borrowed but, to give her credit, she never claimed to have originated them herself with the exception of one for Oxford Sausages and another for Soup for Benevolent Purposes. She did, however, test

competitive market. It subsequently appeared in volume form, prefaced with a quotation from Milton: "Nothing lovelier can be found In Woman, than to study household good". Consisting of a mammoth 1,296 pages and illustrated with full-colour plates which put the book in a class by itself compared with its rivals, it weighed in at a hefty three pounds. The project appears to have been entirely her idea, pursued with determination despite the death of her second child during the course of its composition. The preface is a clarion call against mismanagement: "... there is no more fruitful source of family discontent than a housewife's badly cooked dinners and untidy ways. Men are so well served out of doors — in their well ordered taverns and dining places, that in order to compete with the attraction of these places a mistress must be thoroughly acquainted with the theory and practice of cookery."

the recipes she published and amended them as she thought fit. In presenting each she "attempted to give an intelligible arrangement to every recipe, a list of the *ingredients,* a plain statement of the *mode* of preparing each dish and a careful estimate of its *cost,* the *number* of people for whom it is *sufficient* and the time when it is *seasonable.*" She also glossed her prescriptions with admonitions of domestic hazard: "the aged, delicate and children should abstain from ices and iced beverages; even the strong and healthy should partake of them only in moderation ... the taking of these substances during the process of digestion is apt to provoke indisposition. It is also necessary to abstain from them when persons are very warm, or immediately after taking violent exercise, as in some cases they have produced illnesses which have ended fatally."

The year after Isabella's own death Sam Beeton was wiped out by the collapse of his bankers, Overend Gurney & Co. in the great crash of 1866. His asssets were bought up by the publishing firm of Ward Lock, which kept him on as a salaried editor. Although he eventually regained his status as a publisher, Sam was unable to regain control of his previous publications and died of consumption in 1877. Ward Lock, meanwhile, recognised the value of 'Mrs. Beeton' and ensured that it was kept updated and regularly reprinted and promoted. It sold 60,000 copies within a year of its publication, half a million by 1890 and has never been out of print. Regrettably, although perhaps understandably from a commercial point of view, the text, including many recipes, was extensively 'revised' to mirror changing tastes, moving far from the domestic simplicities of a mid-Victorian household to mimic the grandiose style of Escoffier *(see p. 70)*. Purists should therefore seek out a facsimile edition of the original.

42. *George Augustus Sala, by Ape, in* Vanity Fair, *September 1875. "Careless of money matters, he gave too liberal a scope to his tastes as a gourmet ..." (DNB)*

FAIR ROAD TO RUIN

By his later middle age George Augustus Henry Sala (1828-95) had become not so much a Fleet Street 'character' as a Fleet Street institution, instantly recognisable by his immaculate white waistcoats, bulging stomach and a nose both prominent and rubicund, the product of long indulgence. Born of Italian descent and educated in Paris, Sala by twenty had been a clerk, draughtsman, scenery-painter, illustrator and editor. A hustling promoter of Soyer's financially disastrous essay into mass-catering *(see p. 61)* and a regular contributor to Dickens' *Household Words,* he also covered the Crimean

War before becoming a stalwart of the *Daily Telegraph,* contributing an average of ten articles a week. Earning £2,000 a year but spending lavishly on his passions – rare books, ceramics and good living – Sala was constantly in debt and eventually kept ahead of his creditors by travelling abroad and turning his foreign exploits into travel books.

Described by the *Catholic Encyclopaedia* as "a man of social and convivial habits who prided himself on his extensive knowledge of cookery", Sala also possessed an intimate knowledge of his native city, bringing the two together in *Twice Round the Clock, or The Hours of Day and Night in London* (1859). In this he described in detail how such a simple human activity as breakfast reflected the complexity and contrasts of life in the capital. While most of London had breakfasted by nine am., he observed, in the ultra-respectable squares of Bloomsbury and Marylebone the bourgeoisie were still battling with "frizzled bits of bacon ... muffins ... sodden in yellow butter-pools ... dry toast, shrivelled and forbidding". The "upper fifty thousand" waited till ten or even noon and there were yet "sundry listless members of fast military clubs whose broiled bones and devilled kidneys shall scarcely be laid on the damask" until sunset. Other sketches in this volume covered Billingsgate, Covent Garden, Dining London, a Charity Dinner and Evans's Supper Rooms. Sala finally left the *Daily Telegraph* to start his own journal, which failed disastrously, forcing him to sell off his library of 13,000 volumes. Writing frantically to keep ahead of creditors, Sala in his last two years produced a volume of memoirs, a survey of London life, a two-volume autobiography and, last of all, drawing on a lifetime's experience of eating from Andalucia to Australia, *The Thorough Good Cook* (1895), covering soups, fish, entrées, poultry, curries, sauces, vegetables, cheese, hors d'oeuvres, eggs, salads and sweets. The recipes were more distinguished for their brisk enthusiasm than their precision, the

instruction "throw in" occurring regularly and quantities being left unspecified. They were also interlarded with literary references where a connection suggested itself to the author, as in his prescription for 'Kickshaws' of rabbit, which he explained as a corruption of '*quelque chose*' and referred to its use by Justice Shallow in *Henry IV Part I*. The entire text of the book is accessible online at www.eatdangerously.com/thorough cook. Prime Minister Lord Rosebery arranged a lifeline in the form of a Civil List pension of £100 but Sala died shortly after, a broken man, in Brighton.

ICE QUEEN

While Mrs Beeton attained an immortal reputation and Rosa Lewis *(see p. 69)* an (undeservedly) immoral one, the name of Mrs Agnes Bertha Marshall (1855-1905) has been largely forgotten. Yet she not only wrote, like Mrs Beeton, and was a celebrity cook, like Rosa Lewis, but also ran a cookery school at 30-32 Mortimer Street from 1883 until her death, as well as a domestic staff agency and a kitchenware business. In addition to this she invented the edible ice cream cone, patented an ice cream maker and freezer and in 1886 started a magazine *The Table,* in which she campaigned for better standards of food hygiene. Especially noted for her skill in making ice-based dishes, Mrs Marshall published 117 recipes in her *Book of Ices* (1885) and a further 222 pages of different ones in her *Fancy Ices* (1894) as well as *Mrs A.B. Marshall's Book of Cookery* (1888) (which sold over 15,000 copies in its year of publication) and *Mrs. A.B. Marshall's Larger Cookery Book of Extra Recipes* (1891). *Fancy Ices* included recipes for Banana, Gooseberry and Rose sorbets, Bismarck Rhubarb, Brown Bread soufflé with fruits, Duke of York apricot meringues and Parisian cucumber cream. These delights were intended not only for the formal dinner party but also for such quintessentially late Victorian occasions as the garden party and its newly-born younger sibling, the tennis party. Mrs

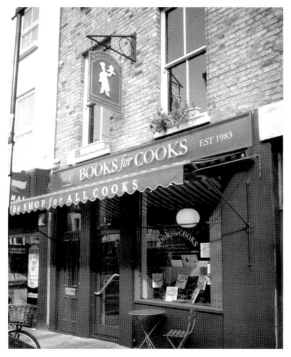

43. Books for Cooks at 4 Blenheim Crescent W11 started in 1983 and was managed for three years by Clarissa Dickson Wright. Famed for its in-house test-kitchen, the bookshop also runs practical workshops and culinary tours of Tuscany.
(See www.booksforcooks.com)

Marshall died from a riding accident before her fiftieth birthday and her family failed to capitalise on her extraordinary career and achievements, allowing Ward Lock, publishers of Mrs Beeton, to buy out and thereby suppress the copyrights of her publications. An exact facsimile edition of *Fancy Ices,* limited to 300 numbered copies, was produced in tribute in 1999.

DOMESTIC SCIENCE
Schooling in England did not become free and compulsory until 1891 but 1870, when W.E. Forster's Education Act first provided funds for non-sectarian schooling, marked the beginning of a major expansion in educational provision and attendance. In 1876 Macmillan published on behalf of the School Board of London *The Scholar's Handbook of Household Management and Cookery*, compiled at its

request by W.B. Tegetmeier. whose *Manual of Domestic Economy*, intended "for the use of students in female training colleges" was by then in its 9th edition. The purpose of the new publication was to give female pupils a grounding in the principles of cooking and housecraft which would give them a headstart in domestic service, beyond mere skivvying. Chapters systematically covered the nature, value and uses of meat, fish, eggs, dairy products, flour, pulses, condiments and beverages in fifty pages – of which a bare *five lines* were allocated to fresh fruits. The second half of the book was devoted to health in the home in terms of its water supply, ventilation, heating, lighting and cleaning. Appended to the book was a compendium of 150 recipes in twenty chapters which formed the core curriculum at the National Training School of Cookery in South Kensington. These included not only such predictable favourites such as Norfolk Dumplings and Toad in the Hole (made with ox kidney) but also more unexpected dishes such as Brazilian Stew (cheap meat cuts, vinegared, with vegetables), German Pea Soup (with grated sausage) and Poor Man's Goose (pork chitterlings). Interestingly an entire chapter was given over to the various possible uses of Australian (i.e. tinned) meat. Another was devoted to invalid cookery, including a prescription for raw beef tea (for Typhoid Fever) – throughout the emphasis was on economy and digestibility.

The instruction and advice imparted was soundly guided by an understanding of basic nutritional science but assumed a vocabulary which would nowadays be thought sophisticated in an early teenager. The opening section on The Nature and Uses of Food, for example, uses such terms as saline, gelatine, gluten, albumenoid, nitrogenous and oleaginous. The author's foreign name implied a familiarity with cuisines other than English – confirmed by an enthusiasm for offal, soups, omelettes, ready-skinned Ostend rabbits and French coffee-pots and criticism of such common

44. A cookery class at a Board School in Kilburn Lane, early 20th century.

English practices as over-boiling vegetables, salting meat and a too ready recourse to roasting – "an advantageous mode of cooking only in cases where the joints are large and where the cost of a large fire is not of importance. Consequently it is not best suited to the circumstances of the working classes." Further confirmation came from the observation that "it is only prejudice or ignorance which prevents the English housewife ... using the French plan of always having a stewing pipkin or *pot-au-feu* by the side of the fire", to which off-cuts and left-overs could be constantly added to provide nourishing stews and soups – in other words the peasant pottage long since displaced by puddings (*see p23*). The great Careme himself (*see p55*) was then quoted to endorse the value of this practice. Apart from French practice, there was also approval for Scottish cookery and the inclusion of specific regional recipes, such as a Channel Islands soup made from conger eels.

A similar publication for the London School Board of 1890, Miss E Briggs' *Cookery Book and General Axioms for Plain Cookery,* was, if anything, even more obsessed with the need for hygiene, safety and economy in the kitchen, with numerous recipes for the recycling of left-over scraps of meat, breadcrumbs etc. Dull instructions for the preparation of dull dishes revealed an obsession with the prevention of food poisoning rather than the slightest enthusiasm for the preparation and consumption of food. The author also shared the general prejudice against ingredients that might cause bad breath (or worse) such as leeks and onions. Briggs' recipe for gravy states that "if the onion is not liked it can be omitted" and is coupled with the admonition that "great care must be taken ... or it will be indigestible." Indigestion, like constipation, was another major fear.

"MRS LEWIS IS COMING TO COOK THE DINNER"

According to Colonel Newnham-Davis *(see p. 163)* this simple statement invariably proved decisive in assuring the attendance of a wavering guest. Firstly, it was as good as a guarantee that the meal would be superb and secondly it carried the unspoken implication that the Prince of Wales *(see p. 183)* might be among the other guests. Any hostess who managed to secure his acceptance of a dinner invitation would be well advised to have first secured the services of Rosa Lewis (1867-1952). On the day appointed this legendary cook would be at Covent Garden market at 5 am. to select her produce personally. Having then prepared whatever she could in her own kitchen, in the afternoon she would repair to the home of the hostess for that evening, accompanied by her 'girls', clad alike in chef's white, complete with tall hats and – a stylish touch – high-laced black kid boots. The regular servants would be banished and Mrs Lewis would commence to work her regular magic, and in due course receive a fee which matched the substantial feast she had conjured up. Having become the indispensable hidden ally and secret weapon of society scalp-hunters, Rosa Lewis moved on to become the proprietor of the Cavendish Hotel in St James's, an establishment which she made notorious for its discretion. How did this all come about?

Rosa's origins were humble but respectable. She was born in Leyton, then still in Essex, beyond the burgeoning East End and on the edge of Epping Forest. The fifth of nine children, she was the daughter of William Ovenden, a watchmaker, later an undertaker, who could afford to let her gain a basic education at the local board school – attendance was not yet compulsory and not always free. Rosa left at twelve to become a general servant in return for her keep and a shilling a week and might have remained her whole life in suburban obscurity had not a fortunate personal recommendation enabled her at sixteen to take

45. *Rosa Lewis sampling a dish. She was banned from the Ritz for insulting her former customers there. Evelyn Waugh was banned from her hotel after caricaturing her as Lottie Crump in* Vile Bodies.

service in the household of the exiled Comte de Paris at Sheen House, Mortlake. There she worked her way through the unforgiving hierarchy of culinary tyrannny to become head kitchenmaid. When the Prince of Wales dined there he was so delighted with the meal that he asked that the chef be sent for so that he could congratulate him. He came accompanied by Rosa, whose cheery banter greatly amused the heir to the throne, whose penchant for touring the East End incognito by night ('slumming') had given him a first-hand acquaintance with cockneydom. When Rosa's employer 'loaned' her to the Duc d'Aumale at Chantilly her independent career may be said to have begun. From his service she went on to take charge of the kitchens of the Duc d'Orleans at Sandhurst. Not surprisingly, Rosa's cuisine was basically French – and royal French at that – but her ability to resist the characteristic Gallic temptation to over-elaborate dishes brought a distinctive simplicity to, for example, her version of quails stuffed with *foie gras*. In 1887, still only twenty, Rosa began to go out to cook in private houses, starting with Lady Randolph Churchill, American wife of the ambitious Tory maverick who had just resigned from the government of the day. She was soon taken up by the Asquiths, who brought her to the notice of the Liberal elite, and then by Captain Charles Duff a member of the 'Marlborough House set' which revolved around the Prince of Wales. In 1893 Rosa married, for calculated reasons of her own, a butler whose most impressive feature was his name – Excelsior Tyrel Chiney Lewis. They set up in a house in palatial Eaton Terrace. Just how they were able to afford this remains something of a mystery, though Rosa cannot have lacked contacts with wealthy backers by then. There they took in lodgers and Lewis, having little to do, drank. They divorced after ten years.

In 1899 Rosa took on the catering at exclusive White's Club but the experiment proved unsuccessful. The demand for her services as a caterer in private houses, however, continued to grow. She also gave lessons to the cooks of the wealthy, such as the arriviste American millionaire W.W. Astor. Her fee was a surprisingly modest half a guinea but Rosa seldom did anything without a shrewd reason and the experience doubtless enabled her to make contacts, look, listen and learn.

By 1902 Rosa was able to buy the Cavendish in Jermyn Street. Already fashionable, it gained added cachet from Rosa's unanticipated flair for furnishing and decoration. Converting rooms into a series of suites, each with its own private dining-room and bathroom, she created the ideal venue and ambience for the conduct of discreet liaisons. Not for nothing did the Cavendish have four separate rear exits.

Rosa Lewis presided over her new establishment as though she were herself a society hostess and could without apparent irony rebuke discourteous guests with the reproof "You treat my house like an hotel." (Notice that "*an* hotel".) The wealthy Lord Ribblesdale kept a permanent suite at the Cavendish and Sir Wlliam Eden was a long-term resident. Anglophile American plutocrats were also accepted. Meanwhile Rosa continued to cater for such prestigious corporate clients as the Foreign Office and the Admiralty. The Great War killed off Rosa's catering-out activities. With only the Cavendish to occupy her Rosa turned herself into a patriotic Robin Hood, putting up impoverished young officers on leave, refusing to charge them and relying on the receipts from her wealthy clients to cover the gap. This became a practice which she continued into the post-war years.

As the years passed Rosa's legend grew. In *Vile Bodies* (1930) the youthful Evelyn Waugh, never one for flattery, portrayed her as "a warm-hearted, comic and totally original woman", and still a beauty in her sixties. The sometimes raffish behaviour she tolerated in others did not necessarily provide a key to her own behaviour or beliefs. She was an informal, if intermittent, member of the Church of England, only being confirmed shortly before her death, at the Cavendish, in 1952. The extraordinary career of Rosa Lewis later inspired two biographies and a television series, *The Duchess of Duke Street.*

'EMPEROR OF CHEFS'

Auguste Escoffier (1846-1935) gained his title from Kaiser Wilhelm II of Germany, when the Frenchman was in charge of the kitchens aboard the Hamburg-Amerika Line's steamer, *Imperator.* Escoffier got an early head-start in his career when he was taken on at thirteen by his uncle, who ran a famous restaurant in Nice. After working in Paris, Lucerne and Monte

Carlo, Escoffier came to London in July 1890 to work with Cèsar Ritz at the newly-opened Savoy Hotel. Together they rapidly raised the Savoy to a pitch of excellence which established its reputation for luxury and elegance, inaugurating such novelties as after-theatre suppers. In the kitchens, to speed service to diners, Escoffier divided his staff into five specialist squads responsible respectively for cold dishes and supplies, soups, vegetables and desserts, roasts, grilled and fried dishes, sauces and pastry. He also banned smoking and drinking in the kitchen, decreed that orders were no longer to be shouted and improved the ventilation to make the heat more bearable. Cooks were also required to change out of soiled working clothes before going out on the streets lest they be seen by members of the public.

Although Escoffier professed that his motto was '*faites simple*' his dishes were often highly complex as well as extravagantly rich. The restaurant critic Col. Newnham-Davis *(see p. 163)* managed to persuade the chef to divulge his recipe for *Timbale de filets de sole Savoy* which consisted of sole fillets cooked in white wine, served on a pastry case lined with a layer of macaroni in Béchamel sauce, covered with a sauce made from crayfish and truffles and surmounted with yet more crayfish. On the other hand Escoffier routinely obtained the essential stock for his sauces by reducing the water, wine or milk in which meat, fish or vegetables had been cooked to produce a fragrant concentrate.

Escoffier's flair for showmanship and publicity stimulated him to develop his most famous dish, named in honour of Australian soprano Dame Nellie Melba (née Helen Porter Mitchell) (1859-1931), then singing *Lohengrin* and craving a dessert which would soothe and relax her throat. The original version consisted of a swan carved from ice, carrying peaches on a bed of vanilla ice cream, surmounted by a net of spun sugar. This '*Peach Melba*' was far too labour-intensive and time-consuming to become part of even the Savoy's regular

46. *Auguste Escoffier – now immortalised at www.fondation-escoffier.org/*

restaurant menu. In 1900 Escoffier devised a much simpler version in which the ice swan was discarded in favour of a sauce made of sweetened raspberry purée with kirsch and almonds. By 1907 Escoffier's Melba sauce was on sale as a commercial product. He eventually produced nine such sauces and eight varieties of soup, although he derived only a small portion of the fortunes they made for their manufacturers. He also endorsed Maggi products. Escoffier's other celebrity creations included a dish made of frog's legs in a jelly of cream and white wine, flavoured with paprika, for the Prince of Wales *(see p. 183)* with the appropriately erotic name of *cuisses de nymphe aurore; chaud-froid Jeanette* (inspired by the fate of a ship which had become trapped in polar ice); *Rejan salad* and *Rachel mignognettes* of quail, in homage to two celebrated actresses; *soufflé Tetrazzini* for a diva of that name; and *poularde Belle Helene* for superstar Sarah Bernhardt. For Victoria's Diamond Jubilee in 1897 he created *cherries Jubilee à la reine.*

Escoffier and Ritz both left the Savoy in 1898 after an unseemly row over kickbacks from suppliers, which yielded a 5% commission through false accounting. Escoffier regarded this a normal trade practice but the Savoy's owner, Gilbert and Sullivan impresario Richard d'Oyly Carte, took a contrary view. Escoffier was forced to sign a confession and pay back £500 of an estimated £8,000. Another £8,000 was recovered from complicit traders. Ritz and Escoffier then briefly departed to Paris to establish a new hotel there, returning to create the elite Carlton at the bottom of Haymarket in 1899. Escoffier's kitchen staff there consisted of no less than sixty cooks, serving up to five hundred diners per meal. To mark Allied victory in 1918 Escoffier supervised a celebratory dinner at the Carlton for 712 diners, beginning with *potage à victoire.*

Escoffier wrote extensively about his art. His best-known works were *Le Guide Culinaire* (1903) and *Le Livre des Menus* (1912) and, in retirement, *Ma cuisine* (1934). The *Guide,* written for other professional chefs, contained over a thousand recipes and was recognised as a classic summation of the classic French tradition.

In 1920 Escoffier was honoured by his elevation to the rank of Chevalier of the Legion of Honour. He retired in 1921, on a pension of one pound a day, after a professional career of more than sixty years. during the course of which he had cooked for Napoleon III, Wilhelm II, three British monarchs and three French presidents. The house in Villeneuve-Loubet in which he was born became a museum of the

47. *The Ritz Hotel in Piccadilly, built in 1906, based on specifications by Cèsar Ritz, who by then had retired. One of London's first steel-framed buildings, its basement served as a bomb-shelter for the wealthy in World War Two.*

culinary art in 1966.

"To know how to eat is to know how to live," Escoffier once declared, "No man should have less than two hours for the chief meal of the day." Escoffier's own meals were always cooked for him by his wife. He attributed his longevity to a nightly draught of a concoction of his own devising — egg yolk, sugar and champagne in hot milk.

PART THREE

Supply and Demand

LONDON'S LOST MARKETS

"...an open market seems indispensable ... open shambles are essential to the poor and the poorer description of tradesmen who cannot pay large rents." *John Nash (1752-1835)*

Despite John Nash's sympathetic opinion, many of the capital's markets were to disappear within a half century of the architect's death. The Fleet Market had already gone in Nash's own lifetime, having itself been a reincarnation of a much older one – the Stocks market, which dated from the thirteenth century: this yielded rents for the maintenance of London Bridge. By the fifteenth century Stocks market specialised in fish and flesh but, rebuilt after the Great Fire, became a general market, described by Strype in 1720 as "surpassing all other markets in London." But in 1737 it was cleared to make way for the building of the Mansion House and relocated on the decking over of what had been the Fleet Ditch. It was finally cleared in 1829 to make way for the construction of Farringdon Street.

Hungerford Market was built in 1682 as a rival (largely unsuccessful) to Covent Garden *(see p. 78)*. Although it was rebuilt as a two-storey building in 1831-3, it was demolished in 1862 to make way for the building of Charing Cross station. Newport Market, dating from 1686, was already described in 1720 as "much eclipsed" by Clare Market *(see below)*, although Defoe still considered it important. By the

1850s, however, it had become a squalid slum. It was closed in the 1880s as part of the redevelopment of the Soho area to allow for the construction of Shaftesbury Avenue.

Newgate Market in Newgate Street predated the Great Fire, the thoroughfare being originally known as Bladder Street. In 1720 Strype described it as follows:

"there was a Market House for Meal and a middle row of sheds, which afterwards were converted into houses and inhabited by butchers, tripesellers etc. And the country people which brought provisions to the city were forced to stand with their stalls in the open street, to the damage of their goods and danger of their persons, by the coaches, carts and cattle that passed through the street."

Cunningham in 1850 referred to the market as "not unaptly likened to one continuous butcher's tray." Newgate Market closed on the construction of the Central Meat Market at Smithfield in 1869.

Established in 1682, Spitalfields Market was soon boosted by an influx of French Huguenots *(see p. 100)*. Industrious and thrifty, the Huguenots made Spitalfields the focal point of London's silk-weaving industry. The founder of the market, John Balch, sold it on to the Goldschmidt family and in 1856 they sold it to Robert Homer, who had once worked there as a porter and who invested some £80,000 in new market buildings. The City of London Corporation acquired the market in 1920 and spent £2,000,000 on a modernisation programme which was completed in 1928.

48. Old Hungerford Market, by Frederick Shepherd, c.1839. The old building was cleared away c.1830 and Shepherd (born 1819) probably relied on the sketches that his father, Thomas Hosmer Shepherd, had made in earlier times, to compile this view.

Intended to specialise in the handling of fruit and vegetables, this revamped Spitalfields included heated cellars for ripening bananas. When the City Corporation relocated the market eastwards to state-of-the-art premises at Leyton in the 1980s, it was feared that the old market buildings might be flattened to make way for yet more office development. Spirited resistance – doubtless assisted by a downward blip in the commercial property market – saved the Victorian complex for redevelopment as a recreational and retailing refuge on the City's doorstep. Apart from Spanish and Thai restaurants, Spitalfields also boasts a food court offering a choice of Indian, Tex-Mex, South East Asian and Middle Eastern dishes, not to mention Bubba's Arkansas B-B-Q, which offers

'lamburgers' made from the produce of the Prince of Wales's farm.

The Oxford Market in Great Titchfield Street was developed in the 1720s to the designs of local resident James Gibbs, architect of St Martin-in-the-Fields, to serve the then emerging suburb of Marylebone. It was demolished in 1876 to make way for flats. The Grosvenor Market in South Molton Street was closed c.1890 to allow for the extension of Davies Street.

Clare Market *(ill. 7)*, which now survives only as a street name, was established in 1657. In 1720 Strype described it as being "very considerable and well served with provisions, both flesh and fish: for besides the butchers in the shambles, it is much resorted to by the

49. *Newgate Market in 1856, from a watercolour by Thomas Hosmer Shepherd.*

50. *Columbia Market (see p. 76), built at great expense by Baroness Burdett-Coutts, was unsuccessful. It is seen here at the end of the 19th century, when it had ceased to be a market.*

51. Live poultry for sale at Caledonian Market, c.1950.

country butchers and higglers." It was from Clare Market that the highwaymen and wonder prison-breaker Jack Shephard stole a butcher's smock and apron as disguise; he was still wearing it when recognised and captured at Finchley. As late as 1850 sheep and oxen were still being slaughtered at Clare Market and there was also provision for a Jewish slaughterer. By the late Victorian period Clare Market was described as "crowded, noisy and unsavoury". Part was demolished in the 1870s to make way for the construction of the Royal Courts of Justice in the Strand and the rest was swept away for the Kingsway-Aldwych scheme around 1900.

Out in the rapidly growing East End new markets came into being, though not always successfully. Randall's Market in Poplar was established in 1850 but defunct by 1930. The imposing Columbia Market, designed by Henry Darbishire for the philanthropist Baroness Burdett-Coutts, was built in 1864-9 at an alleged cost of £200,000. It was intended to encourage

better standards of hygiene and honest trading but local vested interests ensured that it proved to be a gigantic white elephant almost from the first. Taken over briefly by the City Corporation, it was returned to the Baroness in 1874, briefly reopened in 1884 and closed the following year. Parts of the premises were subsequently let as workshops. Columbia Market was finally demolished over the years 1958-1966.

Shadwell Fish market was opened in 1885 a mile and a half east of Billingsgate. It closed during World War One.

Caledonian Market (properly the Metropolitan Cattle Market) was established on a thirty-acre site in Copenhagen Fields, Islington in 1855 to handle the livestock trade of Smithfield. Six times larger than Smithfield and capable of processing fifty thousand animals, it also handled all slaughtering. A bric-a-brac market developed among the pens when they were empty on Fridays. By 1930 this off-shoot had over two thousand stalls but was closed in World War Two and not reopened.

52. *Smithfield Market at the end of the 19th century. Modelled on the Crystal Palace, it opened in 1868.*

53. *Billingsgate Market c.1809, drawn by Rowlandson and Pugin. The building itself was rebuilt by the City Surveyor, Sir Horace Jones in 1877.*

The cattle market finally closed in 1965. Billingsgate, dating back to the eleventh century, as famous for foul language as for fish, was rebuilt in 1849-53 and again in 1874-7 to the designs of City Surveyor Sir Horace Jones, architect of the rebuilt Smithfield and Leadenhall markets. Billingsgate remained in business until relocated to Docklands in 1982.

COVENT GARDEN

Covent Garden was originally the convent garden, orchard and burial ground of the monks of Westminster Abbey. Following the dissolution of religious houses it was granted to the Russell family *(see p. 168)*, who built themselves a London residence facing onto the Strand. Francis, 4th Earl of Bedford, commissioned Inigo Jones to lay out the area to the rear as London's first square, intended as a residential enclave for London's elite. Built between 1631 and 1639, it was dominated on the west side by the imposing portico of St Paul's church but it was against the south side

of the piazza, against the rear wall of the back garden of Bedford House, that a booth is first mentioned in 1644. In 1670 the 5th Earl received a royal charter to establish a market for the sale of fruit and vegetables, but it was limited to weekdays and to the area of the piazza. In its first year the market lease yielded the Russells just £5, but by 1705 it was worth a hundred times as much and by 1741 was yielding £1,200. This growth reflected the enlargement of the market but that in turn diminished the attractiveness of Covent Garden as an enclave, except perhaps for artists, who valued its centrality and the lively company of the many local coffee-houses. Illustrious painterly residents included royal portraitists Sir Peter Lely and Sir Godfrey Kneller, Sir James Thornhill and his son-in-law, William Hogarth.

Defined, and as it were framed, by fine rows of arcaded houses, the bustling market remained a favourite subject for generations of genre and topographical artists, although Hollar's etchings of 1647 completely ignore its existence. In the

54. Covent Garden Market, early 19th century, by Rowlandson and Pugin, before the erection of the handsome market buildings still standing today.

55. Pea shellers in Covent Garden, early 20th century.

words of Celina Fox "it was a quintessential London location, where a range of characters could be portrayed together in the midst of colourful still-life displays and a distinguished architectural setting."

By 1700 the inhabitant of Bedford House had become a Duke and saw fit to vacate it and build Tavistock Row along the south side of the piazza, forcing the market traders to relocate to a central railed-off enclosure. Strype in 1720 described the location in favourable terms:

> "there is a small grotto of trees, most pleasant in the summer season; and on this side there is kept a market for fruits, herbs, roots and flowers every Tuesday, Thursday and Saturday; which is grown to a considerable account and well served with choice goods, which make it much resorted to."

The closure of the Stocks Market *(see p. 73)* brought a great boost in demand. In 1748 a major upgrading of facilities provided for 106 new shops and 299 stands. By the late eighteenth century Covent Garden was acknowledged as the finest market in all England for fruit, herbs and flowers. By the early nineteenth century, as the works of Pugin, Rowlandson and Scharf illustrated, the market was bursting its bounds, benefiting from the closure of the Fleet Market *(see p. 73)*. New market buildings, designed by Charles Fowler, were built between 1828 and 1830 and glazed in 1874-5. Peter Cunningham in his 1850 *Handbook of London* advised visitors "to enjoy the sight and smell of flowers and fruit, the finest in the world, any time from 10 am. to 4 or 5 pm. will answer. The centre arcade at mid-day is one of the prettiest sights in London. Saturday is the best day." The 9th Duke of Bedford sold his interest in the market to the Covent Garden Estate Company, which was owned by the Beecham family. In 1961 an Act of Parliament transferred control of the market to the Covent Garden Market Authority and it was relocated to Nine Elms, near Vauxhall Bridge, in 1973. The Covent Garden area, however, remains rich in gustatory delights, ranging from cookware shops to restaurants specialising in the cuisines of Africa and New Zealand.

56. Established in the 1840s, Soho's Berwick Street market is the only surviving fruit and vegetable market in the heart of London's West End.

MARKET GARDENS AND MARSHLAND

What would now be called market gardening developed continuously from the sixteenth century in areas along the South Bank, in what is now Lambeth and Wandsworth, and on the north side of the Thames, to the west and towards Chelsea and beyond, to sustain London's prodigious growth in population. Gardeners working within a six mile radius of the city organised themselves into a guild, which obtained its charter in 1605. By 1617 it claimed to be employing "thousands of poor people, old men, women and children in selling of their commodities, in weeding, in gathering of stones etc". Immigrants from the Low Countries, where a similar pressure of population on food supply had encouraged the intensification of horticulture even sooner, brought with them new methods of cultivation. Voluntarily removing stinking piles of human and animal waste from the streets of the capital,

doubtless to the puzzlement of the inhabitants, they dug deep pits in which to bury this unlikely treasure, thereby creating 'hot beds' which enabled them to force vegetables for sale weeks ahead of their normal seasonality.

In 1633 it was estimated that some twenty thousand cartloads of root crops such as carrots, parsnips and turnips were being brought into London annually from its western outskirts alone. Richard Bradley, Professor of Botany at Cambridge and author of The *Country Housewife* (1727/32) estimated that whereas in 1600 there had been some 10,000 acres around London given over to market gardening, by 1721 the figure had risen to 110,000. Newly fashionable residential areas, such as Kensington, retained their semi-rural aspect but witnessed the substitution of nurseries for vegetable plots as householders became gripped by the new fashion for urban gardening. Although the relative stagnation of London's population in the early eighteenth century may have eased the situation temporarily the secular trend was towards ever increased demand, thrusting the incentive to switch from arable to horticulture ever further outwards into Surrey, Middlesex and Essex. The thrust westwards went from Chelsea out as far as Ealing where by 1800 there were an estimated 250 market gardens. On the south side of the river horticulture dominated from Lambeth out to Battersea, a district which became famed for its asparagus.

Other specialities were cherries, strawberries, mulberries, melons, apricots and figs. Suppliers sustained a nightly traffic, by cart and barge, which converged on Covent Garden in the early hours of the morning. Whether their produce was dew-fresh by the time it reached its ultimate consumer is another matter. In *The Expedition of Humphrey Clinker* (1771) Tobias Smollett described with fascinated loathing a stall-keeper "cleaning her dusty fruit with her own spittle; and who knows but some fine lady of St. James's parish might admit into her delicate mouth those very cherries which had been rolled and moistened between the filthy and perhaps ulcerated chops of a St Giles' huckster." A French visitor, writing a year later, complained that all the vegetables grown on the fringes of the capital "cabbage, radishes and spinnage, being impregnated with the smoke of sea-coal, which fills the atmosphere of the town, have a very disagreeable taste ... I ate nothing good of this sort in London but some asparagus." Perhaps he should have followed local custom and smothered his vegetables with butter, bacon fat and pepper.

Out to the east growing vegetables for the London market had begun in Barking by at least the mid-eighteenth century. Writing in 1796, the Revd Lysons noted 300 acres planted with potatoes in the Barking area. By 1801 the potato acreage was just over a thousand, plus 330 acres planted with turnips or rape, 88 with peas and 51 with beans. Agricultural reformer and propagandist Arthur Young in 1807 declared that the largest potato-grower in Essex, possibly in England, was Mr T Pittman of Barking, who farmed from two to three hundred acres. His enterprise was skilfully integrated to take advantage of the opportunities open to him. Stable manure was brought from the capital by road and river to enrich his fields. Surplus potatoes were fed to a hundred oxen, accommodated in the largest 'bullock house' in the county. He also spent two hundred pounds on digging a well to provide water to wash his potatoes before sending them to market. Pittman's fields followed a varying rotation of potatoes, clover and wheat. Other major Barking crops were cabbages, turnips, asparagus, onions, cucumbers, strawberries, apples, plums, rhubarb and walnuts. Pruning, digging and trenching provided valuable off-season employment for locals. At harvest-time, when demand for labour was at a peak, girls were brought in from North Wales. Young also noted that inhabitants of Barking still enjoyed and exercised an ancient right to pasture cattle in Hainault Forest. Osiers were also still gathered in the marshlands for weaving into baskets. Nor were the most progressive approaches universally followed. Amazingly in 1847 there was still a medieval open-field near Porters, on the Barking side of the Barking-Dagenham border. Its twenty-five acres were divided into eight strips, with three separate owners, although the whole area was actually farmed by Joseph and Philip Choat. These strips continued to appear on Ordnance Survey maps down to 1921.

In 1848 the continuing importance of agriculture to the local economy of Barking was attested by the number of subsidiary occupations which depended on it – five corn dealers, six blacksmiths, three wheelwrights, three basket-makers, two leather cutters, a saddler, a millwright, a marshman, a tallow chandler, a cowkeeper and a cattle dealer. At Upney Farm, which extended over 102 acres in 1866, farmer Thomas Circuit introduced a style of cultivation, developed in Bedfordshire, of inter-cropping cucumbers and onions (some grown for seed) between rows of rye. In 1879 the 208-acre farm of William Wallis Glenny won second prize in a competition organized by the Royal Agricultural Society to encourage farmers in the London area to grow more vegetables. Although the expansion of housing would inexorably diminish the cultivated area around Barking with increasing rapidity from the 1880s, it was not until the construction of the gigantic Becontree estate in the inter-war period that the last substantial farms in the immediate area would disappear under the flood-tide of bricks and mortar.

TWININGS

The Twinings were originally Gloucestershire weavers. In 1684 recession in the textile trade led them to forsake Painswick in the Cotswolds

57. The first illustrated advertisement for Twinings Tea.

for the chance of a better life in London. When he grew up Thomas Twining (1675-1741) opted to abandon the family craft in favour of the tea business and in 1706 bought Tom's coffee-house in Devereux Court, just off the eastern end of the Strand.

In addition to the usual offerings of coffee, brandy, rum and arrak, Twining's also offered fine teas – at a price. 'Gunpowder Green' (the leaves were rolled into little pellets, like lead

58. The Twinings tea warehouse in 1800. The lantern has gone but the famous doorway remains.

shot) sold at the modern day equivalent of £720 a pound. The clientele for such products was correspondingly distinguished and included courtiers such as the Master of the Buckhounds and a Gentleman of the Bedchamber. Thomas became wealthy enough to live in fashionable Twickenham and commute to the Strand. By 1717 he had expanded the business into three adjacent houses, one of which directly fronted the Strand and is now numbered 216 but was then known by the sign of the 'Golden Lyon'. By 1734 Thomas was content to sublet the coffee-house and focus entirely on the tea side of the enterprise. Thomas's son, Daniel, began exporting tea to the American colonies. His customers included the governor of Boston – but his products were not among the ones which were to end up in the harbour.

In the next generation Richard Twining became chairman of the London Tea Dealers and in 1784 successfully persuaded Prime Minister William Pitt that slashing the high duties on tea was the best way to combat widespread smuggling, which was depriving the government of revenue. In 1787 Richard had the famous doorway installed at 216 Strand, surmounted by a golden lion, two Chinese figures and the family name in a distinctive typeface – without an apostrophe. This now appears on packets of Twinings tea and the firm claims that it is the oldest logo in continuous use in the world, just as the shop at 216 Strand is the oldest in London owned by the same family and in the same original business. In 1825 Twinings diversified into banking, with premises at 215 adjoining. Twinings bank merged with Lloyd's in 1892. In the year of her accession, 1837, eighteen-year-old Queen Victoria awarded the firm a royal warrant as 'Purveyor in Ordinary to Her Majesty'. In 1874 a second branch was opened in the City. Twinings became not only a blue riband brand but a national institution. During World War Two Twinings supplied tea to the Women's Voluntary Service, YMCA canteens and for Red Cross prisoner-of-war parcels. The Twining

family still heads the business, now in its tenth generation, although it became part of Associated British Foods in 1964. In 1972 Twinings became the first tea company to win the Queen's Award for Export.

FORTNUM & MASON

William Fortnum arrived in London in 1705 and initially stayed with his cousin, a Stepney builder who had done well out of the rebuilding of London after the Great Fire. Fortnum soon found lodgings with Hugh Mason, who kept a small shop in St James's Market. In 1707 Fortnum found employment in the household of Queen Anne as a footman. Being responsible for the lighting of candelabra, he received the perquisite of disposing of the used candles. This prompted him to master, in very short order, an understanding of the needs of the royal establishment and he suggested to his landlord that they should go into partnership. Fortnum increasingly took charge of the retail side of the business while Mason, who had quickly established stables in nearby Mason's Yard to receive deliveries, supervised the buying.

Although the business established by the founders proved sound major progess waited on the success in 1761 of Charles Fortnum, William's grandson, in entering the service of Queen Charlotte, recently-wed consort of the new monarch George III. By the time he ended his service he had risen to the post of Groom of the Chamber, having all the while retained a guiding hand over the progress of the business. The royal connection undoubtedly gave the flourishing grocer an invaluable insight into changing consumer tastes at the highest level. The other vital connection was with the East India Company, prime source of teas, spices and exotic gourmet delights, in which several Fortnums were also employed. Situated between the court suburb of St James's and the exclusive residential area of Mayfair, where making an impression on guests was not to be achieved by penny-pinching, it was logical that what one

59. The Fortnum & Mason building, Piccadilly, in 1837. Note the ultra-large display windows.

might call luxury convenience foods should be developed as a speciality — game in aspic, ready-boned poultry and a range of potted foodstuffs. In the following century this concept was extended to supply the growing picnic market and take advantage of demand for user-friendly treats on special London occasions such as Victoria's coronation, royal reviews of troops and the Great Exhibition of 1851. Thus was the famed Fortnum & Mason hamper born. Charles Dickens, himself a regular patron, said that if he had a horse to enter for the Derby, "I would call that horse Fortnum and Mason. Public opinion would bring him in somehow", observing that on Derby Day, Epsom Downs "burst into a blossom of lobster salad" as "the hampers fly wide open". The like scene was annually re-enacted at other great sporting fixtures when London was 'out' for the day — Ascot, the Boat Race, Henley or the Eton and Harrow match. On such occasions the whole of the firm's staff would be on duty at 4 am. to be ready to load hampers into carriages as they formed a queue down Piccadilly. Since those leisured days the Fortnum's hamper has been relied upon as a standby against the hazards of railway or airline catering.

The long wars against the French (1792-1815) opened up another new market among officers serving overseas, who longed for a taste of home. Largely drawn from the aristocracy in the army, and frequently enriched by prize money in the navy, they could afford to pay for their indulgences or, more modestly, for items to supplement and vary the often dull or coarse fare available to them on campaign. There was therefore a considerable expansion in the firm's range of preserves and foodstuffs which would last and could be eked out over a long period — cereals, dried fruits, honey and

60. The present Fortnum building, erected 1923-5. The famous articulated clock, depicting Mr Fortnum and Mr Mason, was installed in 1964.

now famed F & M stencilling on the outside because it virtually incited pilfering. Queen Victoria, an ardent supporter of Miss Nightingale's efforts to set the provisioning of her hospitals on a sound basis, had Fortnum's send out to her a huge consignment of beef tea concentrate.

In 1886 Fortnum & Mason extended the range of its potential offerings by taking on an enterprising new supplier from across the Atlantic – H J Heinz *(see p. 97)*. When the shop celebrated its 250th anniversary in 1957 H J Heinz II was there in person to tender his congratulations and gracious thanks for its early support in launching his company's products as an international brand. Britain's far-flung empire and constant colonial wars kept the market for tinned beef stew and Scotch salmon buoyant for almost another century. As a by-product of its experience in meeting the needs of clients in adverse climates in 1908 Fortnum & Mason opened a new department to provide camping and other equipment for overseas expeditions and cruises. In the same year, for the stay-at-home market, it began to offer a complete home entertaining service supplying not only food and wines but flowers, table

61. The celebrated cheese shop of Paxton & Whitfield in Jermyn Street, which has traded here since 1797.

spices, all stoutly packaged in well-made boxes and baskets. Service officers constituted a conservative caste and, once convinced of the soundness of an institution, were likely to patronise it loyally, becoming a core market which continued into peace-time. In 1819 Sir William Parry's preparations for his expedition to find the North-West Passage included placing an order for two hundredweight of the Fortnum's ready-sweetened cocoa-powder. During the Crimean War Florence Nightingale turned to Fortnum & Mason as a key supplier. She was confident that their well-packaged goods would survive the worst voyage and any amount of rough handling. Serving officers, however, wiser perhaps in the practicalities of campaigning, advised the firm to omit the by decorations, chefs and serving staff. Completely rebuilt in 1923-5, Fortnum & Mason reopened with brand new departments offering kitchenware, perfumes, ladies' fashions and children's clothes. Subsequent make-overs in 1981 and 1996 have seen the extension of departments to include crystal and china, menswear, bed linen, bathroom accessories and an auction room. Even David Piper, doyen of London guide-book writers, having enthused over this "Mecca for the moneyed shopper, its windows fascinating as a tropical aquarium with all varieties of rare food in all variety of rare packaging", felt it necessary to inform his readers that "It is quite free to go in" but warned them that "there is a slight risk of being mesmerized ... by so much of so much...". Festooned with Royal Warrants, Fortnum & Mason remains, despite its diversification, still undisputedly the Grocers to the Posh.

LONDON'S FISHING PORT

The earliest reference to salt-water fishing by Barking men dates from 1320. The Barking Abbey Rental of 1456 makes several references to a 'Fisshamles' – i.e. Fish Shambles – which implies that the sale of fish was by that date sufficiently important to have a part of the market area specifically devoted to it. Daniel Defoe, passing through Barking in 1722 in the course of collecting material for his *Tour through the Whole Island of Great Britain,* characterised it as "a large market-town, but chiefly inhabited by fishermen, whose smacks ride in the Thames, at the mouth of their river, from whence their fish is sent up to London to the market at Billingsgate, by small boats ...".

Defoe was also aware that more than economics was involved:

> "these fishing-smacks are very useful vessels to the public on many occasions; as, particularly, in time of war, they are used as press-smacks, running to all the Northern and Western coasts to pick up seamen to man the navy when any expedition is at

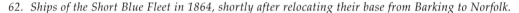

62. Ships of the Short Blue Fleet in 1864, shortly after relocating their base from Barking to Norfolk.

hand that requires a sudden equipment. At other times, being excellent sailors, they are tenders to particular Men of war; and, on an expedition, they are made use of as Machines for the blowing up of fortified ports and havens..."

Barking's position as the nation's biggest single fishing port was assured by its proximity to the enormous market London represented. In the right conditions smacks could sail right up to Billingsgate itself, offering London dealers the chance to buy the freshest catch available to them. At worst the capital was a brisk cart ride away. Fishing ports which would become important in the future, such as Grimsby or Brixham, had as yet only a small and relatively impoverished hinterland to sell into and, before the coming of railways, no means of reaching big inland cities while the catch was still fresh.

During the nineteenth century Barking was to be dominated by the Short Blue fleet created by Scrymgeour Hewett (1769-1850), a Fife-shire man, who married Sarah Whennell, daughter of the owner of two smacks. Hewett went into business with his father-in-law, retaining the square blue house flag flown on the mast of his smacks but greatly enlarging their number. Nevertheless, in deference to his senior partner, he insisted that the Short Blue, which was to become in its time the largest single commercial fishing fleet in the world, dated not from their partnership but from 1764, when the first boat had been acquired. During the Napoleonic wars Scrymgeour obtained letters of marque and sailed as a privateer. Returning home, he found that his second son Samuel (1797-1871) had himself run away to sea. Taking him on as an apprentice, Scrymgeour gave his son his first command at the age of nineteen: it was appropriately called *Liberty's Increase* and he soon turned the effective direction of the business over to him. This confidence was not misplaced. By the time of Scrymgeour's death his fleet had grown to 220 ships, crewed by 1,370 men and boys. Of the latter many were orphans, recruited from the Foundling Hospital (see p. 172) in Bloomsbury. Apprentices made up half the crew on most smacks, which must have kept costs down.

By the time Hewett and Whennell went into partnership it was already an established practice for the farmers of the Barking area to allow their low-lying lands to flood in winter to make ice. Harvesting the ice in winter and carting it off to storage afforded welcome employment to many who might be unemployed during severe weather. Samuel Hewett systematised the business and around 1846 built two large ice-houses with walls thick enough to keep the tons of ice right through summer. He also set up Britain's first artificial ice-making plant but this proved too expensive and the experiment proved abortive.

In 1837 a fishing ground for sole, known as the Great Silver Pits, was discovered out in the North Sea. Its potential seemed limitless and the London market offered an equally limitless demand. The problem was getting the catch there fast enough from so far north. Samuel Hewett also realised that holding the catch in the traditional 'peds' – round-ended wicker baskets – was not best calculated to optimise the carrying capacity of a boat. He also fretted that smacks returning to Barking to unload or make repairs were using time that could have been more profitably spent catching more fish. Hewett therefore organised his fleet into two classes of vessel. One type stayed on station for four to eight weeks, catching fish, the other acted as a carrier, plying backwards and forwards between fleet and market, carrying the catch, pre-packed by the catching crews, in square boxes, which were stacked in tiers in their holds, with a layer of ice between each tier. Carriers sailed out with fresh provisions for the catching crews plus eighteen tons of ice on board and returned with forty tons of fish layered between the ice. Meanwhile Hewett developed a ship-repairing base at Gorleston on the Norfolk coast, which was a hundred and twenty miles nearer the fishing-grounds. This was not only a thriving fishing community in its

By Royal Warrant to H.M. The King.

LEA and PERRINS' ·SAUCE·

IS EXCELLENT WITH ALL KINDS OF ·GAME·

THE ONLY ORIGINAL & GENUINE WORCESTERSHIRE

own right but, more important, offered space for further expansion of support services.

In 1862 Samuel Hewett relocated his fleet headquarters to Gorleston. The following year Barking's remaining fishing community suffered a terrible blow when sixty fishermen were lost in a gale off the Dutch coast. In 1865 the railway reached Great Yarmouth, beyond Gorleston. The existence of fast rail links to London and the ability to buy ice cheaply from Norway effectively nullified Barking's previous locational advantages. Many Barking families followed the Short Blue to Suffolk and by the time of the 1881 census Barking born people accounted for an eighth of the population of Gorleston. Other Barking families moved up to Grimsby and developed the industry there. Only three smack owners were listed in Barking in 1870. By 1903 the last of the Barking fleet had been sold off. Meanwhile the Hewett business had switched from Gorleston to Yarmouth and in 1929 relocated to Fleetwood.

63. (Above) An advertisement for Lea & Perrin's Worcestershire Sauce.
64. (Below) The stables of Crosse & Blackwell in what is today Charing Cross Road.

CROSSE & BLAC
OFFICES 21 SOHO SQ

65. Advertisement for Liebig's meat extract. In 1899 the firm launched OXO.

HOUSEHOLD NAMES
Keen's Mustard
Keen's original mustard factory was reached via Jack's Alley, off Great Trinity Lane, itself a turning off Garlick Hill. The ultra-hot condiment became famed throughout the British empire, its ardently fiery impact giving rise to the proverbial phrase 'keen as mustard'.

Peek Freans
In 1857 James Peek and George Freans went into partnership as biscuit-makers at Dockhead. Their riverside location led them almost inevitably into the export market and their products had reached Australia as early as 1861. Argentina, India, Egypt and Canada were to follow. Expansion brought relocation to Bermondsey in 1866. In 1921 the firm merged with Huntley & Palmer of Reading to form the Associated Biscuit Manufacturers Ltd. Overseas factories were opened in India (1924), Australia (1931) and the USA (1949). Peek Freans became renowned for its decorative biscuit tins which have become collector's items. In 1982 Associated Biscuits was purchased by Nabisco, a subsidiary of the US tobacco giant Philip Morris and in 1989 by the French firm Danone which renamed it Jacob's Bakery Ltd.

Crosse and Blackwell
In 1830 Edmund Crosse and Thomas Blackwell acquired for £600 the firm of Jackson's, founded in 1706 as a produce supplier to English colonies, which they had joined eleven years previously as apprentices. The firm reoriented its business towards preserving foodstuffs for use on ships and in tropical climates. One of its earliest lines was a mustard pickle. In 1862 the firm pioneered the sale of canned soups and in 1866 a mango chutney and a marmalade. For decades the firm had a major works on the north-east side of Soho Square, its principals being very active in the affairs of the local Soho community. In 1919 Crosse & Blackwell was to acquire the celebrated Dundee marmalade manufacturer James Keiller and Sons. It subsequently developed a portfolio of brands, including Branston Pickle, Gale's honey. Typhoo Tea, HP baked beans, Rowntree's jelly and Sarson's vinegar, which became peculiarly beloved by Britons living in culinary exile abroad.

In 1960 Crosse & Blackwell was itself acquired by Nestlé who passed it on to Premier International Foods in 2002, having failed "to establish the brand as a major food marque" on account of its "portfolio of peculiarly British foods."

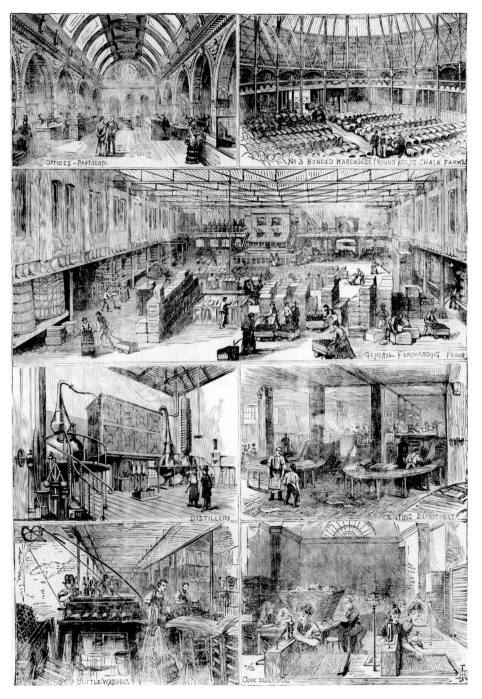

66. *The development of the railway system transformed the distribution of food and drink. Gilbey's the well-established wines and spirits merchant developed a distribution complex at Camden Town, where it was serviced by the London & North Western Railway and by the Regent's Canal.*

LYONS' ROAR

The Saga

The corporate career of J. Lyons & Co. is a dramatic parabola of unstoppable rise and precipitate fall. In between the two it became a national institution which seemed as durable as the Tower or St Paul's and quite naturally the inevitable caterer for Buckingham Palace, the Chelsea Flower Show and Wimbledon. As early as 1895, within a year of its formation as a public company, Lyons provided all the equipment, from tents to horse-drawn vans, for the Guards Officers' Mess while the regiments were on manoeuvres for six weeks. Lyons would acquire its own printing-works, box-making factory and overseas tea estates and employ so many musicians in its restaurants that it needed its own Orchestral Department. During World War Two the company managed one of the country's largest bomb-making factories, made components for Bailey bridges and packed three million ration packs for troops fighting in Asia, as well as Red Cross parcels for POWs. In the course of its expansion the firm acquired such brands as Horniman's Tea, Tetley Tea, Findus, Symington's Soups, Baskin-Robbins Ice Cream, Dunkin' Donuts and Luncheon Vouchers Ltd. One of its seven hundred associates and subsidiaries became Europe's largest laundry and developed its own subsidiary lines of linen hire and workwear manufacture. In Margaret Hilda Roberts the Lyons' research laboratories employed Britain's first female prime minister. J Lyons introduced the British public to frozen food and it built the world's first business computer, LEO (Lyons Electronic Office) and then manufactured computers for others. Between them the firm's chairmen in the course of the century were honoured with an OBE, three CBEs and two knighthoods.

Origins

Although it became strongly centred in London, the firm's origins lay not in the capital but in the north-east where in 1887 Joseph Lyons, Barnett Salmon and Isidore and Montague Gluckstein joined together to supply the catering for the 1887 Royal Jubilee Exhibition in Newcastle-upon-Tyne. So successful were their (mostly Lyons') efforts that they took on the catering at exhibitions in Glasgow and Paris and took over the concessions at London's Olympia and Crystal Palace. Trading under the name of J Lyons, the catering, hotel and food empire which evolved from this venture was to remain completely under the control of the Salmon and Gluckstein families until its demise.

Isidore Gluckstein (1851-1920), educated in the East End and without formal accountancy qualifications, was nevertheless the firm's financial genius. It was Montague Gluckstein (1854-1922) who persuaded his family to take capital out of their tobacco business and move into catering. Joseph Lyons (1847-1917) brought artistic taste, theatrical flair and an extrovert personality to the founding partnership. Barnett Salmon (1829-97), another tobacco salesman, died before the firm's rapid expansion.

Teashops

The first Lyons teashop was opened at 214 Piccadilly in London's West End in 1894, the year in which the firm purchased its headquarters site at Cadby Hall *(see below)*. Eventually there would be over two hundred teashops nationwide, liveried in a simple but elegant and distinctive white and gold, with a front shop for bakery sales and a cafeteria within. At one time there were seven on Oxford Street alone, the headquarters of the teashop branch of the business being located in Orchard House, near Selfridges. Teashops offered a wide range of light meals including pies, patties, sausages, fish cakes, hot snacks ('Spaghetti on Welsh Rabbit'), hot and cold sweets, ice cream sodas, sundaes and parfaits and beverages – both hot ('Grapefruitade') and cold ('Bovril with Milk'). The teashop tariff routinely carried advertisements for well-known brands such as

67. A Lyons teashop at 329 High Holborn, c.1907. Workers in local offices and shops provided a buoyant clientele

Colman's Mustard, Cerebos Salt, Lea and Perrins and Hovis Bread, an acknowledgment from the advertising industry of how many people would handle a Lyons' menu card in the course of a day. The menu also boldly featured the company policy of NO GRATUITIES. Teashop waitresses, known as Nippies, were paid on commission. The Nippy became such a nationally well-known figure that children would dress up as one for a local fete or pageant. Waitress service failed to survive World War Two and teashops switched over to slickly-designed self-service counters.

Restaurants

As the teashop network developed it was matched by a restaurant chain. The first became a London landmark – the Trocadero, opened in 1896 on an historic site at the junction of Shaftesbury Avenue and Windmill Street. Lunch was three shillings and a nine-course dinner half a guinea. The 'Troc' also offered

68. The Lyons Corner House in the Strand, in 1915. Imposing architecture on a prime site.

69. An evening of Table D'Hôte at the Trocadero – haute couture gowns, white tie and tails, champagne on ice and coffee served by a waiter wearing a fez.

70. 'The Corner House', watercolour by Elfrida Hughes, 1917. Note the number of off-duty officers wearing khaki and Sam Brown belts.

the unique service of taking forward bookings and orders for specific dishes by telephone. In its first year it turned a profit of £200 a week, by 1900 of £800, almost twice as much as all the then teashops put together. The Troc's famous, exclusively male, Long Bar opened in 1901. Cabaret was introduced in the 1920s but this gesture towards a more informal style of dining implied no compromise on standards. The wine list by then included 560 varieties, including the entire output of Chateau Belair St Emilion from 1895 to 1916.

In 1909 Lyons opened their first Corner House on Coventry Street and inaugurated a new concept in the restaurant business – a four- or five-storey outlet built on a commanding site and employing on average four hundred staff. Others were opened on the Strand and at Tottenham Court Road, while Marble Arch and Shaftesbury Avenue were home to a variant form, Maison Lyons. Each floor had a different style and usually its own orchestra. The ground

floor was usually a vast Food Hall. Some Corner Houses were open twenty-four hours. Others featured hairdressing salons and ticket agencies. There was a twice daily food delivery service anywhere in the capital. Corner Houses became another casualty of changing taste and were closed in the post-war period. The Trocadero finally closed in 1965 as the company sought a new market level through its chain of licensed suburban Steak Houses, aimed at the aspirant and expanding lower ranks of the middle class and Wimpy Bars, aimed at teenagers, which proved a huge success.

Hotels
The opening of the first Corner House was matched in the same year by the opening of the first hotel, the Strand Palace, managed by Barnett Salmon's youngest son, Julius. In 1915 the firm opened the Regent Palace, with 1,280 rooms the largest hotel in Europe. In 1919 came the Royal Palace on Kensington High Street and in 1933 the Cumberland at Marble Arch, built by Lyons' own Works Department and opened by the future King George VI.

The Food Business
Success in catering soon led on to manufacturing the food and drink products that the firm sold. Initially this facility was located at Cadby Hall. In 1921 a state of the art factory opened at Greenford on a site with direct access to the new Western Avenue and Great West Road, Grand Union Canal and Great Western Railway, as well as its own canal basin and railway sidings. Powered by electricity and set in landscaped grounds planted with roses, the Greenford works was deemed worthy of a royal inspection by the King and Queen. Here tea and coffee were packaged and ketchup, salad cream and convenience foods such as jellies, cake mixes and custard powder, were manufactured. A major ice-cream factory was added in 1954.

Lyons headquarters complex, Cadby Hall, on the Hammersmith Road, combined both manufacturing and administrative functions and eventually employed ten thousand people, working round the clock. It came to comprise separate bakeries for bread, cakes, Swiss rolls and pies, an ice cream factory and a supermarket, as well as laboratories, training and medical facilities and residential accommodation. At its peak of production the weekly output included 750,000 muffins, 2,000,000 Vienna rolls and 36 miles of Swiss roll. The other London facilities included a factory at Abbey Road, Park Royal for making counter and kitchen equipment for the teashops and another at Rannoch Road, south of Hammersmith Bridge and with its own wharf, which prefabricated fittings for Lyons' premises and also at various times turned out jams, suet, mincemeat, purées, canned fruit, frozen food and, most important, cordials, fruit juices and other soft drinks, many for sale under supermarket labels.

Nemesis

In the post-war era Lyons seemed to go from strength to strength. Its pioneering computer, LEO, was a symbol of its far-sighted 'can do' outlook, having been built by a specially assembled in-house team, without the benefit of any prior corporate experience in electronics. In 1953 LEO began to work out the weekly payroll; calculating an individual employee's weekly take-home pay which had formerly taken a clerk an average of eight minutes now took 1.5 seconds. New manufacturing facilities were built in the provinces and new hotels at Heathrow and St Katharine's by the Tower of London. In the early 1970s the company went on a buying spree, spending $100,000,000 to acquire holdings in nine French, Dutch, American and Italian food companies, most notably Tetley Tea and Baskin-Robbins Ice Cream. As this expansion was largely financed by US borrowing the 1973 oil crisis and subsequent economic contraction brought disaster. In 1976 the Wimpy hamburger chain was sold off to United Biscuits. A take-over by Allied Breweries followed in 1978. Most of the Cadby Hall site was demolished in 1983.

71. John James Sainsbury and his wife Mary, founders of the Sainsbury empire, in 1896.

Components of the business were sold off to finance drinks trade acquisitions such as Hiram Walker of Canada and Pedro Domecq of Spain and the last vestige of the once mighty Lyons empire finally disappeared in 1998.

SAINSBURY'S

John James Sainsbury (1844-1928) started in the grocery trade, aged fourteen, in a shop near Waterloo Station. He married Mary Ann ('Polly') Staples, whose father owned a chain of dairy shops. Together they set up their own business, selling milk, butter and eggs, at 173 Drury Lane in 1869, one of some fifty food retailers in that congested thoroughfare. A second branch was opened at 159 Queen's Crescent, Kentish Town in 1873; by 1885 Sainsbury's had three branches in that street alone. The rapidly growing new suburbs of north London, unlike the East End, were poorly served with shops and markets and customers came from as far away as Hendon. In 1881 Sainsbury took over from his brother-in-law, Edward Staples, a shop at 68 Watney Street, Stepney and in 1882 opened a depot to receive bulk deliveries and another branch at 48 Chapel Street, Islington, where his fascia modestly proclaimed that "J. Sainsbury's Shilling Butter is the Best Value in the World. Quality Perfect. Prices Lower". Other offerings included pickled pork and Ostend rabbit. After taking a record £400 on a single Friday Sainsbury was encouraged to open a further branch specialising in game and poultry. These early branches were routinely fronted by stalls to encourage custom – and add as much as 50% to the sales area. One of the first jobs that boy apprentices were sent on was 'barking' – cry the virtues of eggs from these vantage-points. The first branch outside central London, opened in its most populous commuter suburb, Croydon, in 1882, was a showpiece notable for the lavishness of its decor, featuring gilded lettering, mahogany counters, marble surfaces, mosaic floors, Minton tiles and stained-glass pictures. Success at Croydon led to further expansion in burgeoning white collar residential districts with branches at Balham, Lewisham and Brondesbury. Such outlets offered a wider product range, such as foreign cheeses and luxury game like ortolans and quails, and extra services, such as home delivery and monthly accounts. This contrasted with the strategy of the infant firm's larger rivals. Maypole dairies sold only five working-class staples – eggs, tea, margarine, butter and condensed milk. The Lipton's range was little larger *(see p. 98)*.

In 1890 a major new riverside depot was opened for Sainsbury's at 11 Stamford Street Blackfriars, enabling the firm to accept deliveries virtually direct from ships arriving from France, Denmark and the Netherlands. This depot became the springboard for further rapid expansion. Between 1890 and 1900 Sainsbury's trebled its outlets from 16 to 48 and extended its coverage from Watford to Redhill and from Ealing to Ilford. The five

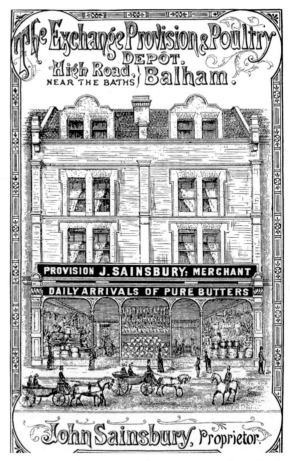

72. *The ninth Sainsbury shop, at 87-89 Balham High Road. It was opened in 1888.*

original products of 1869 had become 130 and the number of staff risen from two to just short of a thousand. By 1903 the number of branches had more than doubled to pass the hundred mark. Sainsbury's early history reflects the way in which food retailing was becoming an increasingly male-dominated business. Whereas the formerly close link between the preparation and sale of many foodstuffs placed a premium on domestic skills and had therefore made it feasible for many females, especially widows, to run food shops, the trend to factory processing and bulk buying broke this link. Perhaps ironically in view of the fact that it was Mrs Sainsbury who worked in their first shop before he did, male staff were invariably appointed as managers while females worked as counter-hands, clerks, cleaners, and where large staffs lived in, cooks. During World War One the absence of male staff in the armed forces (a third joined up in the first three months) gave females the chance to achieve managerial positions and take on new roles, such as delivery drivers. There were, however, demotions when the men returned and the rule against employing married women was upheld. Sainsbury's was glad to have them back during World War Two. The advent of self-service in the 1950s opened up opportunities for part-time employment as cashiers, pricers, packers and shelf-stackers ('gondola girls'). In 1955 Sainsbury's opened Europe's largest self-service food store in Lewisham. By then the company was poised to transcend its core in the capital to become a national institution.

Beanz meanz Heinz

Henry J. Heinz (1844-1919) made his first sales trip to London in 1886, having founded his American food-processing business in 1869. Its first product was his mother's grated horseradish, presented in a clear glass jar to highlight its purity, a visual assertion of his own aphorism that "quality is to product what character is to man". Other makers 'extended' their horseradish by mixing in turnip, leaves or even wood fibre, disguising the deception by packaging the product in green glass. This commitment to quality gave Heinz the confidence to pioneer the 'public factory tour' to demonstrate the hygienic working conditions in which goods were produced. Henry Heinz embodied the optimistic American 'can do' philosophy epitomised in another of his maxims, "To do a common thing uncommonly well brings success."

Heinz arrived in London with a range of samples in a Gladstone bag – but no prior appointment. As a result of his persuasive endeavours Fortnum & Mason *(see p. 83)* agreed to stock his entire range of seven products. Heinz, exalted by success, returned home

proclaiming "Our field is the world". In 1896 Heinz opened its first representative office, near the Tower of London and by 1898 they had fifty staff in the UK. In 1905 the company acquired Batty & Co., makers of the Nabob Pickle, and opened its first British plant, at Peckham. In 1914 Heinz launched its own brand of salad cream. In 1919 the firm acquired a site at Harlesden in north-west London; its second London factory opened there in 1925. It began making baked beans in 1928.

By 1939 Heinz was employing 579 salesmen to service over 80,000 accounts. The Harlesden factory was bombed twice during World War Two. One of its most important products at this time was a self-heating range of canned foods for use in the field by British and American troops. The middle of the can held a metal tube filled with smokeless chemical fuel. When the protective cap was prised off and the fuse lit the contents were heated in under five minutes. By 1954 Heinz annual product output exceeded two million tons. In 1967 the company launched its memorable 'Beanz Meanz Heinz' advertising campaign.

Threats to close Harlesden first emerged in 1985 and were confirmed in 1999. By 2002 with a utilisation rate of only 52% it was the least utilised of the company's half dozen UK plants. The labour force had been cut from 2000 to 450.

Heinz itself continues to display a healthy corporate appetite. In the 1990s it acquired Liverpool-based fish canning company John West, best known for its tinned pink salmon, the Frozen and Chilled Foods Division of United Biscuits (including the Jane Asher desserts brand), Farley's the baby-rusk manufacturer and Complan, the slimming aid; Weight Watchers International is also a subsidiary. In 2000 Heinz marked the millennium with a special limited edition of spaghetti hoops in which a quarter of the hoops were replaced by a pasta number 2.

GLASWEGIAN MAKES GOOD

Sir Thomas Johnstone Lipton K.C.V.O. Bart (1850-1931) was born in a Glasgow tenement the son of a refugee from the Irish potato famine. Employed in his father's grocery shop at nine, Lipton ran away to America at fifteen. He would later claim that the five years he spent there taught him all he ever needed to know about retailing. Lipton returned to Glasgow to open his first shop when he was just twenty-one. Like other successful food retailers he realised that rigorous attention to cleanliness and a willingness to put in long hours were necessary but not sufficient conditions for success. Lipton made the acknowledged fact that the bulk of a grocer's turnover comes from half a dozen staple lines into a fundamental principle of business. Cutting out the middleman by buying his provisions in bulk in Ireland, he was able to beat his rivals on such basics of working-class diet as bacon, butter, cheese and eggs. He also displayed an unrivalled flair for publicity and a willingness to spend lavishly on advertising. A millionaire by the age of thirty, Lipton continued to devote all his energies to expanding his retail empire through a strategy of vertical integration which made him the proprietor of a hog-slaughtering factory in Chicago, tea plantations in Sri Lanka and fruit farms in Essex and Kent as well as the operator of a substantial printing and packaging business. Lipton opened his first English shop, in Leeds, in 1881 and his first London store in 1888. This was bang opposite Whiteley's Bayswater emporium, whose prices Lipton undercut by an average of twopence in the shilling. Lipton moved his entire headquarters – and a thousand Scottish staff – to London in 1889-91, rapidly expanding a major office and warehouse complex at the junction of City Road and Bath Street.

In 1892 the provisions depot and manufactory for coffee and chicory essence were moved to a nearby site at Old Street. A huge fire necessitated a major rebuilding in 1894-6, creating a headquarters worthy of the

73. *Lipton's store in Green Lanes, Palmers Green, near to Lipton's 'country home'. Note the proud display of Royal warrants on the fascia and clinically white staff uniforms, implying spotless hygiene.*

world's greatest grocery empire, which occupied the entire area bounded by Old, Bath, Cayton and Peerless Streets. Lit by electric light and fully equipped with telephones, it even had its own telegraph office and printing works. At the rear of the main building separate factories, employing some 800 staff; manufactured tea, cocoa, chocolate, coffee essence, pork pies and sausages – ten tons a week. Another factory, out at Bermondsey, made jam. In the year of Victoria's Diamond Jubilee Lipton began to devote his formidable energies and fortune to philanthropy. When Alexandra, Princess of Wales, launched a scheme to provide subsidised meals for the poor Lipton donated £25,000 of the £30,000 needed. When a few years later she wanted to establish a restaurant for the poor, Lipton donated the entire £100,000 required. Knighted in 1898, Lipton was created a baronet in 1902 by his friend, Edward VII. He spent the next thirty years – and £1,000,000 – on fruitless attempts to win the America's Cup for ocean yacht racing.

PILE IT HIGH! SELL IT CHEAP!

The only begetter of the Tesco chain of supermarkets was 'Jack' Cohen (1898-1979), the fifth of six children of an immigrant Polish-Jewish tailor, Avroam Kohen. Educated at a London County Council elementary school, he left school at fourteen to join his father as an apprentice tailor. Volunteering for the Royal Flying Corps at eighteen, he used his tailoring skills to stitch canvas for aircraft and balloons, serving in the Middle East and narrowly escaping death when his troop carrier was sunk by a mine off Alexandria. A malarial infection brought Cohen an early discharge and a demob gratuity of £30 which he used to buy surplus foodstuffs from the armed forces. Setting up a stall in a Hackney street market, he soon began trading in a different market each day of the week. Moving into the wholesale trade, he specialised in tea and invented his brand-name by joining the initials of one of the partners in his supplier's business – T.E. Stockwell of Torring and Stockwell of Mincing Lane – with the first two letters of his own name. In response to the pleas of his bank manager, whose staff had difficulty in distinguishing between several Jacob Cohens, 'Jack' changed his name to John Edward by deed poll. The first indoor stall was opened in Tooting Arcade. In 1931 Cohen opened his first shop – on the world's biggest housing estate, at Green Lane, Becontree. Another was opened in Burnt Oak the same year. London's booming suburbs offered ever new retailing opportunities and by 1939 there were over a hundred Tesco stores in London and the Home Counties. In 1935 the headquarters operations moved out of an aged warehouse in Upper Clapton Road and into purpose-built premises at Angel Road, Edmonton. Deliveries from depot to branches, however, still relied on a fleet of converted ambulances, later replaced by charabancs. Over the next four years new store openings averaged one a month. Site expansion stopped during the war but Cohen compensated by acquiring his own nurseries at Enfield and Cheshunt, fruit farms in Essex and a canning business. After the war and a visit to the USA he pioneered American-style self-service and check-outs. The first Tesco supermarket opened in Maldon. By 1959, 140 of the 185 Tesco stores were self-service, and in 1960 Tesco went nationwide. By 1968 Tesco, with 834 outlets was the UK's fourth largest chain. 'Sir Jack' was knighted the following year.

In 1977 Tesco used Jubilee weekend to launch 'Operation Check-Out', slashing hundreds of prices in an opening assault on the supremacy of Sainsbury's. From price wars the rivalry spread to competition for out-of-town sites and product challenges in the form of the first Healthy Eating range. In 1992 a new strategy was initiated with the opening of the first Tesco Metro in Covent Garden. In 1995, the year in which Tesco launched its loyalty Clubcard, it was declared the nation's No. 1 supermarket. In 1996 it became the first supermarket chain in Britain to offer online shopping. By 2001 Tesco profits had hit £1 billion and in September 2003 it was reported that one in twelve of all purchases in the High Street are at Tesco's.

PART FOUR

Foreign Flavours

THE FRENCH CONNECTION

"Paris is the culinary centre of the world. All the great missionaries of good cooking have gone forth from it, and its cuisine was, is, and ever will be the supreme expression of one of the greatest arts of the world."

Lt.Col. N. Newnham-Davis: *The Gourmet Guide to Europe* (1903)

"A hardboiled people, the French ... hardboiled; over-cooked; over-praised for their cooking. When people professed a love of France, they meant love of eating."
    Evelyn Waugh: *Put Out More Flags* (1942)

The French have long regarded their cuisine as a major contribution to world civilization and while the majority of their neighbours across the Channel may have deferred, or, as in the case of Col. Newnham-Davis *(see p.163)*, endorsed it warmly, the claim has sometimes provoked a degree of Britannic dismissal. As early as the 1570s aristocratic enthusiasm for a proliferation of dishes was blamed on their cooks, "for the most part musicall-headed Frenchmen." French-style eating establishments, such as Pontack's *(see p.124)* were known in London from the Restoration onwards, offering such novelties as ragout and morells. In 1667 Pepys recorded dining with his wife on impulse at an 'ordinary' run by his French wig-maker "in an ugly street in Covent Garden", who "in a moment almost had the table covered and clean glasses and all in the French manner, and a mess of potage first, and then a couple of pigeons *à l'esterve*, and then a piece of *boeuf-à-la-mode*, all exceeding well-seasoned, and to our great liking; at least it would have been anywhere else but in this bad street ... but to see the pleasant and ready attendance that we had, and all things so desirous to please, and ingenious in the people, did take me mightily. Our dinner cost us 6s."

The court at Versailles and the fashionable *quartiers* of Paris, then Europe's largest city, were the normal source of French influence on London cuisine. The advent of the Huguenots, Protestant refugees who fled persecution to find refuge in London from 1550 onwards, brought a humbler tradition to bear. For the most part skilled and thrifty craftsmen, they were exponents of the waste-not-want-not approach to cooking and it is to them that Londoners were to owe what were to become two quintessentially English dishes – the saveloy and ox-tail soup. Saveloy is an anglicization of the French *cervelas* which in turn comes from the French for brains (*cervelles*), originally a major ingredient along with pork, pork fat, garlic or pepper. Smoked or unsmoked, saveloys were eaten, after being simmered, with vegetables or cold in a salad with an onion vinaigrette dressing, or fried. A meatless version based on pike, potatoes, butter and eggs, was originally prepared for Lent but this was obviously not incumbent upon

Protestants. By Dickens' time the saveloy had become a standard treat among the working-classes and in a debased version – containing few knew what – a standard item of street-side fast-food. The addition of saltpetre as a preservative made it bright red, thus providing a convenient disguise for the adulteration of its contents. Currently it appears to have become more of a joke icon than a genuine item, Cockney actress Kathy Burke, profiled in the press as an enthusiastic vegetarian cook, being characterised as "more Saveloy than Savoy" and a commentator referring to Tony Blair choking on a saveloy as an image of the politically surreal. The culinary use of the ox-tail, either to make soup or as a dish in its own right, was likewise unknown in London before the advent of the Huguenots. It was simply thrown away. Interestingly the modern *Larousse Gastronomique* declares that "Oxtail soup is a classic English soup which ... could have been introduced into Britain by refugees from the French Revolution." Londoners have been generally content to defer to French culinary eminence but there have been a few notable exceptions, though their basis has been more ideological than gastronomic. William Hogarth (1697-1764) was a classic beef and beer patriot who couldn't stand the French, an attitude that may have been aggravated by their proximity. When he was an appprentice engraver in Cranbourne Street he lived on the edge of the Huguenot community in Soho, where a quarter of the population habitually spoke French. The only time Hogarth went to France he managed to get himself arrested as a spy. Being an artist he naturally made sketches of his surroundings – which included the local fortifications. Hogarth had his revenge in a satirical painting, *Calais Gate, or The Roast Beef of Old England.* The central figure is a fat French monk slavering over a massive piece of beef being carried to the English inn – anti-clericalism was the flip side of English Protestant bigotry – while a sentry makes do with a dish of watery gruel. To the left of them the artist is seen having his

74. *Self-portrait of William Hogarth (publ. 1817). A pugnacious critic of foreign affectations.*

collar felt. Slumped on the ground to the right an exiled Jacobite contemplates dining on an onion, or garlic – some foreign muck, anyway. Thomas Rowlandson was to recycle the image of the French as emaciated munchers of onions and snails in 1792, at the outbreak of war with France's revolutionary regime. To the British the fact that the average French peasant could not afford to eat beef was proof of his oppression and therefore of the manifest superiority of the British constitution, hence the foundation of the Sublime Society of Beefsteaks under the slogan 'Beef and Liberty' *(see p.137).* Hogarth's anti-Gallicanism was shared by the (in the circumstances ironically named) Louis-Philippe Boitard, a fellow engraver of London life, whose panorama of *The Imports of Great Britain from France* (1757) excoriated the flow of cheeses from Normandy and vilified a band of 'high liv'd epicures' waiting at the dockside to greet their new French chef. Unsurprisingly the engraving is dedicated to the Society of Anti-Gallicans.

75. *The Hotel de la Sablonière at 29-32 Leicester Square, one of half a dozen London hotels which primarily served foreign visitors.*

et de Provence (1890), the Hotel de Paris (1896) and the Grand Hotel and Café de l'Europe (1899), which housed a brasserie. Soho meanwhile prospered on the success of Kettner's *(see p. 157)*, whose eponymous *Book of the Table* proclaimed the many superiorities of French cuisine and gustation. One was the superiority of bread over potatoes in acting "upon the palate as a sponge to prepare it for a new experience." Another was the diligence of French cooks in puréeing vegetables – "the English cook is content with slovenly work; hence mashed potatoes full of lumps and spinach full of strings and coarse. The English cook shirks the labour of the sieve." Another Soho institution, dating from 1871, was the patisserie Maison Bertaux. In 1894 George Gaudin founded L'Escargot Bienvenu, later L'Escargot, in Greek Street, Soho. Its name proclaimed not so much a speciality dish as a philosophy – the diametric opposite of 'fast food' – a meal that was worth eating was worth waiting for. In 1906 Randall and Aubin opened England's first charcuterie in Brewer Street.

The outbreak of the Great War in 1914 meant that, as 'enemy aliens', German proprietors forfeited their businesses. One beneficiary was Victor Berlemont who took over the York Minster in Dean Street, Soho. It swiftly became known as 'The French' and during World War Two served as a regular watering-hole for Free French forces in London. Victor in due course was succeeded by his son, Gaston. The pub and its upstairs restaurant, which supplied French provincial cooking with few concessions to the unconverted, was patronised by a Bohemian set which included Brendan Behan and Dylan Thomas and such exotic birds of passage as Salvador Dali. The redundancy of its formal designation led eventually to the re-badging of the York Minster as The French House. In 1955 Gaston founded the annual Soho Festival and its associated waiters' race. With a truly Gallic flair for historical resonance the Berlemont connection was finally sundered after seventy-five years

That said, in the aftermath of the bitter wars against France, the Hotel Sablonière opened in Leicester Square and was hailed for its *table d'hôte* which "affords the lovers of French food and French conversation an opportunity for gratification at a comparatively moderate charge." Before the opening of the Sablonière, according to the bon viveur Captain Gronow, the only public hotel "where you could get a genuine French dinner" was the Clarendon, kept by a chef named Jacquiers who had served Louis XVIII in exile. The highest echelons of London society were eager to employ French chefs such as Ude *(see p. 58)*, Careme *(see p. 55)*, Soyer *(see p. 59)* and Escoffier *(see p. 70)*, several of whom came as refugees from French political instability. Wine merchant Daniel Thévenon came as refugee from bankruptcy. His success with the Café Royal *(see p. 149)* inspired a cluster of French restaurants in the Leicester Square area, including the Sablonière

76. *Georges Gaudin, the original founder of L'Escargot in Greek Street, Soho bestrides a snail – a house speciality and a symbol of his belief that food worth eating was worth waiting for.*

77. *The French House, formerly the York Minster, in Dean Street, Soho. The restaurant to the right was once La Terrazza, the first in the Mario and Franco chain specializing in regional Italian dishes.*

on Bastille Day 1989 – the two hundredth anniversary of the French Revolution.

In 1925 (Xavier) Marcel Boulestin (1878-1943) opened his Restaurant Français in Panton Street, Leicester Square, and then moved to Southampton Street, Covent Garden 1927 as the Restaurant Boulestin. Two visits to London had made Boulestin sufficiently anglophile – not to say anglomane – to experiment with Sir Kenelm Digby's mead recipes *(see p. 53)* and to eulogise the curry served at Romano's *(see p. 109)*, as well as acquiring an alleged penchant for mint and mince pies. While living in a flat in Southampton Row, Boulestin had become friendly with Dorothy Todd, editor of *Vogue,* and began to cook his favourite French dishes for her. After he had arranged a spectacularly successful lunch for Virginia Woolf the assembled guests all agreed that it would be marvellous if Marcel could open a restaurant. One of them, wealthy Leo Myers, offered to put up the money. Boulestin, who had himself been a professional interior decorator (and music critic, picture dealer, novelist and war-time soldier), installed contemporary Parisian decor featuring fabrics designed by Dufy and painted panels by Marie Laurencin and Jean Laboureur. A striking contrast to the overblown and dated Belle Epoque style of established rivals, this avant-garde approach was copied by Quaglino's *(see p. 111)* and Prunier's, which opened in 1934 as a branch of the celebrated Parisian establishment. Boulestin's self-imposed patriotic mission was to bring true French *haute cuisine* to a capital too frequently bamboozled by Italianate Soho variants. Apart from running his restaurant Boulestin ran cookery classes at Fortnum & Mason and wrote columns for *Vogue* magazine and the *Evening Standard.* Believing that "food which is worth eating is worth discussing", he also reached a wider audience via a stream of widely influential cookbooks, to which he brought a designer's eye – large type, thick paper, stout binding and a jacket designed by the artist Laboureur. His *Simple French Cooking for English Homes* (1923, reprinted 1923, 1924, 1925, 1928, 1930 and 1933) was written at the invitation of its publisher and it was that book's success which enticed the author into the restaurant business, for which he had had no professional training. The book was followed by the aptly titled A *Second Helping* (1925) and succeeded by *What Shall We Have Today?* (1931), *127 Ways of Preparing Hors-D'Oeuvre* (1932) plus two companion volumes on eggs and potatoes, *What Shall We Have To Drink?* (1933) and the *Evening Standard Book of Menus* (1935), which contained a lunch and dinner menu for every day of the year, with recipes for every dish. But he had to write. His restaurant was one of the most expensive in London but still did not pay. Perfection may have too high a price.

In 1937 Boulestin gave the first ever TV cookery demonstration, on BBC's *Cook's Night Out* programme. You can't get more modern than that, but Boulestin still maintained the mystique of Gallic creativity with such pronoucements as "It is not really an exaggeration to say that peace and happiness begin, geographically, where garlic is used in cooking" and "Cookery is not chemistry. It is an art. It requires instinct and taste, not exact measurements." *Panache,* anyone?

In 1936 Boulestin published an autobiography *Myself, My Two Countries,* but for all his Anglophilia Boulestin never considered naturalization and died in Nazi-occupied France. In 1952 his publisher, Heinemann, honoured him with the posthumous accolade of an anthology *The Best of Boulestin.* Unlike his campaigning countryman, André Simon *(see p. 198),* whose name is perpetuated in a prestigious book award, Boulestin's is largely forgotten.

THE ITALIANS

Neither White's, the most exclusive of gentlemen's clubs, nor Gunter's, the top people's confectioner for over two centuries, betray Italian origins in their names.

White's began in 1693 as a chocolate house, whose founder, Francesco Bianco, anglicised his name to Francis White. It originally stood on the site of what became Boodle's but crossed the road to become part of Arthur's Club, John Arthur being White's assistant and, after the death of Mrs Arthur, his successor as proprietor. Steele, Gay, Pope and Swift all referred to it as an institution of note – or notoriety – being famed for wit and excessive gambling. Nevertheless every British prime minister from Walpole to Peel was a member of White's, as were such luminaries as Beau Brummel and the Duke of Wellington.

Gunter's was founded by an Italian confectioner, Domenico Negri, in 1757 and initially traded under the sign of the Pineapple, then a symbol of luxury and hospitality. The first Gunter was Negri's assistant, then partner, then successor in his own right, running his own business on the east side of Berkeley Square. Famed for ices and sorbets, Gunter's attracted an elite clientele which habitually consumed these treats while sitting in their carriages outside the shop or in Berkeley Square itself, the waiters dodging in and out of the traffic to serve them. Gunter's other speciality was elaborate, tiered wedding-cakes for high society nuptuals. Gunter's moved to Curzon Street in 1936 and closed as a tea-shop twenty years later, though the catering business survived for a further twenty years.

Not until after World War Two would the most high-profile Italian restaurants actually serve mainly Italian food. Those who had initially done so a century before represented something of a 'find' to the cognoscenti as the outrageously snobbish Donald Shaw ("One of the Old Brigade") implied, writing in 1908 of 'London in the Sixties':

> "to get an unpretentious Italian eating-house in Old Compton Street ... was as good as attending the opera − if one was in the magic circle. Here ... congregated the leading exponents ... of Italian opera ... while below viands of the strictest Italian type were being consumed ... osso-buco, minestrone and spaghetti ... as undiluted as at Savini's in Milan ... No abominations in imitation of French cookery were to be found here. No half-crown dinners of half-a-dozen courses, with their deadly accompaniments of artichokes fried in tallow (au Cardinal) ... no New Zealand mutton garnished with turnip-tops (*ris de veau garni aux truffes*) ... and shop-boys and shop-girls knew their places too well to venture into such reserved pastures ..."

If anyone can be blamed for starting the supposed rot it was pragmatic Carlo Gatti, a Swiss-Italian from the impoverished and mountainous province of Ticino, who arrived in London in the late 1830s. At that time the city's Italian residents were too diverse, in terms of social standing and region of origin, to constitute a single community in a meaningful sense. They ranged from eminent political exiles, like Rossetti, first Professor of Italian at King's College and father of the poets Dante Gabriel and Christina, to seasonal migrants working the streets as musicians. Carlo Gatti also worked the streets, initially selling coffee and waffles. As he prospered he opened stalls, kiosks and cafés, staffing them with fellow Ticinese − eventually more than a thousand of

them. To these outlets he added a chocolate-making business and then opened a large café in Hungerford Hall, where "a little light music" was played in the background and the British public was introduced to the delights of the penny ice cream. By the 1850s Gatti had become an ice-importer on a large scale, bringing in thousands of tons from Norway and storing it in a canal-side icehouse at Islington. This not only supplied the needs of his own business but became a major business in its own right, serving butchers, fishmongers, restaurants and the wealthier private homes. By the 1860s Gatti was able to diversify still further, buying two music halls, which became known as Gatti's in the Road and Gatti's in the Arches (now the

78. Agostino and Stefano Gatti, c.1875, nephews of Carlo Gatti.

79. Gatti's restaurant (with music hall behind), in Villiers Street c.1885.
Rudyard Kipling lived opposite and could recall the "the smoke, the roar and the
good fellowship of relaxed humanity" there.

Players' Theatre, underneath Charing Cross station). In 1862 Gatti opened a restaurant in the Royal Adelaide Gallery in the Strand, which had served by turns as a concert hall, a dance hall and a casino. The cuisine, interestingly, was not Italian but English or Anglo-French. Carlo Gatti himself lived in some style in Bedford Square and by the time he died in 1878 had become a millionaire. The business was carried on by his daughter, Rosa, and nephews Agostino and Stefano. They acquired control of the Royal Adelphi Theatre in the Strand. Stefano carried on the Strand restaurant until 1939. The ice business finally closed in 1981 –

the former ice house is now home to the London Canal Museum.

The Café Monico was founded by former Gatti employees of that name, in Tichborne Street in 1876. The building of Shaftesbury Avenue in 1888-89 allowed a major expansion, the imposing new premises including a restaurant, grill-room and large banqueting suites and was still under the control of the Monico family half a century later, when it was hosting such events as a formal dinner for the London Welsh rugby club. Monico's was demolished in the 1950s to make way for a Piccadilly Circus reconstruction scheme which was then scrapped.

Pagani's in Great Portland Street began as a humble coffee-shop, kept by Mario Pagani in 1871. Much frequented by Italians, by a perhaps natural cultural extension it became a favourite with musicians generally. From 1874 onwards distinguished patrons of the upstairs 'Artists' Room' were encouraged to autograph the walls. Some added bars of music associated with them. Musical stars whose names were thus recorded included Tchaikovsky, Dame Nellie Melba, Paderewski and the tenor Enrico Caruso, whose after-dinner party trick was to swallow an entire peach whole. Other signatures included those of Sarah Bernhardt, H G Wells, Lillie Langtry, George Robey, Sir Henry Irving and Mrs Patrick Campbell, the original 'Eliza Doolittle'. The wall panels, preserved under glass, are now in the Museum of London. By 1881 London's Italian population had risen to about 3,500. During the course of that decade they came to monopolise the street trade in ice cream, served in small glasses with a conical bowl, called 'licks' – hence 'a penny lick' became a huge favourite with cockney children. Tempting buyers with the merest dab of this tasty treat, offered with the phrase 'ecco un poco' – 'here's a little bit'- the Italian ice-cream seller became known as the 'hokey-pokey man'. Invariably referred to as 'Jack', he would often be trailed by a small troupe of hopefuls whining the appeal to "Giss a taster, Jack!" By 1900 there were an estimated nine hundred ice cream barrows radiating daily onto the streets of working-class districts from the Clerkenwell homes where the ice cream was made to allegedly jealously guarded family recipes. In 1886 an 'Italian Society of Mutual Aid and Employment among Hotel and Restaurant Employees' was established in Gerrard Street. In 1890 Terroni

80. An Italian ice-cream seller in Clerkenwell. The royal portraits on the cart impart a touch of class.

81. *The splendid delicatessen of Camisa & Son at 61 Old Compton Street. Despite the existence of such old-established businesses in Soho and Clerkenwell as late as the 1950s, suburban shoppers might still find themselves seeking olive oil in a chemist's.*

82. Pinoli's Restaurant at 17 Wardour Street before the First World War. The Magic Circle was founded here in 1905. Pinoli's was still in business in 1956.

and Son's delicatessen opened in Clerkenwell Road, then the heart of the capital's 'Little Italy'. In 1901 it was followed by G Gazzano and Son's establishment in nearby Farringdon Road. On Goswell Road Adolfo Santuzzi, Giuseppe Caraccio and Vincenzo Doritis were confectioners. Elsewhere in Clerkenwell the Necchi family ran another confectionery; the Locatellis were cheese factors and Amata Benaventa ran a greengrocery.

The other main area of Italian presence was Soho, a neighbourhood "savoury with macaroni and oils... There are 'albergos' and wine shops where you may obtain a quarter of a fowl for 9d and a bottle of marsala and you can get olives and brandied cherries, as

dessert, for a few pence." The Del Lugo family had a pasta factory on Gerrard Street. Sherlock Holmes by this date was supposedly dining regularly at a fictional restaurant called 'Marcini's'. Oscar Wilde favoured the Florence in Rupert Street, quite fittingly, since it was well known to theatregoers. Although the rooms were small they were frescoed and a four course meal with wine could be had for an unbelievably modest two shillings.

Romano's at 399 Strand – 'The Home of Bohemia' – stood between the Vaudeville and the Adelphi theatres, which provided much of its clientele. Founded in 1885 by a former waiter at the Café Royal, Nicolino Alfonso Romano ('Old Roman'), it was located in a

83. Manzi's on Lisle Street, Soho, is now famed for fish but was once a German hotel, patronised by Johann Strauss the Elder and refugee Karl Marx, who was ejected with his family for failing to pay the bill.

former shooting-gallery and was consequently very narrow. Enlarged by taking in an adjacent shop, it burned down in 1891 but was reopened with a fanciful Moorish decor. George Edwardes, the enterprising manager of the nearby Gaiety Theatre, arranged for his famed Gaiety Girls to dine at Romano's at half-price.

Needless to say, this attracted a large number of young, and not so young, men-about-town. Much favoured by writers and sportsmen as well as 'theatricals', Romano's was sold on to new management on the death of its founder in 1901. Rebuilt in 1911, it finally closed in 1948.

Frascati's original building at 26-32 Oxford Street was completed in 1893 to designs by T E Collcutt, architect of the Imperial Institute, and given a glitzy gold make-over by Stanley Hamp in 1928. The main restaurant, known as the Winter Garden, featured a spectacular domed roof and balcony and was always noted for its impressive displays of flowers, regardless of season. Much favoured for formal banquets and Masonic dinners, it was demolished in the

early 1950s to make way for the Language Tuition Centre. Oddenino's Imperial Restaurant was opened in 1901 by Cavaliere Augusto Oddenino, who had been a manager with the Gattis and also worked at the Café Royal and the Criterion. The original restaurant was demolished and reconstructed as part of the 1920s' redevelopment of Regent Street. The rebuilt premises featured "an out-of-doors café reminiscent of the Continent." During the inter-war period both the Lew Stone and Syd Roy bands played there. In 1950 Oddenino's was chosen to host the celebratory banquet at which the London Lions Club received their Charter. Oddenino's closed in 1955.

Signor Gaspare Antonio Pietro ('Luigi') Gatti (1875-1912) was not a member of the famous catering dynasty but an immigrant from Montalto Pavese who had married a British girl, become a naturalized Briton and named his Southampton home, Montalto. A graduate of the Ritz and Oddenino's, he then ran two Ritz Restaurants – Gatti's Adelphi and Gatti's Strand – before becoming manager of an *à la carte* restaurant aboard the liner *Olympic,* sister ship to the *Titanic.* Gatti then transferred to manage the *A la Carte* restaurant aboard the *Titanic,* taking many of his Olympic staff with him. The *A la Carte* was run as an independent concession with its own kitchen and a staff of sixty-eight, including ten of his cousins. Three only of the entire staff survived the sinking of the ship. Gatti's body was recovered and buried in Halifax, Nova Scotia. Among his personal effects were his gold watch and chain, silver match case, initialised cuff-links, a diamond ring, and a knife marked 'Imperial Restaurant'.

Bertorelli's opened in Charlotte Street in 1913. As it had no liquor licence the customers' drinks were brought across from the Fitzroy Tavern opposite on a tray. Its Bohemian 'Fitzrovia' location normally appealed to the more raffish end of the literary and artistic world but in the 1970s it was regularly favoured by the very un-raffish novelist Anthony Powell and his right-wing chums – Kingsley Amis,

84. Dinner at Quaglino's, sketched by Francis Marshall before the last war.

Robert Conquest, Bernard Levin, Tibor Szamuely and John Braine. In 1998 Bertorelli's Senior Waitress, Mrs Gloria Lucia Guiditta Bittante, was awarded the MBE for her services to tourism.

The Ivy was opened at the end of the Great War by Abel Giandellini. Initially no more than a modest café, it soon became a favourite with the theatrical profession, one of whom gave it its name. When the actress Alice Delysia overheard 'Monsieur Abel' apologising to a customer for the inconvenience caused by building works, she butted in to reassure him that his customers would always remain faithful, quoting a line from a popular song of the day – "we'll cling together like the ivy". The Ivy's success was largely the product of its Mâitre d'Hôtel Mario Gallati. He finally left at the end of World War Two to open Le Caprice in 1947. Le Caprice folded in 1975 following Gallati's retirement but was reopened by 1981 by Chris Corbin and Jeremy King with an uncompromisingly contemporary black and white decor, complemented by a gallery of David Bailey photographs. In 1950 M. Abel sold the Ivy to Wheelers and it was later owned by Joseph Melatini, Lady Grade and the Forté organisation before it was acquired by Chris Corbin and Jeremy King in 1989 and relaunched in 1990.

85. A successful modern chain of restaurant-delicatessens has been pioneered by the Italian chef, Antonio Carluccio, appealing to those who cook as well as dine. Pictured here is the branch in Upper Street, Islington, in 2003.

Quaglino's, opened in 1929 in Bury Street, was named for the former head waiter at Sovrani's. The chef, M. Rossignol, formerly of Ciro's, presided over "no less than twelve highly-qualified specialists in each branch of cooking." A typical dinner menu offered a choice of caviar, turtle soup, mousseline of salmon with prawns, chicken, asparagus salad and a dessert – at twenty-five shillings for two; though the suggested accompaniments – vodka, a 1916 Chateau Margaux, vintage champagne and Napoleon brandy – would have bumped up the reckoning somewhat. Quaglino's swiftly established itself as one of the smart society restaurants. Like Odoni's, it had its own dance band, led by Frank Gregori, which played until 2.00 am., but was "to be congratulated on not troubling ... guests overmuch with cabaret". While he was studying at the London School of Economics the Hungarian-born financier and philanthropist George Soros funded himself by working as a waiter at Quaglino's. In 1961 the aged Sir Winston Churchill joined in celebrations at Quaglino's to mark the 'coming out' of his granddaughter, Celia Sandys. In 1993 a totally rebuilt and greatly enlarged Quaglino's was reopened on the original site by Sir Terence Conran. Commentators dubbed it a 'gastrodome' or megabrasserie.

Another inter-war newcomer was the San Marco, opposite the Ritz. The presiding spirit. Umberto, was also a Ciro's alumnus. True to type, the menu offered such specialities as Dublin Bay prawns with an Italian name in French – Scampi Venetiens.

Running parallel with the development of these high-profile 'name' restaurants were the simple but stylish *trattoria* which brought Italian food to customers who paid out of their own pockets. Post-war immigrant Otello Schipioni, initially a waiter at the Savoy, opened his Trattoria Toscana in Frith Street, Soho in 1954. The Fraquellis, also post-war immigrants, began with a coffee-shop at Golders Green and launched their Spaghetti House chain in Goodge Street in 1955 with the slogan 'Spaghetti, but not on toast!". At the top end of the range was the Romilly Street establishment, La Terrazza, started by ex-waiters Mario and Franco in 1959 to offer Italian regional dishes. In 1962 they followed this with Tiberio in Carnaby Street, offering ten soups, fifteen types of pasta and dishes which were then either new to most Londoners, such as sea bass, or represented an alien sophistication of some traditional English fare, such as tripe or duckling, or like baby lamb with truffles, sounded as though it had come straight out of the pages of the Roman gourmet Apicius.

NORTH BRITONS

The Act of Union of 1707 (north of the border known as the Treaty of Union, a subtle but significant difference), dissolved Scotland's separate Parliament in return for disproportionately favourable representation at Westminster and encouraged a southward migration of talented Scots, prompting Dr Johnson to remark with typically English self-assurance that the fairest prospect before any young Scotsman was the highway to London. Better educated than his English counterpart, in the land of his birth the average Scotsman had more restricted economic opportunities than could be found in England, Europe's largest free trade area, which was increasingly benefiting from the expansion of its global commerce and the first phases of industrialisation. Edinburgh, epicentre of the Scottish Enlightenment, led Britain as a centre of medical education. Glasgow gave the nation James Watt. Between the two of them these cities also produced Adam Smith. The Scots had much to offer, but the offer was not always welcomed. London's established elite found them pushy and referred to them disparagingly in code as 'North Britons'. Frequently marginalised, they did what enterprising Scots have learned to do throughout their diaspora, networked and helped each other at such locations as the appropriately named 'British Coffee-House' in Cockspur Street. With them Scots brought tastes unfamilar to their new compatriots, rejecting the current English addiction to gin for the 'water of life' – *usquebaugh* in Gaelic, anglicised as whisky; although it took until the 1880s for this to become generally available in most pubs. Salmon was well enough known in England but smoked haddock was something of a novelty, especially boiled in milk ('seethed') in the Scottish (originally French) style. Haggis was unlikely to attract many converts but Scotch broth – in its homeland barley broth – evidently did. Hannah Glasse *(see p. 53)* included a recipe for it in her 1747 *Art of Cookery. The* first known printed recipe for Scotch Eggs dates from 1809. Although it has subsequently become a convenient picnic favourite, at that time it was eaten hot with gravy.

As the English prided themselves on eating white wheaten bread as a mark of national superiority *(see p. 16)* the Scottish proclivity for oats, eaten as bannocks or porridge and better suited as a crop to their less benevolent climate, was equally mystifying, though it did provide one of the few occasions on which Johnson's Scottish acolyte and biographer, James Boswell, had the better of the great man in repartee. In his *Dictionary* Johnson defined oats as a grain which in England was fed to horses but in Scotland to men. To which Boswell riposted – "Ah!, but where did you see such horses – or such men?" Years before meeting Johnson, in the course of his first sojourn in London in 1762-3, Boswell had determined to undertake a self-imposed crash-course in anglicisation:

> "The enemies of the people of England who would have them considered in the worst light represent them as selfish, beef-eaters and cruel. In this view I resolved today to be a true-born Old Englishman. I went into the City to Dolly's Steak-house in Paternoster Row and swallowed my dinner by myself to fulfill the charge of selfishness; I had a large fat beefsteak to fulfill the charge of beef-eating; and I went at five o'clock to the Royal Cockpit in St James's Park and saw cock-fighting for about five hours to fulfill the charge of cruelty. A beefsteak-house is a most excellent place to dine at. You come in there to a warm, comfortable, large room, where a number of people are sitting at table. You take whatever place you find empty; call for what you like, which you get well and cleverly dressed. You may either chat or not as you like. Nobody minds you and you pay very reasonably. My dinner (beef, bread and beer and waiter) was only a shilling....
>
> At five I filled my pockets with gingerbread and apples ... put on my old clothes ... laid by my watch, purse and pocket-book and with oaken stick in my hand sallied to the pit. I was too soon there. So I went

into a low inn, sat down amongst a parcel of arrant blackguards and drank some beer ... I then went to the Cockpit ... Thus did I complete my true English day and came home pretty much fatigued and pretty much confounded at the strange turn of this people."

THE JEWS

J. Lyons *(see p. 91)*, the greatest Jewish contribution to feeding London – indeed, the nation – was Jewish only in its top management. Such Jewish 'ethnic' restaurants as did develop catered for a specifically Jewish clientele, who accounted for perhaps as much as 90% of their customers. Quite possibly the strength of the Jewish traditional emphasis on family meals and the observance of kosher practices militated against the development of a restaurant culture geared to the tastes of a Gentile market. Jewish entrepreneurship was, however, evident in other market niches. In the 1850s Henry Mayhew observed a virtual Jewish wholesale monopoly operating in the squalid Houndsditch area where costermongers came to buy their oranges, lemons, grapes and nuts. He also recorded a dozen Jewish pastry-cooks in Whitechapel as the main suppliers of the biscuits, cakes and tarts hawked on London's streets by itinerant vendors. In late Victorian Clerkenwell Nathan Levy and Samuel Isaacs ran fried fish shops on the Goswell Road and Sam had another one on Pentonville Road.

The heart of London Jewry in the Victorian period was to be found in Aldgate and Whitechapel. Rothschild Buildings (1887), the product of elite Anglo-Jewish philanthropy, was built to house the influx of refugees fleeing pogroms in the Tsarist Russian empire. Many of the incomers brought to this densely populated urban location the habits of peasant life in the *stetl,* keeping a rabbit or even chickens in their apartments. Fed on kitchen scraps, these would make a small but welcome addition to the family food supply. Perhaps surprisingly it was also still possible for them to buy milk fresh from the cow from one of the three dairies surviving in Whitechapel, the

86. Tubby Isaacs' shellfish stall at Aldgate, 2003. Note the pub's offering of recently ubiquitous Thai food.

largest being licensed for forty-six cows. Rinkoff's bakery in Thrawl Street sold *matzos* and black bread and also served as a community cookshop for the Saturday midday meal, typically a substantial *cholund,* a meat and vegetable casserole. Kosher meat and poultry were readily available, with fifteen kosher butchers and poulterers in Wentworth Street alone. As far as meat went families gave priority to the Sabbath meals. During the week they would expect to rely on filling soups made from barley, potatoes, broad beans or 'soup greens', penny bundles of mixed vegetable scraps sold from market stalls for the purpose.

Although degrees of religious observance varied, even the lax and the sceptical regarded the ritual celebration of a Friday night family meal as central to their identity as Jews. A common religious heritage co-existed with differences, sometimes marked, in styles of cooking, with the newcomers hailing from regions as far apart as Rumania and the Baltic.

A Lithuanian remembered his amazement at the seasoning habits of Polish neighbours: "We used a great deal of pepper and seasoning. The Polish used sugar ... when you had boiled fish. Ours was peppery and theirs was sweet ... I went into Grodzinsky's family and they were having black bread with cream cheese and they sprinkled sugar on it. And I thought what on earth are they doing that for?" Large families and low incomes compelled some to shop for food daily, buying small treats in tiny quantities, like a saucer or jam jar of pickles, a single herring from a large tin or jam by the 'ha-porth' at tea-time. Broken eggs and broken biscuits were also regularly on sale. Children hapless enough to lose a father and therefore reliant on a widow's earnings were particularly pinched. One remembered breakfast as a bit of hard bread, the rest of which made do for lunch. Another, whose mother toiled long hours, came home every day to an empty room with a banana left out for her supper. (Fruit about to turn would have been cheap in the street markets.) This was surely better than the bread in salt water which another mother proffered as a stomach-filler. Yet another former resident recalled being simply packed off to bed at five o'clock because there was no supper. The poor yet remained aware of the poorest:

> "... if you ever had any lunch over you'd wrap it in paper and hang it on the railings outside so that somebody would come along and take it. If we had half a loaf left over it would be left out like that for the ultra-poor, the beggars."

The Jewish sense of community responsibility also ensured the establishment of charitable institutions, such as the soup kitchen, originally in Fashion Street and from 1902 in handsome new premises in Brune (then Butler) Street. This fed a thousand people. The circumstances of each family were assessed by an investigating officer. Those deemed worthy of relief were given an official soup-kettle proportionate to the size of their family. In addition they would also be entitled to a dole of bread, which was reputedly much better than the soup. The Jewish Free School also provided bread and milk for breakfastless children if they arrived early. At Commercial Street school there was hot milk in winter. A journalistic description of Whitechapel around 1900 declared that eating well was one of the first priorities for a by then increasingly prospering community:

> "Kosher restaurants abound in it; kosher butcher shops are clustered in thick bunches (seven of them at the junction of Middlesex Street and Wentworth Street), and if the expert handling of the fowls on the stalls by ill-clad Jewesses is not a revelation of epicureanism in humble life then, most assuredly, things are not what they seem."

Despite the seeming chaos of the street-markets their operations were strictly supervised and regulated to maintain Orthodox standards:

> "Now and then something like a shiver of horror passes over the Ghetto when it is disovered that a

traitor has been palming off *trifah* (non-kosher) meat on his customers as kosher. Then the Board for the Affairs of Shechta, which attends to such matters, pastes a solemn warning on the walls to the faithful and the offending stall is promptly forsaken."

During the inter-war period, especially, many West End pubs were managed by Jewish publicans, who would routinely put out pickles and bite-size portions of traditional fish and meat delicacies as bar-snacks. The Bohemian Fitzroy Tavern in Charlotte Street was presided over by Judah Kleinfeld. Goody's of Berwick Street was said to be the oldest kosher restaurant and Folman's, off Wardour Street, was said to be the largest but the most famous was Bloom's at Aldgate, opened in 1952 by Sidney Bloom and famed for the excellence of its salt-beef sandwiches and the surliness of its elderly waiters. Modestly proclaiming itself as "the most famous Jewish restaurant in the world", Bloom's finally closed its Aldgate establishment in 1994, though another branch survived in Golders Green. The Jewish tradition of catering in the East End was represented thereafter by the twenty-four hours a day, 365-days-a-year Bagel Bake in Brick Lane – much favoured by the capital's Jewish cab-drivers – and Tubby Isaacs' seafood stall at Aldgate.

BEST OF THE WURST

Considering its weight in Europe and its strong relationship with the British royal family, the German-speaking world has had a relatively limited, if various, impact on London's gastronomy. Folklore credits George III's German wife, the notoriously parsimonious Charlotte of Mecklenburgh-Strelitz, with making her own personal contribution to English cuisine by inventing Apple Charlotte as a way of using up stale bread. Chemist Friedrich Accum *(see p.190)* made an invaluable contribution to combating the problem of food adulteration. Germans, almost from its origins, took charge of the sugar-baking industry in the East End. Throughout the nineteenth century

87. *The proprietors of this Portobello Road snack stand clearly assume that customers will not understand the German names of what they offer.*

they were renowned as specialist pork butchers and makers of sausages. The ultra-respectable German colony in the Denmark Hill area, mostly consisting of wealthy bankers and merchants, had its own bakery to supply familiar types of bread and pastry. Visiting Germans were doubtless grateful to take advantage of offers of hospitality from these comfortable bourgeois. In 1904 Mrs Alfred Sidgwick, the German-born author of *Home Life,* summarised what was to her the fundamental culinary difference between the land of her birth and her adoptive country:

"If you like cold mutton, boiled potatoes and rice pudding, most days in the week ... to cook for you requires neither skill nor pains, while to cook for a German family, even if it lives plainly and poorly, takes time and trouble ... In well-to-do English households you get the best food in the world as far as raw material goes, but it must be said that you often get poor cooking. It passes quite unnoticed, too."

The marriage of Prince Albert of Saxe-Coburg to Queen Victoria in 1840 may have inspired the term 'Coburg' for a round loaf with two cuts made in the top at right angles, so that it opens out when baked. There may have been a punning intention as a round loaf without the cuts was known as a cob. The first known use of the word is in a letter of Dante Rossetti's of 1843. Parti-coloured Battenberg cake is supposed to have been named in honour of the marriage in 1884 of Queen Victoria's grand-daughter, Princess Victoria of Hesse-Darmstadt to Prince Louis of Battenberg.

Kettner's in Romilly Street, Soho was established by the Austrian ex-chef of French Emperor Napoleon III in 1867. *Kettner's Book of the Table* (1877) contains the first mention in English of the 'Frankfurt sausage'.

In 1908 Austrian Rudolph Stulik founded the Restaurant de la Tour Eiffel at 1 Percy Street, off Tottenham Court Road. As the name implies it served French rather than German food. It was patronised by the Vorticist group of avant-garde artists and poets including Percy Wyndham-Lewis and Ezra Pound. One of their gatherings, to launch their magazine *Blast,* is memorialized in a 1962 painting by one of their number, the English Cubist, William Roberts, now in the Tate Gallery collection. After Stulik retired in 1937 the Tour Eiffel subsequently went through several incarnations featuring Greek *(ill. 88),* French-Vietnamese and Thai cuisine.

In the late nineteenth century London acquired several café-patissiers, which offered the Central European seductions of coffee, confectionery, chess and newspapers. Most notable were the Vienna Café at 24-8 New Oxford Street near the British Museum, opened *c.*1885 by the Anglo-Austrian Confectionery Company. There were also German Hotels in Lisle Street and Greek Street, Soho. German and Austrian proprietors of many cafés and hotels were dispossessed as enemy aliens in 1914. The café-confectionery concept was reincarnated on a mass-scale by J. Lyons & Co. Rumpelmayer's survived the war and is mentioned by Virginia Woolf as supplying the catering for the evening entertainment which represents Mrs Dalloway's social climax. In the inter-war period there was a luxury basement restaurant in Bond Street, Fischer's. At the other end of the market, from 1901 onwards Schmidt's in Charlotte Street supplied cheap, filling food for generations of students and the Fitzrovian Bohemians who could not afford Bertorelli's *(see p. 110).* It was also favoured in

88. Formerly the Restaurant de la Tour Eiffel, at 1 Percy Street, it became an early Greek restaurant, the White Tower, between the wars. The proprietor, Yanni Stais, poses at the door.

the 1960s by left-wing intellectuals like Michael Foot and the historian Isaac Deutscher.

THE CURRY CONNECTION

When the East India Company was founded in London in 1599 to exploit the hugely profitable Asian spice trade, India was reluctantly accepted as its main focus of activity as second best to Indonesia, where the Dutch had successfully established themselves. The voyage to India was long and hazardous and the ships built for the Company in its docks at Blackwall were as much men-of-war as trading vessels. Storms, scurvy and pirates were as much hazards as the predatory ships of competing European nations with which Britain was, overtly or covertly, often in conflict. But the profits of this perilous commerce were potentially immense as the palatial estates created by East India merchants like Sir Josiah Child demonstrated. It took the best part of a year and a half for a ship to reach India and return but a safely returned ship stuffed with pepper and cloves, nutmeg and mace, brought a return on capital of hundreds

per cent, sometimes even more.

British traders were at first basically supplicants in a much richer country and were dazzled by the opulence of the Mughal court and Indian cities. They were also in rivalry with the French, Portuguese and Danish for royal favour. The British founded Calcutta in eastern India as a fortified trading-base and established themselves likewise at Madras and Bombay.

Following the death in 1707 of Aurangzeb, the last great Mughal emperor, the Mughal empire rapidly disintegrated. The authority of the later emperors extended little further than their decaying capital of Delhi. To protect its trading interests the East India Company built up its private army and navy and began to get sucked into local political disputes. Meanwhile Britain began to achieve a decisive technical superiority in military and naval power. The East India Company became the *de facto* government of much of India. The resident British population adopted Indian lifestyles, took Indian mistresses and acquired a taste for curries, kedgeree, shampoos, punch, pyjamas

89. *Opened in 1982, the Bombay Brasserie in Courtfield Road, set a standard of luxury which was a novelty for the Indian restaurant trade at the time.*

and polo. British merchants and officials returned home as fabulously wealthy 'nabobs' (from 'nawab', the title of a native ruler). Some brought their Indian servants back with them so that they could continue to placate their palates with dishes of which they had become inordinately fond. (One returnee's longings inspired the invention of Worcestershire sauce as a universal flavour-all.) Hannah Glasse *(see p. 53)* included a recipe for "Currey the Indian way" in her 1747 cookery classic, although actually it was a chicken fricasee spiced with ginger, turmeric and pepper "beat very fine". As early as 1773 a coffee-house in Norris Street, off the Haymarket, was offering curry on its menu and the first commercial curry powder was on sale by 1780. Even boobies like the gross and ridiculous Jos Sedley in Thackeray's *Vanity Fair* made a parade of having Indian

dishes served at their table. (Thackeray himself was a fan and in 1846 published a *Poem to Curry* in a volume *of Kitchen Melodies.)* Although published in 1847-8, *Vanity Fair* is set a generation earlier, at which time Jos could have satisfied his gustatory nostalgia by patronising the Hindostanee Coffee House run by Dean Mahomed from 1810 at 34 George Street, Portman Square. There he could have joined "the Nobility and Gentry where they might enjoy the Hookha with real Chilm tobacco and Indian dishes of the highest perfection and allowed by the greatest epicures to be unequalled to any curries ever made in England." The business soon expanded into no. 35 but this proved unsustainable and Mahomed went personally bankrupt in 1812. The business, however, survived his departure (to become a successful 'shampooing surgeon' in Brighton) and carried on for another twenty years. From 1824 onwards the Oriental Club would have given him another possible venue. A book on *Indian Cookery* was published by its chef, Richard Terry, in 1861, including recipes "gathered not only from my own knowledge of cookery but from Native Cooks".

Eliza Acton's *Modern Cookery for Private Families,* published in 1845, not only included Indian dishes in its concluding chapter on 'Foreign and Jewish Cookery', but also devoted a separate chapter to 'Curries, Potted Meats Etc.' By the mid-Victorian period both curry powder and curry paste were commercially available but quite correctly Eliza Acton argued that:

"the great superiority of the oriental curries over those generally prepared in England is not .. .altogether the result of a want of skill or experience on the part of our cooks, but is attributable ... to many of the ingredients, which in *a fresh and green state* add so much to their excellence, being here beyond our reach."

Eliza further cautioned against heavy-handed over-use of turmeric and cayenne and urged greater use of cocoa-nut. Deferring to the expertise of a Mr Arnott, she quoted his formula for 'currie-powder' – by ounces, turmeric (8), coriander seed (4), cumin seed (2), fenugreek (2) and cayenne (0.5) but noted that as "the preparing is rather a troublesome process the task might be delegated to a 'high-caste' chemist." Mr Arnott's recipe for a curry starts with a cabbage heart "about the size of an egg", chopped fine, plus two thinly sliced apples, half a dozen onions, a clove of garlic, lemon juice, black pepper, curry powder, butter, flour and "one pint of strong mutton or beef gravy". To this may be added "a fowl that has been roasted and nicely cut up or pork chops, a rabbit, a lobster or the remains of yesterday's calf's head". Other recipes are offered for curried macaroni, eggs and sweetbreads and, in the last chapter, for 'The King of Oude's Omlet' (which included cream, salt, cayenne, mint, leeks and onions) and kedgeree.

Anthony Trollope's wife is known to have served curried salmon and there is also a contemporary recipe for curried oysters. During the Irish famine of the 1840s the Duke of Norfolk suggested that its victims be relieved with curry powder in water, apparently in the belief that if Indian peasants could survive on this ....

Although personally uninterested in the pleasures of the table and strongly preferring the plainest of food, Queen Victoria, having assumed the title Empress of India, deemed it appropriate that Indian servants in the royal kitchens should prepare a curry to appear on the royal table every single day of the year, presumably to anticipate the needs of any maharajah who might be passing through. It was invariably returned whence it came, untouched. Whatever the familiarity (or, in the case of the Duke of Norfolk, unfamiliarity) of Londoners with Indian-style foods the fact remains that when Mohandas Gandhi (1869-1948) came to study law in London in the 1880s, he had a hard time of it until he encountered a missionising band of vegetarians *(see p. 161)*. When Gandhi was a student in the capital he was one of only about a hundred

Indians pursuing higher education. By 1931 there would be 1,800. In theory these would constitute a substantial market when added to the small resident elite of Indian officials, lawyers and businessmen, the retired Anglo-Indian community and the thousands of lascar seamen who passed through the port of London annually. Unfortunately these constituted such very contrasting social types that they could not cohere into a single culinary constituency. The Anglo-Indians and Indian elite might conceivably dine in the same sort of place (the Savoy very daringly employed an Indian cook) but neither were likely to welcome the students as fellow-diners. And the students, many of whom had little more cash to spare than a lascar, lived too far from the dock areas to find common culinary cause with them. By the 1920s former ships' galley-cooks from Sylhet in what is now Bangladesh were, however, opening cafés and lodging-houses for other sailors.

In 1911 the Salute Hind restaurant opened in Holborn but failed to make a durable impression. The first high-profile South Asian restaurant, Shafi's at 18 Gerrard Street, opened in 1920, employing ex-lascars in the kitchen and attracting students as customers (together at last). Veeraswamy's in Regent Street, opened on the strength of success with a food counter in the Mughal Palace at the 1924 Empire Exhibition at Wembley *(see p.145)*. The founder, Edward Palmer, was the great-grandson of a British general and an Indian princess. Soon recognised as the preferred haunt of former British Raj officials, its patrons also included the Prince of Wales, to be followed in due course by numerous Indian princes, the king of Sweden, Nehru, Indira Gandhi, King Hussein of Jordan, Charlie Chaplin and MarIon Brando. The kitchens, meanwhile, served as a *de facto* training academy for restaurateurs who were to spread the curry crusade into the provinces. A tandoor was in use at Veeraswamy's as early as 1959, quite possibly the first in Britain. During extensive renovations in 1997 it was discovered that the original floor-plan, long since obscured by subsequent alterations, was laid out in accordance with the principles of Vastu Shatra, the ancient Vedic science which is the Hindu equivalent of feng shui.

Veeraswamy's was followed by Bir Bahadur's Kohinoor in Rupert Street, the Durbar and Bengal in Percy Street, the Shalimar on Wardour Street and the Dilkush in Windmill Street.

By the 1930s Bengalis, initially employed in the Jewish-run clothing industry, were already established in Brick Lane. Shirref's opened in Great Castle Street in 1935. In 1938 ex-sailor and community leader Ayub Ali 'Master', opened the Shah Jolal at 76 Commercial Street. Halal opened in St Mark's Street in 1939. In 1941 the East London Mosque was established in Commercial Road. During the war also the Green Mask and the Anglo-Asian restaurant both opened in the Brompton Road. By 1946 there were estimated to be about twenty Indian restaurants in London.

In 1947 the partition of the British Raj into India and Pakistan brought migrants from the disputed Punjab and Kashmir and also from Gujarat and Sylhet. In the 1950s South Asians came as industrial replacement labour to the factories of the East End and West London. In 1951 there were 350 Asians in Southall; by the 1960s they accounted for 12% of its population. In 1967 came the arrival of Asians expelled from Kenya and in 1972 more from Uganda. The 1970s and 1980s witnessed a process of family reconstitution as all-male households in lodging-houses give way to owner-occupied family households with females, children and older relatives. There was a corresponding growth of family enterprises, especially into grocery stores and restaurants.

A decade before the expulsions L G Pathak arrived from Kenya with a wife, six children, five pounds and a life insurance policy. Starting out in 1956 by selling samosas made in his own kitchen, he accumulated enough to buy his first shop, at 134 Drummond Street, just north of Euston station, a thoroughfare later to be lined with Indian restaurants and shops. By word of mouth recommendation Pathak's shop won a reputation for quality products, especially pickles and chutneys. Soon Pathak was catering for functions at the Indian High Commission and, in 1958, for the Queen's Garden Party at Buckingham Palace. By 1962 Pathak's — anglicised to Patak's — had opened its first factory in the east Midlands. In 1976 the founder's son, Kirit, on a buying trip in India met his future bride, Meena, who had just graduated with a degree in food technology and hotel management. Within three months of their marriage she had created a commercially viable tandoori paste. Success soon obliged the company to relocate its operations to Lancashire.

The Bangladeshi presence in London was greatly enlarged by the civil war in East Pakistan which led to its successful secession to become an independent Bangladesh in 1971. Over half of all Bangladeshis in the UK are in London, making it the largest Bangladeshi community outside Bangladesh. Brick Lane, Aldgate, officially designated since 1998 as 'Banglatown', stands at the heart of the community. The decision of Taj International Hotels in 1982 to open its Bombay Brasserie in Courtfield Road, SW7, adjacent to the historic Bailey's Hotel, set new standards in luxurious surroundings and threw down a gauntlet to the rest of the trade. Led by the flamboyant and enterprising Amin Ali, creator of Last Days of the Raj (1977), Lal Qila (1981) and Red Fort (1983), Bangladeshi restaurants began to move up-market. The fact that some four-fifths of all Indian restaurants were actually Bangladeshi was initially concealed by their proprietors in the belief that Indian culture had a higher perceived status in British eyes. Over the last decade Bangladeshi restaurants have increasingly 'outed' themselves as such, an indicator of growing cultural self-confidence. Nationally the Bangladeshi catering industry now has an annual turnover of £2 billion and employs 70,000 people, far more than steel,

90. Design on a grocer's bag of P H Benn, of 277 Mile End Road. A stereotypical view of traditional China could still be exploited commercially well into the twentieth century.

coal and shipbuilding combined. While restaurants continue to experiment with fusion cuisines, such as Thai-Bengali, a 'curry crisis' has emerged at the kitchen level as younger Bangladeshis with alternative employment options have begun to prove reluctant to move into the family business.

CHINOISERIE TO CHINATOWN

Direct British trading contacts with China began in 1637, focusing on porcelain and silks and then tea. Eighteenth-century Londoners subscribed to the European cult of *chinoiserie,* which affected decorative taste and led to the establishment of porcelain factories producing imitations of Chinese blue and white wares at Chelsea, Vauxhall, Limehouse and the 'New Canton' works at Bow, which benefited from the simultaneous rise in the fashion for tea-drinking.

91. *Gerrard Street, Soho, the heart of London's officially designated 'Chinatown', has over twenty Chinese restaurants and several supermarkets. Loon Fung's sign obscures the first plaque marking the home of poet John Dryden (see p.134) – actually fixed to the wrong house.*

The East India Company developed a profitable counter-trade export in opium to offset its purchases of tea and other Chinese products. When the Chinese banned the opium trade in 1839 the British were swiftly victorious in the subsequent 'Opium War'. The 1842 Treaty of Nanking ceded Hong Kong to British control and it became a major centre for British trade and finance in Asia. Chinese migrated there from the mainland as traders and labourers. In 1949 Britain recognised the Communist regime in China and accepted refugees into Hong Kong, from where they could move on to Britain. Most Chinese in Britain therefore speak Cantonese or another southern dialect, as opposed to the majority ('Mandarin'/ putonghua) speech of northern China. Chinese sailors, especially cooks and laundrymen, had begun to settle in Limehouse in the 1880s.

Their concentration, physical difference and maintenance of a distinctive culture gave them a visibility quite out of proportion to their numbers. In 1913 there were only about 400-500 in Limehouse, London's main Chinatown, where they had established some 30 cafés and laundries. The popular fiction of the period demonized Limehouse as an abode of nameless horrors and white slavery, epitomised from 1913 in Sax Rohmer's novels (later filmed) of the evil master of crime Dr Fu Man Chu. There was opium smoking and illegal gambling but the other calumnies were baseless fantasies.

Chung Koon, a former ship's chef on the Red Funnel line, who had married an English girl, opened two up-market restaurants in the West End, Maxim's in Soho in 1908 and the Cathay, in Glasshouse Street, soon after. Then there was a long gap. Choy's opened in the

King's Road, Chelsea in 1937. The Old Friends, appropriately located in Mandarin Street, Limehouse was in existence by World War Two.

As a dockside district Limehouse was severely damaged during the Blitz, dispersing members of the Chinese community there. The run-down area around Gerrard Street and Lisle Street in Soho was offering short leases for business premises which British entrepreneurs were unwilling to take up. Cheap Chinese food, served until late, found a market among West End pleasure-seekers and ex-servicemen who had served in the Far East. One particularly prominent group in the restaurant trade was the Man clan from the Hong Kong New Territories village of San Tin, where agriculture had been undermined by environmental deterioration. At the same time the advent of the laundrette and the domestic washing-machine sounded the death-knell for the traditional Chinese laundry.

Perhaps as much as 75% of the economically active Chinese labour force is still employed in catering and related trades. The shift of emphasis from laundry work to catering was assisted by a fundamental British cultural perception. Whereas it was widely thought for two centuries that an acceptable adaptation of Indian cooking could be approximated by liberally dousing a random assortment of ingredients with curry powder, no one thought, before the advent of the wok, that there was an equivalent way of appropriating Chinese cuisine. There was, however, also a substantial downside. Working long hours in restaurants and take-aways has hindered Chinese restaurant workers' contact with mainstream British society, inhibiting participation in politics at local or national level. Concentrating on the demands of business and family may have retarded the development of broader community institutions by starving them of leaders and volunteers. The Chinese community has, however, exhibited a strong commitment to the maintenance of cultural identity, especially through language. The Chinese Chamber of Commerce in London sponsors what is claimed to be largest of Europe's Chinese language schools with 900 pupils. The 1991 census counted 156,938 Chinese in the UK, of whom a third were in London.

Chinese restaurants, like their Indian counterparts, have moved upmarket since their initial proliferation in the 1950s. At that time their willingness to stay open late attracted a clientele, after pub closing hours, which was often less than desirable. Increasing public familiarity with Chinese culture, from martial arts to acupuncture and feng shui, however, has enabled the restaurant trade to entertain higher aspirations with regard to both custom and offerings. In 1957 Chung Koon's son, John, took over the Cathay and in 1958 opened the stylish Lotus House. He then moved the entire trade into a new direction by opening the first ever take-away on Queensway. In 1963 Mr. Kuo, the chef at the Chinese Embassy, defected and started Britain's first non-Cantonese Chinese restaurant, in Willesden.

Since 1973 an annual festival has been held in Chinatown to welcome in the Chinese New Year. In 1980 Kenneth Lo opened *Memories of China*. In 1984 Westminster City Council officially recognised south Soho as 'Chinatown'. At the time of writing there were over sixty Chinese restaurants there and over twelve hundred more in the rest of London, with luxury standard outlets in the City, Mayfair and Queensway, plus supermarkets in Park Royal, Barnet, Haringey, Hackney and Croydon.

PART FIVE

Eating Out

NOT SO ORDINARY

London's largest inns became noted for their provision of a daily 'ordinary', a fixed-price table d'hôte meal. Unlike restaurants, therefore, they did not offer a choice of dishes from a menu. Nor were they socially exclusive or, usually, places of fashionable resort, although they might be resorted to by the fashionable if they were located near enough to the court. Nor was the food they offered very elaborate, consisting mostly of roasts and chops and sometimes pies or puddings. Misson's late seventeenth-century account can stand for most:

> "Generally four spits, one over another, carry round each five or six pieces of butcher-meat, beef, mutton, veal, pork and lamb; you have what quantity you please cut off, fat, lean, much or little done; with this a little salt and mustard upon the side of the plate, a bottle of beer and a roll; and there is your whole feast."

Some ordinaries were, however, less ordinary than most.

Pontack's was London's most celebrated eating-house from the year of the Great Fire until it passed out of the hands of the de Pontac family eighty years later. Arnaud III de Pontac (1599-1681) inherited the chateau and vineyards of Haut-Brion, married advantageously and became the richest and most powerful man in Bordeaux. Although he lived extravagantly, he also had the wit to grasp the huge potential of the London market for quality claret. Haut-Brion – anglicised as Ho Bryan – was being drunk with relish by Samuel Pepys by 1663 and has the unique historical distinction of being the first wine to be marketed under the name of the estate on which it was produced, rather than under the name of its owner or of the parish in which it was located. In 1666 Arnaud despatched one of his sons, the multi-lingual François-Auguste (1636-94), to open a tavern in Abchurch Lane, complete with a French chef, whose exotic offerings would tempt in the capital's more discriminating palates to become acquainted with, and hopefully enslaved to, the family vintage. The decade was propitious for such a venture. Charles II had returned to his throne from years of exile in France. French fashions and French tastes were the order of the day among the capital's elite. The specific year was less happily chosen. The first premises must have perished in the Great Fire of September 1666, which started in Pudding Lane, less than five minutes walk away. Undeterred, François-Auguste persisted and was rewarded with immense success. Initially using a portrait of de Pontac *pere* as a trade-sign, the house was at first known as Pontack's Head. Literary references confirm its rapid acceptance as a fashionable venue, noted as such in Congreve's *Love for Love* (1695) and also being referred to in plays by Southerne, Sedley and Mrs Centlivre. Pontack's clientele included Wren, Pope, Swift and Evelyn, despite the latter's intense irritation at the host's ebullient and knowing manner,

Chop Room.
Ye Olde Cheshire Cheese

92. Ye Olde Cheshire Cheese, just off Fleet Street beween the wars, a popular place to eat an Ordinary. The pub has changed very little since then. A sign in the passageway outside records the eminent literary figures who have made a pilgrimage to this ancient hostelry.

opining that "much learning hath made him mad". According to Defoe in 1722 a meal could be had at prices ranging from four shillings to a guinea and the name of Pontac was still synonymous with "the best French clarets". Pontack's was also the preferred venue for the annual dinners of the Royal Society until the business passed into English hands in 1746. The new proprietress, Mrs Susannah Austin was said, nevertheless, to have made a considerable fortune by continuing to serve such delicacies as ragout of snails and chicks not two hours out of the shell.

The original Lockett's was a Charing Cross ordinary which took its name from proprietor Adam Lockett, who died in 1668. It provided meals at regular hours and fixed prices. During the reign of James II it provided a take-out service for "officers of the Horse Guards that are in waiting". In Vanbrugh's *The Relapse*

(1696) Lord Foppington commends it – thinly disguised as Lacket's – on the grounds that "there you are so nicely and delicately served, that, stap my vitals, they can compose you a dish, no bigger than a saucer, shall come to fifty shillings...". Lockett's is also mentioned in Congreve's *Way of the World* (1700) but appears to have lost its cachet by the time of the Hanoverians. The modern Lockett's restaurant is much favoured by politicians and political journalists. One of its house specialities is a savoury consisting of toast topped by water-cress, thinly sliced pears and Stilton, lightly baked and topped with freshly ground black pepper.

Established in Covent Garden in the reign of Charles II, Chatelain's, another French 'ordinary' became sufficiently celebrated to be mentioned in fiction. Pepys patronised it on at least two occasions in 1668. His first experience

93. 'An Ordinary on Sundays at two o'clock' afterDighton – a somewhat jaundiced view of the Georgian
'Age of Elegance'

94. Scene in a chop-house, by Thomas Rowlandson, early 19th century. Benches and booths, rather than chairs and isolated tables, fostered an atmosphere of conviviality as well as maximising space.

was less than satisfactory – "a base dinner which did not please us at all" – but on the second occasion he was enlivened by "musick and good company and mighty merry till ten at night".

The 'ordinary' survived, especially in the City, to become the 'chop-house'. F D Byrne, writing in 1909, praised their conservatism and simplicity:

> "there is nothing 'Frenchy' about them and never could be ... place me in a comfortable bay of the old wooden partition; set before me my generous yet homely steak – for, believe me, it is the excellence of its steak, and not of its chops, which is the glory of the true old chop-house."

Half a century later Raymond Postgate *(see p. 199)* praised The George and Vulture, off Cornhill, with similar enthusiasm:

> "This is an old City chophouse as once it was in its old glory. You pick your own chop or steak and it is grilled in front of you; you may take a good roast

duck or such, or fish. In 1956 a grilled steak, potatoes, bread and a tankard of beer cost a member 10/-; there was good cold beef and salmon (but not mayonnaise) and fine cheese. Very good draught Bass. You sit in pew seats, as in Dickens' day and finish off with a glass of port – a large wine glass full up to the brim and good port, too."

COFFEE COMES TO LONDON

Originating in Ethiopia and Sudan, the use of the coffee berry to produce a refreshing drink crossed the Red Sea to Yemen, where it was used by the Muslim mystic Sufis as a stimulant to a heightened spiritual awareness. The use of coffee had reached the sacred city of Mecca by 1511, when it was banned by the *muhtasib,* the Islamic official appointed to enforce public morality. It may have been the circumstances of its consumption as much as the product itself which provoked the prohibition. As a contemporary Turkish observer, Katic Celebi, noted "the fact that it is drunk in gatherings passed hand to hand is suggestive of loose living." Despite this official disapproval, however, consumption of the narcotic berry spread northwards along the caravan routes to Egypt, Syria and Turkey. By 1554 members of the Ottoman Sultan's crack shock-troops, the Janissary Corps, were using coffee-houses as their regular off-duty meeting places. Early in the following century an Italian traveller noted how coffee had been taken up by scholars and students as an aid to combat drowsiness. The English traveller Sir Henry Blount (1602-82) attested to its medicinal value as a relief from deprived or squalid circumstances:

95. *Today's plaque that commemorates Pasqua Rosee's first London coffee house in St Michael's Alley off Cornhill.*

> "most of the eastern world ... acknowledge how it freeth them from crudities caused by ill diet or moist lodging, insomuch as they, using coffee morning and evening, have no consumptions, which ever come of moisture, no lethargies in aged people or rickets in children and but few qualms in women with child .... when a Turk is sick he fasts and takes coffee, and if that will not do, he makes his will and thinks of no other physic."

Another English traveller, George Sandys (1578-1644) was less enthusiastic, describing coffee as "black as soot and tasting not much unlike it." Coffee-houses continued to be regarded with suspicion by the Ottoman authorities, on grounds to be echoed decades later in London. In 1633 Sultan Murad IV ordered their demolition as a fire hazard, but they were certainly back in business a decade later. In 1656 they were closed on the command of the powerful vizier Mehmed Koprulu as centres of political intrigue.

The use of coffee became first known in England rather haphazardly. As an undergraduate at Oxford in 1637 the diarist John Evelyn (1620-1706) knew a Greek who regularly drank it and it was in Oxford that England's first coffee-house was opened by 'Jacob the Jew' at the Sign of the Angel in 1650. Two years later the first London coffee-house was opened in St Michael's Alley, off Cornhill, at the sign of Pasqua Rosee's Head. Pasqua Rosee was by birth a native of the

walled trading city of Ragusa (now Dubrovnik) and would therefore in terms of modern nationality be reckoned a Croat. He had become the servant of an English 'Turkey merchant' named Edwards, who had been based in Smyrna (now Izmir) and who had seen a coffee-house in Leghorn (now Livorno) on his way back to London. Edwards, who had himself acquired the taste for regular infusions of coffee, brought Pasqua Rosee back with him and decided to set him up in business. When the local ale-house keepers of Cornhill petitioned the Lord Mayor against Pasqua Rosee on the grounds that, not being a Freeman of the City, he was legally barred from conducting a business within its jurisdiction. Edwards simply inserted his father-in-law's coachman, who was a Freeman, as Rosee's partner. The times were especially propitious for the launch of the new venture. The civil wars were over. Commerce was picking up and with it a degree of socialising in public places. But the Puritans had closed down the theatres and clamped down on taverns whose landlords permitted overt drunkenness or disorderly behaviour. An alternative type of venue, geared to the taste of the man of affairs, offered a novel and attractive alternative. As if to affirm their conformity to the prevailing mood of moral censoriousness the anonymous author of *The Character of a Coffee House* averred that

"Coffee and Commonwealth both came in
    Together for a Reformation
  To make's a free and sober nation."

Coffee, moreover, was warmly promoted by its partisans as "a very good help to digestion, quickens the spirits and is good against sore eyes, dropsy, gout, King's Evil etc.". It was also claimed, even less plausibly, as a panacea against scurvy.

Such claims were, however, endorsed by one of the highest medical authorities of the day. William Harvey (1578-1657), physician at St Bartholomew's Hospital and discoverer of the circulation of the blood, proclaimed coffee an effective antidote to the excess consumption of alcohol. He bequeathed his own coffee-pot to his brother, with the death-bed assertion that "this little fruit is the source of happiness and wit." He also left half a hundred-weight of coffee-beans to the College of Physicians with instructions that they should commemorate his passing by means of a monthly coffee-morning.

A second London coffee-house, Bowman's, soon opened in St Michael's Alley, its proprietor, Christopher Bowman, coming from the same background as Pasqua Rosee, having been coachman to a Turkey merchant. Another early coffee-house proprietor, one Farr, a former barber, soon found himself the object of a hostile petition "for making and selling a drink called coffee, whereby in making the same he annoyeth his neighbours by evil smells, and for keeping of fire for the most part night and day, whereby his chimney and chamber hath been set on fire, to the great danger and affrightment of his neighbours." Such protests proved futile. By 1662 there were eighty-two coffee-rooms in the City alone. A system of licensing was introduced the next year. In the course of the following decade yet more houses were established which were to become institutions with a distinct character and functions of their own — Garraway's *(see pp. 130-1)*, the Jamaica, which was patronised by traders with the

Will's Best Coffee Powder at Manwarings Coffee House in Falcon Court over against S.t Dunstans Church in Fleet Street

96. *The exclusivity of coffee as a product is implied in this advertisement by the dress of its consumers and the formality of the setting.*

Caribbean, and the Amsterdam, where the East India Company hired seamen.

For once London was ahead of Paris in gastronomic trend-setting. Not until 1669 was coffee introduced to the court of Louis XIV, appropriately enough by the Turkish ambassador, who might well be suspected of harbouring hopes of fostering a new export. If so, it was not to be. In 1672 one Pascal, an Armenian, tried opening a coffee-house in Paris. It failed and he transferred his operations to London. Only a decade later, following the lifting of the siege of Vienna by the Turks in 1683, did a former prisoner of theirs, inspired by their abandoned stores of coffee, successfully open a coffee-house in the Habsburg capital. It was this Viennese example that finally inspired the emergence of that most characteristic of Parisian institutions — the café.

97. The Coffeehouse Mob, an engraving used as a frontispiece to Ned Ward's 'The Fourth Part of Vulgus Brittanicus', published in 1710.

Meanwhile in London brewers and vintners joined forces to attack the unwelcome competition represented by the coffee-houses. Punching below the belt, as one might say, in 1674 they sponsored a pamphlet which alleged that coffee-drinking caused impotence:

"The Women's Petition Against Coffee Representing to Publick Consideration The Grand Inconveniences accruing to the SEX from the Excessive Use of the Drying, Enfeebling LIQUOR Presented to the Right Honourable the Keepers of the Liberty of Venus by a Well-willer."

On December 29th 1675 King Charles II, himself a prominent libertarian in the court of Venus, peremptorily ordered the suppression of coffee-houses on quite other grounds as "the great resort of idle and disaffected persons. In such houses divers false, malicious and scandalous reports are devised and spread abroad to the defamation of His Majesty's Government and to the disturbance of the peace and quiet of the realm." It was an uncharacteristically assertive gesture for a monarch whose youth in exile had taught him the unwisdom of antagonising his subjects. Such was the outcry at the attempted prohibition that the ban was summarily withdrawn on 8 January 1676.

COFFEE AND COMMERCE

According to gossipy James Howell (?1594-1666) – diplomat, debtor, prisoner, poet, pamphleteer, hack and historian – coffee was good for the conduct of commerce,

"for whereas formerly apprentices and clerks with others used to take their morning's draught in ale, beer or wine, which by the dizziness they cause in the brain make many unfit for business, they use now to play the good-fellows in this wakeful and civil drink"

Other and very varying factors also combined to boost the commercial role of the coffee-house – the invention of the coffee-mill in 1687, which much improved the quality of the drink; the founding of the Bank of England in 1694, which provided a focus for financial operations on a scale hitherto undreamed of; the abolition in 1695 of newspaper licensing, which prompted the appearance of twenty new newspapers, bearers of much commercial information, by 1710.

The City's first coffee-houses having been established just off Cornhill, they soon spread to the surrounding streets at the heart of London's commercial activity. Garraway's, established in Exchange Alley in 1669, had an upstairs sale-room where the proprietor pioneered the selling of tea and the auction of wines. Writing in 1722, Daniel Defoe, himself a businessman, considered it the prime resort of "the People of Quality, who have business in the City, and the most considerable and wealthy citizens." Garraway's continued to be favoured as an auction house for the disposal of coffee, textiles, sugar, spices, ships and salvaged goods. The bill of fare was enlarged to feature such house specialities as sherry, sandwiches, punch, pale ale and cherry wine. Mentioned in three of Dickens' novels, Garraway's finally closed in 1872.

Jonathan's, also in Exchange Alley, was established by Jonathan Miles around 1680 and soon became the favoured haunt of stock-jobbers. It consequently served as the epicentre of the frenzy of speculation caused by the share manipulations of the South Sea Company which collapsed so disastrously in 1720. In 1721 the politician Edward Harley wrote to his sister:

> "nothing arises or increases here but uneasiness, discontent and clamour which reigns in every part of the city. The Exchange is the least frequented place of any of it. Jonathan's and Garraway's empty ... nor any trade stirring but what belongs to common necessaries...".

Rebuilt after the Cornhill fire of 1748, Jonathan's failed to arise from a subsequent conflagration in 1778. London's second fire insurance office, fittingly known as the Phoenix, was established in 1682 over the Rainbow coffee-house.

The coffee-house founded by Edward Lloyd was to evolve into a financial institution of not just metropolitan but global significance. Initially located in Tower Street, it relocated to Lombard Street around 1691. Standing at the corner of Abchurch Lane, it became the recognised centre for marine insurance and shipbroking. The enterprising Lloyd secured a novel dominance in these sectors by inaugurating the publication of *Lloyd's News*, a chronicle of shipping and commercial intelligence which appeared up to three times a week between September 1696 and February 1697. Although his newspaper was extinguished by government order, Lloyd continued to prosper and his publication was revived in

98. *Garraway's played a leading role in the commercial life of the City for over two centuries, primarily as an auction house.*

1726 as *Lloyd's List*. In March 1769 an advertisement was placed in the *Public Advertiser* advising those whose main business was shipping to decamp to a new location:

> "To the Merchants in general, Owners ... of Ships, Insurance Brokers etc., etc. – Thomas Fielding, Waiter from Lloyd's Coffee House begs acquaint them that his House in Pope's Head Alley, Lombard Street is now genteely fitted up and will open for the reception of Gentlemen, Merchants etc. Tomorrow the 21st instant by the name of New Lloyd's Coffee House, where he hopes to receive their favours."

The area around St Paul's churchyard was the centre of book publishing in London. Authors, publishers and booksellers frequently met in the appropriately named Chapter coffee-house in Paternoster Row. A contemporary noted in 1754 that the tone of conversation was more commercial than cultural, "when they say a *good* book, they do not mean to praise the style or sentiment but the quick and extensive sale of it. That book is best which sells most ...". Books were also sold by auction at the St Paul's.

The luckless teenage poet and literary forger

99. *A coffee house scene in 1763. The role of coffee-houses as sources of information and venues for literary and political debates led them to be dubbed 'penny universities', from the fee paid for entrance.*

Thomas Chatterton (1752-70) *(see pp 189-90)* wrote reassuringly to his mother that "I am quite familiar at the Chapter coffee-house and know all the geniuses there...". He certainly used the address as a *poste-restante*.

Physicians were another profession who conducted their business in coffee-houses. Child's in Warwick Lane was favoured for this purpose on account of its proximity to the College of Physicians. Royal physician Dr Richard Mead (1673-1754) favoured Batson's, near the Royal Exchange, for consultations with clients but kept his socializing for Rawthmell's in Henrietta Street by Covent Garden. One specialist, having apparently secured for himself the distinction of cutter of corns to members of the royal family,

posted a regular timetable of his availability in various well-known coffee-houses according to the hour of the day.

Coffee houses performed a range of economic functions which would later devolve onto specialised agencies. Tickets for lotteries, concerts and theatrical performances were sold at coffee-houses. Man's, founded at Charing Cross, by Alexander Man, 'Coffee Man' to King Charles II, also served as an employment agency where servants could be hired. Many functioned in effect as travel agencies and postal offices. Anyone desirous of taking passage for Scandinavia or wanting to send letters or parcels there would make for the Baltic coffee house, where captains of appropriate ships would congregate. Lost

100. *Lloyd's coffee house, by William Holland, 1798. By then this City institution was already over a century old. The consumption of coffee is shown to be incidental to the more important conduct of business.*

property office was another common function, regular clients most often seeking the return of stolen watches and runaway slaves. Newspapers were generally available for clients to read at most coffee-houses but some, like Nando's, prided themselves on having 'stop press' items available handwritten, and others kept files of back-numbers of newspapers for reference, thus serving as commercial and current affairs libraries.

COFFEE AND CULTURE

The first generation of coffee-houses was located in the City and their patrons were chiefly concerned with commerce. When a second generation began to emerge in the West End its patrons were primarily preoccupied with culture. It was not necessary that they should be in any way grand to function satisfactorily as arenas for conversation, debate and displays of erudition or pungent wit. Many Londoners lived in single rooms or garrets which would scarcely serve as suitable venues for entertaining friends, even less casual acquaintances whom they wished to impress. The penny that secured their entrance to a fashionable coffee-house − and kept the riff-raff out − also bought them an ambience and setting. A penny paid, one's social status was irrelevant, but gender was not − only males were admitted. Warm, dry and full of company, these meeting-places were immediately welcoming, as Henri Misson de Valburg testified in 1698:

"these houses, which are very numerous in London, are extremely convenient. You have all manner of news there; you have a good fire, which you may sit by as long as you please; you have a dish of coffee; you meet your friends for the transaction of business, and all for a penny, if you don't care to spend more."

At the other end of the scale Tom King's, "a common shed" in Covent Garden run by an eccentric Old Etonian, served as a night shelter for the homeless. Hogarth featured it in his engraving of 'Morning' and it is also described in Smollett's *Adventures of Roderick Random*.

Will's, opened above a woollen draper's at 1 Bow Street, Covent Garden in 1671, took its name, as was usual, from its proprietor, William Urwin; but its celebrity derived from its most famed patron, the poet and dramatist John Dryden (1631-1700), who occupied a seat permanently reserved for him, either at the balcony window, or by the fire, depending on the season. In 1664 Pepys, who knew Dryden from their Cambridge days as undergraduates, recorded having seen him at another Covent Garden coffee house with "all the wits of the town". It was on his way home from Will's that Dryden was savagely beaten up by thugs near the Lamb and Flag tavern in Rose Street. Fifty pounds was offered for their detection but nothing came of it, though the drunken and dissolute poetaster-courtier, the Earl of Rochester, was widely suspected as having hired the ruffians to revenge himself for a literary slight. As was the custom of the day there was little sympathy for the victim. Wycherley and Pope also frequented Will's, although Pope withdrew after a year or so, complaining that the enforced idleness and alcohol were injurious to his health. The very first number of *The Tatler* opined that Will's had lost all its cachet following Dryden's death – "where you used to see songs, epigrams and satires in the hands of every man you met, you have now only a pack of cards." By then the epicentre of the world of wit had shifted to Button's on the other side of the road, where

the essayist Joseph Addison (1672-1719) held court, having set up Daniel Button, his former servant, in the business. Here was erected a post-box in the shape of a lion's head, into whose roaring mouth snippets of scandal and contributions to *The Spectator* could be slipped anonymously. Addison's death had an even greater effect on Button's than Dryden's did on Will's and Daniel Button died in penury in 1731. Button's itself survived the demise of its eponymous founder, attracting some rather less savoury clientele. The highwayman James Maclean was a regular – until he was hanged in 1750.

Another Russell Street coffee-house was Tom's, whose founder Captain Thomas West, demented by gout, jumped to his death from a second floor window in 1722. Writing in that same year Defoe recommended Tom's and Will's as the best places to go after a play to discuss its merits.

The Grecian, originally established in the City by one Constantine, a Greek importer and retailer of "Coffee, Chocolate, Cherbert and Tea" who also offered to teach customers how "to prepare the said Liquors gratis", relocated to Devereux Court off the Strand and became a favoured resort of men of learning such as the scientist Sir Isaac Newton, the astronomer Edmund Halley and royal physician Sir Hans Sloane. The *Tatler* observed loftily that, while news of Marlborough's stunning victories over the French was being toasted in taverns in "other parts of the town ... we generally spend the evenings ... in inquiries into antiquity and think anything news which gives us new knowledge" – such as working out the precise sequence of events in Homer's *Iliad*. Sometimes this pedantry went too far. On one evening two patrons of the Grecian, long boon companions, fell out about "the accent of a Greek word" and resorted outside to settle the matter with rapiers, one being run through and dying on the spot.

Slaughter's, at the Newport Street end of St Martin's Lane, was known for card games, gambling and chess. Established in 1692, it was much frequented by artists such as t Hogarth and the sculptor Louis-François Roubiliac.

The Bedford coffee-house, "under the piazza at Covent Garden", was first mentioned in 1730 and became the haunt of actors such as Quin and Garrick, who lived only a few steps away in Southampton Street. It also attracted literary figures such as Fielding, Smollett and Sheridan and later artists and architects such as Lawrence, Dance and Smirke.

COFFEE AND COTERIES

Many coffee-houses attracted specific social types. Dick's in Fleet Street welcomed country gentry. Anglican clergymen were to be found at Truby's and Child's. The London thronged with Dissenting clergymen and masters of academies and hosted a club for Freemasons, Americans and avant-garde intellectuals like the Unitarian minister and experimental chemist Joseph Priestley. In 1851 millionaire American banker George Peabody hosted a Fourth of July dinner at the London on Ludgate Hill to celebrate the success of the Great Exhibition and the cordiality of Anglo-American relations. His guest of honour was none less than the aged Duke of Wellington. Lawyers and law students were to be found at Nando's, Serle's and Squire's. The schoolmaster father of the artist William Hogarth had the novel idea of opening a coffee-house in which staff and clients would speak only Latin. Believing that fluency in a language required the speaker to "use it or lose it", Hogarth *pere* reasoned that adults would willingly spend a few hours each week in a convivial atmosphere to keep up an accomplishment they had so painstakingly acquired in youth. Of course it ended in disaster, debt and consequent imprisonment. Hogarth was forced to set aside his ambitions to become a painter and apprenticed himself to an engraver – which eventually proved to be the making of his unique career.

Around St James's and Westminster, the home of the court and parliament, the prevailing concerns were inevitably political. The British in Cockspur Street was home to outsiders whose abilities should have made them insiders but for the fact that they were Dissenters, Scotsmen – and Benjamin Franklin. Army and Navy officers favoured the St James's, which also became a stronghold for supporters of the Whig party and additionally numbered Sir Joshua Reynolds, Oliver Goldsmith and Isaac D'Israeli among its patrons. Tories used Ozinda's Chocolate House, which also offered "Several Sorts of Snuffs" and "superfine Liquors" made by the proprietor, a Frenchman, or the Cocoa Tree in Pall Mall, which was also alleged to be a sort of informal headquarters for Jacobites. Bellamy's in Westminster was opened in the late eighteenth century and proved a predictably convenient location for MPs. Also known as Bellamy's Kitchen, it was famed for its steaks and chops. It is said that the dying words of Prime Minister William Pitt the Younger were "I think I could eat one of Bellamy's pork pies."

WHAT BECAME OF THE COFFEE HOUSES

Some of the coffee houses evolved into exclusive gentlemen's clubs. Of these the most eminent was *White's*. The original premises burned down in 1733 and the then proprietor, Arthur, removed to Gaunt's coffee-house in the same street. Rules surviving from 1736 required every member to pay a guinea a year to ensure the employment of a good cook. Paying other members' dining bills was a common sanction for infringing club rules. In 1797 it was ordered that the fixed price dinner should include oranges, apples, olives and 'Malt Liquor'. At certain periods of the year a table of cold meats and oysters was available. *White's* became notorious for gambling, with huge sums being staked on the most trivial of occurrences. Every Prime Minister from Walpole to Peel was a member, as were Robert Clive, Charles James Fox and Beau Brummell.

Tom's in Russell Street became a subscription club with a cardroom in 1768. In 1808 the tax on coffee was cut and in 1824 cut

1850 recorded as being "principally used for temporary public meetings." The Jamaica became a wine house in 1869, and Dick's became a French restaurant in 1885.

A new breed of 'coffee tavern' was promoted in 1874 by a philanthropic company, with Lord Shaftesbury as president, in the "more densely peopled parts of London ... to serve as a counter-attraction to the public house and gin palace"; these were soon leased off to a Mr McDougall, who made a better go of them than the do-gooders had. In 1877 a similar Coffee Public House Association was launched under the presidency of the newly-created Duke of Westminster.

EATING ON PRINCIPLE
Whigs in Wigs

The Kit Cat Club was established in 1703 at the sign of the Cat and Fiddle in Shire Lane, which ran north from Temple Bar. Membership was intended for supporters of the Whig party and a Protestant monarchy and was initially limited to thirty-nine, later to forty-eight. As well as the Dukes of Marlborough and Newcastle and other political heavyweights of the day, the distinguished company included the essayists Addison and Steele and the dramatists Congreve and Vanbrugh. They took their name from their landlord, Christopher Cat, who was "immortal made by his pyes" which were filled with mutton and known as Kit-cats. When their landlord took over the Fountain in the Strand the club moved with him. In summer they also held meetings in the Flask tavern on Hampstead Heath and in a specially built club room at the Barn Elms home in Barnes of Dryden's publisher Jacob Tonson (?1656-1736), who was the club's secretary and moving spirit. A special feature of club meetings was a series of toasts, written in praise of beauties favourable to the Whig cause, whose names were inscribed on special toasting glasses. The members of the club were immortalised over the course of twenty years by one of its own number, the royal portraitist Sir Godfrey Kneller, who

101. A coffee stall in mid-Victorian times. The humble nature of the clientele denotes the demise of coffee as a luxury product.

again, and coffee-drinking lost its elitist associations. By the 1830s there were over three thousand coffee-shops in the capital, catering mainly for working men on their way to or from their employment, and by the 1840s the streets were thronged with stalls selling coffee mixed with chicory or adulterated with baked carrots. Dickens recommended the Covent Garden area for anyone seeking coffee in the early hours.

John's perished in the fire which destroyed the Royal Exchange in 1838. Slaughter's and the Grecian both managed to hang on until 1843, the Jerusalem a decade longer. Survivors among the old-established coffee houses sought salvation by reinventing themselves. The Rainbow in Fleet Street became a tavern. The Turk's Head in the Strand became a hotel in 1838. The British in Cockspur Street, was by devised a specially compact format and pose for his paintings to fit into the low-ceilinged members' dining-room at Barn Elms. This size, 36 inches by 28 and showing only one of the sitter's arms, subsequently became known as Kit Cat. Pope recorded that Tonson got Kneller to paint the portraits for nothing more than presents of venison and wine and much flattery. Perhaps that was just how Tonson got his as the others were gifts from members to him. Tonson published the portraits as mezzotints in 1735 more, perhaps, as a memorial than as a celebration, for Vanbrugh had written to him in 1725 suggesting a meeting that winter "not as a club but as old friends that have been of a club and the best club that ever met". The printed portraits were republished in 1795, doubtless as a coded protest against the anti-libertarian legislation provoked by the wars against revolutionary France. The surviving oil originals can now be seen in the National Portrait Gallery.

'Beef and Liberty'

The original Beef-Steak Society was founded in 1735 by the manager of the Covent Garden Theatre, John Rich and the scene painter George Lambert. Membership was restricted to twenty-four men of gentle or noble birth who met for a beef-steak dinner every Saturday evening from November to June. There was a uniform consisting of buff waistcoats and blue jackets with buttons emblazoned with the slogan 'Beef and Liberty'. The Society originally met in a room in Covent Garden Theatre, but when that burned down in 1808 the Club lost not only its stock of wine but also Handel's organ and most of his manuscript music. The Club transferred briefly to the Bedford Coffee House before moving to the Lyceum Theatre in 1809. When that in turn burned down in 1830 they returned to the Bedford until 1838, then went back to the Lyceum. By then known as the Sublime Society of Beef-Steaks, the club was dissolved in 1867. A re-founded Beefsteak Club first met in King William Street in 1876. Twenty years later it moved to premises in Irving Street. Members

sit at a long table in the order in which they arrive. The steward and waiters are always called Charles regardless of their real name.

The Canada Club

This dining club claims to be the oldest institution connected with Canada, apart from the Hudson's Bay Company. A forum for Anglo-Canadian social and commercial interests, the club has never owned premises. Its early meeting-places included the Freemasons' Tavern, the Albion Tavern, Aldersgate Street, the London Tavern, Bishopsgate and various coffee-houses and restaurants in the City, the Strand, Blackwall, Greenwich and Richmond. In 1856 the club dined at the Mansion House at the invitation of the Lord Mayor. In 1863 its guests included the Hon. John A Macdonald, who was to become Canada's first Prime Minister. Since 1900 the club has favoured West End establishments, especially the Savoy. In 1960 the Duke of Edinburgh. the club's patron, took the chair at a Guildhall dinner to mark the club's 150th anniversary.

GUILDHALL GASTRONOMY

William Harrison, writing in 1577, observed of the Lord Mayor that "there is no public officer of any city in Europe that may compare in port and countenance with him during the time of his office." Public feasting was an essential aspect of affirming this eminence and thus the standing of the City itself.

The City Livery Companies set no mean standard against which Mayoral hospitality was inevitably measured, as Harrison likewise testified:

> "when the companies of every trade do meet on their quarter days ... they be nothing inferior to the nobility ... it is a world to see what great provision is made of all manner of delicate meats, from every quarter of the country, wherein, beside that they are often comparable herein to the nobility of the land, they will seldom regard anything that the butcher usually killeth, but reject the same as not worthy to

102. *A Guildhall banquet, by E. Thöny, published in a German magazine*
between the wars. The artist skilfully conveys a sense of preoccupied self-indulgence.

come in place. In such cases also jellies of all colours, mixed with a variety in representation of sundry flowers, herbs, trees, forms of beasts, fish, fowls and fruits and thereunto marchpane wrought with no small curiosity, tarts of divers hues and sundry denominations, conserves of old fruits, foreign and home-bred, suckets, codinacs, marmalades, marchpane, sugar-bread, gingerbread, florentines, wild fowls, venison of all sorts, and sundry outlandish confections, altogether seasoned with sugar ... do generally bear sway, beside infinite devices of our own not possible for me to remember."

These indulgences, as Harrison further noted, were lengthy affairs:

"merchantmen, especially at great meetings, do sit commonly till two or three of the clock at afternoon, so that with many it is a hard matter to rise from the table to go to evening prayer and return from thence to come time enough to supper."

On Lord Mayor's Day 1761 King George III and his new wife Queen Charlotte were entertained to a majestic formal banquet in their honour. Over 1,200 people were present but a contemporary engraving shows only the male guests actually dining. Female onlookers sat in ranks in temporarily erected galleries either side, beneath which were sideboards arrayed with trays, sauce-boats and plates. Diners are shown ranked on benches at long, wide tables. Dishes were arranged in precise geometrical patterns conforming to the conventions of *service à la Française* which decreed which should be placed in the centre, at the ends, sides and corners. This single course consisted of selections of the dishes offered to the king in four courses. The selection on each table depended, naturally, on the rank of the diners. Soup and fish dishes were eaten first to be replaced by meats, game and 'fine vegetables' such as artichokes and cardoons. Highly esteemed delicacies included venison, turtle, ortolans, ducks' tongues and 'blomanges'. The king's table featured a Grand Pyramid of shellfish flanked by two tiers of delicacies,

encircled with jellies in the shape of temples, grottoes made out of almonds and savoury cakes. These extravagances were the work of Friedrich Kuhff, Confectioner to His Majesty, who also oversaw the other dishes prepared for the king while five other cooks supervised the food for the other diners. Meanwhile, in other less prestigious venues in the vicinity, more than seven hundred servants and attendants were being entertained. The call on the Mayoral purse was to cover not only the costs of food and wine but also waiting staff, musicians and security, lighting and interior decorations, the hire of tablewares and the erection and equipment of a temporary kitchen – and came to £1,605 7s 6d. In 1768 the socialite William Hickey witnessed a rather less decorous Mayoral banquet in Guildhall:

"At six we sat down to a profusion of turtle and venison, followed by all the etceteras of French cookery, with splendid dessert of pines, grapes and other fruits ... The heat from the crowd assembled and immense number of lights was disagreeable to all, to many quite oppressive and distressing. The Lord Mayor's table, at which I was ... was less so than other parts of the hall, from being considerably elevated above the rest. The wines were excellent and the dinner the same, served, too, with as much regularity and decorum as if we had been in a private house; but far different was the scene in the body of the hall, where, in five minutes after the guests took their stations at the tables, the dishes were entirely cleared of their contents, twenty hands seizing the same joint or bird, and literally tearing it to pieces. A more determined scramble could not be; the roaring and noise was deafening and hideous, which increased as the liquor operated ... Such a bear garden altogether I never beheld ... This abominable and disgusting scene continued till near ten o'clock

Completely exhausted I retired to bed, perfectly satisfied with having once partaken of a Lord Mayor of London's feast"

The menu for a Lord Mayor's banquet of the late nineteenth century consisted of the traditional turtle soup, followed by fillets of

103. *The grander dinners of City livery companies compare quite favourably with the extravagant events at Guildhall. Shown above is the dinner of the Licensed Victuallers at Hackney in 1846. Note the picnic baskets in the left foreground.*

turbot, lobster mousse, sweetbread and truffles, baron of beef, partridge, mutton cutlets and smoked tongue with desserts of orange jelly, strawberry cream, Maids of Honour, patisserie and meringues, washed down with sherry, punch, hock, champagne, moselle, claret, port and liqueurs — all for two guineas per head.

EATING OUT OF TOWN
Tea Gardens

If the coffee-house was the rage of the seventeenth century, the tea garden was the fashion of the eighteenth. Unlike the all-male coffee-house, the tea-garden attracted both a mixed and a female clientele, including the wives of prosperous merchants and servants off duty. The favoured location for the tea-garden was in a semi-rural setting within walking distance of residential areas, such as Clerkenwell for the City and Marylebone and Kensington for the West End. More distant locations, such as Islington, Kentish Town and Holloway were noted for the produce of their dairy herds, converted into custards, syllabubs and cheesecakes. The Adam and Eve tea garden, at the junction of today's Euston Road and Hampstead Road, was already in existence by 1718. As well as garden arbours for tea-parties, its facilities included bowling alleys and a long room with an organ, which presumably served as a refuge on showery days. Florida Gardens. established by 1762 on a site now occupied by Stanhope Gardens, near Gloucester Road underground station, was taken over by a German florist and gardener, Rudolf Heim, who diversified its offerings to include confectionery, fresh strawberries and monster cherries, and organized amusements ranging from an orchestra to fireworks, balloon ascents and displays of horsemanship. Another celebrated venue was the White Conduit House at Islington, famed for hot loaves, tea, coffee

104. *Customers at the White Conduit in Islington, by Thomas Rowlandson, early 19th century. In the background volunteer militia chase off a caricature of Napoleon. Militia exercises were invariably followed by enthusiastic attendance at a local watering-hole.*

and liquors "in the greatest perfection". The local cricket team was to metamorphose into the MCC. Tea-gardens fell victim to the explosion of metropolitan building in the early decades of the nineteenth century, most being initially hemmed in by housing, then built over. The White Conduit House, one of the last to survive, went in 1849.

Pie and Bun Houses

Another extramural attraction was the specialist pie or bun house. There were noted eel pie houses at Islington and Bromley and bun houses at Chelsea, Marylebone and Stepney. Under the proprietorship of Richard Hand, the Chelsea Bun House in Jew's Row, Pimlico attracted the patronage of royalty and on Good Fridays crowds, allegedly, of thousands. A local partisan praised Hand's confections

"As flaky and white as if baked by the light,
    As the flesh of an infant soft, doughy and slight"

The Chelsea Bun House was demolished in 1839.

Pleasure Gardens

Pleasure gardens, such as Vauxhall and Ranelagh and some two hundred petty imitators, were primarily intended for an evening clientele and offered cold dishes to be eaten in 'supper boxes' in between strolling through shady groves, watching fireworks or listening to music. The prototype was Spring Gardens, near The Mall, which as early as 1634 was serving "an ordinary of six shillings a meal (when the King's proclamation allows but two elsewhere)" and had already become notorious for "continual bibbing and drinking of wine under the trees".

105. *The Chelsea Bun House in Pimlico, depicted in 1839, the year of its demolition.*

106. *An assembly at Vauxhall, drawn by Rowlandson. Note the dining-booth at bottom left.*

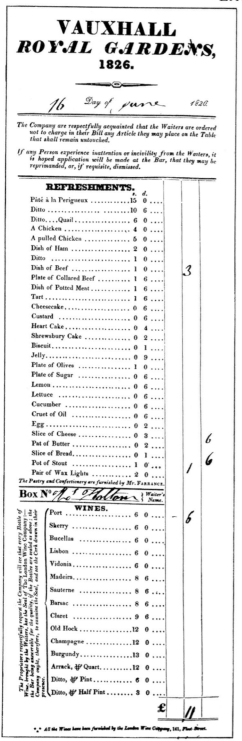

107. *A bill of fare at Vauxhall in 1826. The invitation to report incivility by the waiters suggests it may have been a recurrent problem.*

Closed down by Cromwell, it was reopened after his death and, apart from affording wide scope for 'gallantry' in shady corners, it also offered "trifling tarts, neats' tongues, salacious meats and bad Rhenish".

Contemporary balladeers portrayed the pleasure gardens as arenas of excess:

> Here they drink and there they cram
> Chicken, pasty, beef and ham,
> Women squeak and men drunk fall.
> Sweet enjoyment of Vauxhall.

In fact the proprietors of these establishments appear to have discovered 'portion control' centuries before modern commercial caterers. The suppers at Vauxhall Gardens became notorious for poor quality, high prices, mean portions and ham cut so thin you could see through it. Ranelagh's admission price included refreshments, with "the best Epping butter and milk", but the management was accused of serving "hot water, under the denomination of tea". Nevertheless although Ranelagh went in 1805, Vauxhall survived until 1859.

WHITEBAIT SUPPERS

The ritual consumption of whitebait as the main feature of an evening meal appears to have originated at Dagenham among the commissioners for the engineering projects carried out there between 1715 and 1720 in consequence of the great flood which inundated local marshland in 1713. Breach House, built for the Superintendent of the Works, became a regular meeting-place for the Commissioners of the Levels, who combined their business-meetings with a little angling. From 1792 until 1812 there was a formal club, its founder members including local landowners Bamber Gascoyne and Edward Hulse and such metropolitan illuminati as Admiral Sir Hugh Palliser, Governor of Greenwich Hospital and Sir Joseph Banks, President of the Royal Society. The annual club dinner featured whitebait – among other things. The bill for the last dinner held at Breach House, in 1811, amounted to £26 3s. 6d, of which the fourteen dinners consumed accounted for just eight guineas – less than half the cost of the port, madeira, claret, champagne and hock required to wash them down. By then it had become customary to invite government ministers to these proceedings. In 1812 Earl Bathurst, Secretary for War and the Colonies, was informed that "A vile man has so entirely dismantled the house as to render it quite impossible for the company to dine there. A turtle is therefore sent to the Crown and Sceptre at Greenwich and there will be dinner there on Tuesday, July 2 at six o'clock." Thereafter the dinners were normally held at Greenwich or Blackwall, which had nine inns, five along the riverfront. In the 1830s there were hourly steamer sailings in the summer months to Blackwall so that whitebait could be eaten by "civilized persons, with no little gusto". On 10 September 1835 the *Morning Post* recorded that "yesterday the Cabinet Ministers went down the river in the ordnance barges to Lovegrove's West India Dock Tavern, Blackwall, to partake of their annual fish dinner." By then the meal had become a very substantial repast, featuring not only whitebait (plain fried and devilled) but also a choice of fish soups, lobster rissoles, salmon cutlets, stewed eels, crab omelette and whiting pudding. As "Covers were laid for 35 gentlemen", far more than were in the Cabinet, they must have been accompanied by favoured guests. This ministerial ritual was imitated by others. Richard Doyle's humorous depictions of the *Manners and Customs of ye Englyshe* (1849) also depicts "ye Publick a Dininge on Whytebait" at Lovegrove's. The ministerial whitebait dinners were discontinued in 1868, but revived in 1874 and held for the last time in 1894.

EXHIBITING INITIATIVES

Public exhibitions, a novel phenomenon of the nineteenth century, created a demand for mass-catering on a scale previously only organised by armies. In 1851 Prince Albert's brainchild, the Great Exhibition of the Art and Industry of All Nations, the world's first trade fair, attracted over six million visitors to its 'Crystal Palace' in Hyde Park. Because the sale of intoxicants was forbidden inside the exhibition area Messrs Schweppe's fared very well, selling 1,092,337 bottles of soda water, lemonade and ginger beer. Outside the precincts Schweppe's soda became a favourite mixer with hock to make a refreshing long summer drink. According to Mrs Beeton, the Exhibition was also responsible for popularising the Bath bun – 943,691 were sold over the six months the exhibition was open, well ahead of the 870,027 plain buns, 73,280 'Victoria biscuits', 34,070 Banbury cakes and 28,046 sausage rolls. The popularity of confectionery generally was confirmed by the buoyant sales of biscuits (37,300 lbs), pound cakes (68,428), Italian cakes (11,797), Rich cakes (2,280 lbs) and Macaroons (1,500 lbs). Meat was likewise copiously consumed (113 tons, plus 33 of ham) as well as in its potted form (36,130 lbs) and in pies (33,456 lbs) and patties (23,040 lbs) or enlivened with pickles (1,046 gallons) and mustard (1,120 lbs). Of vegetables, other than potatoes, (36 tons), or of salads or fish the Commissioners meticulously detailed returns make no mention. Fruit was represented only by preserved cherries (4,840 lbs), pineapples (2,000) and jellies (2,400 quarts). Interestingly, far more coffee (14,299 lbs) and chocolate (4,836 lbs) were sold than tea (1,015 lbs). These various disparities may, of course, be accounted for by the fact that many visitors may have wanted no more than a snack, while others were looking for a 'treat', neither category therefore requiring what in other circumstances they would have regarded as a 'proper meal'. Subsequent exhibitions ensured the development and elaboration of this new branch of the catering industry. In the aftermath of the success of Gilbert and Sullivan's *Mikado* the Health Exhibition at South Kensington in 1884 featured a Japanese café. Newcastle's celebraton of Victoria's Golden Jubilee in 1887 gave birth to J. Lyons and Co. *(see p. 91)*. In 1924 that firm was entrusted with the catering arrangements for the Empire exhibition. Erecting 34 restaurants and cafés and eighteen snack bars and kiosks, Lyons served up to 26,000 visitors a day, shipping in 260 tons of bakery products every week from their Hammersmith factory complex. The success of the specialist caterer at the exhibition's Mughal pavilion led to the establishment of Veeraswamy's celebrated Indian restaurant the following year *(see pp. 119-20)*.

'TRADITIONAL ENGLISH'
Rule's

What claims to be London's oldest restaurant was opened in Maiden Lane, Covent Garden in 1798 by Thomas Rule for the sale of "porter, pies and oysters". Its literary clientele has ranged from Dickens and Thackeray to H G Wells,

John Galsworthy and John Betjeman. It was a favourite venue for Edward VII's suppers with Lillie Langtry. It has been referred to in novels by Evelyn Waugh, Graham Greene, John Le Carré, Dick Francis, Penelope Lively and Claire Rayner. But it is with the theatrical profession that Rule's has been most illustriously associated as its unrivalled wall display of portraits, signed photographs and memorabilia testifies – Sir Henry Irving, Laurence Olivier. Charlie Chaplin, Buster Keaton, Charles Laughton, Clark Gable ...

Simpson's-in-the-Strand

In 1828 Samuel Reiss opened his Grand Cigar Divan on the site where the Kit Kat Club *(see p. 136)* had once met in the Fountain Tavern. With their cigars patrons were offered coffee, conversation and chess. At the day rate customers could pay 1/6d (by 1850 1/-) for a

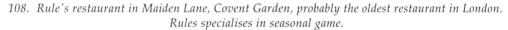

108. Rule's restaurant in Maiden Lane, Covent Garden, probably the oldest restaurant in London. Rules specialises in seasonal game.

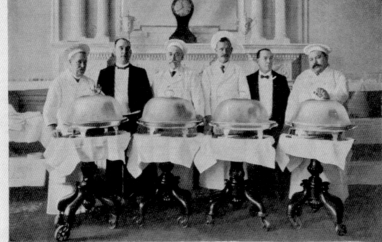

SIMPSON'S IN THE STRAND
The Famous Old English Dining House.

Telephone
Number
4352
Gerrard.

Telegrams:
"SIMPSONS,
STRAND,
LONDON."

VETERAN CARVERS AND SUPERINTENDENTS AT SIMPSON'S.

109. Waiters in the old Simpson's building. The youngest of those shown here had "served there for over a quarter of a century". 110 (below). The old building in the Strand c.1900.

cigar, coffee, newspapers and chess. Alternatively they could subscribe a guinea a year for free admission and coffee. Chess matches were played regularly against other coffee-houses. Caterer John Simpson joined Reiss in 1848, enlarging the range of food and drinks on offer and inaugurating the house custom of wheeling around large roast joints on silver trolleys to carve each customer's portion before his eyes. Cunningham's *Handbook of London* of 1850 recommended the Cigar Divan as providing "the best cup of coffee to be had in London." Simpson's successor, Edmund William Cathie, brought in Thomas Davey as his British Master Cook. As much super-patriot as kitchen autocrat, Davey insisted that everything in the restaurant be British, even replacing the Menu with a Bill of Fare. In 1898 Simpson's was acquired by Richard D'Oyly Carte's Savoy Group. When the Strand was widened in 1903, Simpson's was closed down for redevelopment and reopened in 1904 as Simpson's-in-the-Strand, Grand Divan Tavern.

A fish luncheon consisting of turbot, stewed eels, whitebait, celery and cheese, with a couple of bottles of Liebfraumilch, could be had for three persons at that time for a princely £1 1s 3d. In 1994 Simpson's began serving breakfasts. Forbes, the American businessman's Bible, rates Simpson's as 'Carnivore Heaven ... the best joints of meat in Europe ... Huge helpings! ...gusset-busting puddings. The treacle sponge will give dieters sweaty nightmares."

Scott's
Scott's began in 1872 as an 'oyster warehouse' in the London Pavilion Music Hall. Success led to the expansion of its premises from 18 Coventry Street into nos. 19 and 20 and then to a major rebuilding in 1893. The style was 'Early French Renaissance', the material Bath stone and the designers Treadwell and Martin. For the next half century Scott's was renowned as one of the foremost fish restaurants in London. On Boat Race Night it was especially favoured by the more affluent, and hopefully less rowdy, undergraduates who flooded into the capital to enjoy the annual Oxford *vs* Cambridge confrontation on the river. In the 1950s participants in the BBC's *Brains Trust* programme were first taken to Scott's for "a good lunch with a fair amount to drink." Scott's moved to Mount Street. Mayfair in 1967. In 1975 it was bombed by the IRA.

Sweetings, 39 Queen Victoria Street
Sweetings has always specialised in serving fish dishes to City business types. Only open at weekday lunchtimes, it was noted as much for its peculiarities as the excellence of its fare – most diners sat at high counters, rather than tables, waited on by white-coated 'boys' of pensionable age. Coffee was not served and until 2001 credit cards were not accepted.

Wheeler's
The first Wheeler's, at 19 Old Compton Street, was founded in 1929 by Bernard Walsh, a wholesaler of oysters, whose father had owned a Whitstable shellfish bar known as Wheeler's. The first chef was a Chinese and so have most of his successors been.

CLUBLAND
The gentlemen's clubs which reached their peak of popularity in Victoria's reign traced their origins to the coffee-houses of the previous century. The oldest, White's, began as a chocolate house, taking its name from the anglicisation of its founding proprietor, Francesco Bianco; it had become a private club by 1736. In 1764 William Almack's Pall Mall club split into Boodle's, which early established a reputation for good food, and the equally exclusive Brooks's. The Guards' (1810), initially founded for officers of the Guards' regiments who had served in the Peninsular War, was notable for providing much cheaper and better dinners than were generally available in the West End.

The three decades after the defeat of Napoleon witnessed a proliferation of new establishments. Intended to be exclusive, they were not however, expensive. As not-for-profit enterprises they aimed to provide food, drink and accommodation, newspapers, journals and a library, at little more than cost. They were often housed in palatial surroundings, designed by the leading architects of the day – John Nash, Decimus Burton and Charles Barry among them. Bachelordom need not, therefore, deprive any affluent man of the least creature comforts. Clubs thus helped to perpetuate late marriage among the upper classes but also inhibited the emergence of the sort of large restaurant sector common in other European capitals.

The United Service Club (1815) accepted army, navy and militia officers and commissioned Sir Robert Smirke to design London's first purpose-built clubhouse for its members. The Travellers' (1819) was open to anyone who had been more than a thousand miles from Britain. The Oxford and Cambridge (1821) recruited from graduates of the ancient universities. The Athenaeum (1824), founded

111. *Dinner of the Dilettante Society at the Thatched House Club in St James's Street. The building was demolished in 1843 when the Conservative Club was built on its site. After T. H. Shepherd.*

112. *St James's Street in 1800. Boodle's is on the extreme left, with Brooks's Club opposite.*

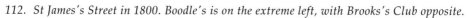

by royal portraitist Sir Thomas Lawrence and scientists Humphrey Davy and Michael Faraday, attracted bishops and heavyweight intellectuals. The Oriental (1824) provided curries for those who had served in India or elsewhere 'out east'.

The Garrick (1831) garnered the actors, authors, artists and journalists eschewed by stuffier circles. The City of London (1832), for businessmen initially met at the George and Vulture, off Fleet Street, of celebrated Pickwickian association, before commissioning a handsome clubhouse in Old Broad Street from Philip Hardwick, the architect of Euston station. The Carlton (1832) became the Conservative Party at table. The Reform (1836) was blessed by the presence of the greatest chef of the era, Alexis Soyer *(see p. 59)*. The Army and Navy (1838) was founded by returnees from India dismayed by the length of the waiting list for the United Service Club.

Although the incarnation of new clubs slackened thereafter their number continued to grow, reaching over a hundred by the end of the century. The Gresham (1843), another club for merchants and bankers and professional gentlemen of 'known respectability', was noted for its port. Pratt's (1857) had just one single basement table, seating fourteen, who were waited on by club servants all known as George. The St James's (1859) was founded for diplomats. The Savage (1857) and the Arts (1863) attracted the same sort of artsy clientele as the Garrick. The shared passion at the Turf (1861) was horse-racing; at the Hurlingham (1869) it was pigeon-shooting, then polo. By 1900 there were at least eight clubs for military and naval officers, five for university graduates and nine for women. By then, however, it was generally acccepted that the fare offered in the capital's great hotels and restaurants was markedly better than what any club could provide. Since then closures and mergers have drastically reduced the number of clubs to a couple of dozen.

THE CAFE ROYAL

Originally a café at 15-17 Glasshouse Street opened by bankrupt Parisian wine-merchant Daniel Nicholas Thévenon (1833-97) and his wife in 1865, the Café Royal expanded to take over prestigious premises fronting onto Regent Street as it attracted a clientele notable for its high profile in the cultural and social life of the capital – Oscar Wilde, James Whistler, Aubrey Beardsley, Bernard Shaw, Frank Harris, Max Beerbohm and Augustus John. Not all onlookers were convinced by the assumed cosmo-politanism of such gatherings. The actor-manager Sir Herbert Beerbohm Tree observed tartly that "if you want to see English people at their most English, go to the Café Royal where they are trying their hardest to be French." By then the amenities included a basement billiard room, a café, luncheon bar, Grill Room and private dining rooms.

The Café Royal offered an enticing combination of opulence, attentive service and

113. Daniel Nicolas Thévenon, founder of the Café Royal. His skills as a wine-buyer led to the creation of arguably London's greatest cellar.

114. *The Café Royal, by Sir William Orpen (1878-1931). Painted in 1912, it now hangs in the Musée d'Orsay, Paris. The Irish-born Orpen, best known as a high society portraitist, was a regular patron at the Café Royal.*

excellent food, but unconstrained by the formality which convention decreed should accompany such delights. The wines, moreover, as fitted the establishment of a former dealer, were outstanding. The noted roué Frank Harris enthused with characteristic hyperbole that "even in 1884-5 the Café Royal had the best cellar in the world. Fifteen years later it was the best ever seen on earth." It was estimated that the cellars, stretching out under Regent Street, contained over 50,000 bottles, the majority fine red Bordeaux. At that time an *à la carte* dinner for two, cooked by the celebrated Oddenino *(see p. 110)* and including caviare, *foie gras,* quails, champagne and liqueurs could be had for £2. 4s. 6d. In *The Adventure of the Illustrious Client* Sherlock Holmes is attacked outside the Café Royal, his assailants escaping through the restaurant and out into Glasshouse Street at the rear. In 1894 a real life mystery occurred at the Café Royal when night porter Marius Martin was founding dying with two bullets in his head.

After the death of the proprietor, who had anglicised himself to become Daniel Nichols, the business was carried on by his widow until her death at the beginning of World War One. Demolished along with Nash's original Quadrant, the premises of the Café Royal were rebuilt in 1923-4, incorporating some of the original decor, such as the celebrated red velvet benches and marble-topped tables of the Domino Room, so long favoured by the capital's artistic elite. Baedeker thought the establishment still worthy of a star and characterised it as "an artistic and Bohemian rendezvous". Regular patrons by then included two future sovereigns, the Prince of Wales and the Duke of York. A standing order in the waiters' instruction book decreed, with reference to the royal princes, "Always plain food. No fuss. Call head waiter at once and notify manager." By the 1930s the Café Royal attracted a new literary coterie – James Agate, Edgar Wallace, A P Herbert, Compton Mackenzie, J B Priestley, Cyril Connolly

and T S Eliot – and a new generation of avant-garde artists – David Bomberg, Paul Nash and Jacob Epstein. Court photographer Cecil Beaton thought the Grill Room the most beautiful dining room in London. In 1948 the Café Royal was uniquely complimented by being selected as the venue for the first Officers' Reunion Dinner of the Army Catering Corps. Bought by Charles Forté in 1954, the Café Royal was given yet another thorough revamp to extend its banqueting and conference facilities through eight storeys. In 1971 Le Relais du Café Royal was opened under the direction of Georges Mouilleron, a former *sous chef at* Le Gavroche and specialist in *charcuterie.* Where Whistler once baited Wilde there now convene the members of the education committee of the Guild of Architectural Ironmongers and participants in conferences on retail automation.

THE GOOD COMPANIONS

Taking his cue from the title of J B Priestley's best-selling novel, Churchill dubbed fish'n'chips 'The Good Companions'. But however inevitable their companionship may now seem it took time for them to get together. The origins of this now classic combination are obscure and disputed, though it seems generally agreed that London and Lancashire are the disputants. The French certainly invented chips, which therefore should indeed be called 'French fries'. It was long known by London street-traders that stale fish could be bought cheaply and that frying arrested its deterioration. Dickens referred to a "fried fish warehouse" in *Oliver Twist,* published in 1839, and described fried fish being offered on the streets of London as a snack, but it was sold cold and accompanied by bread. In *A Tale of Two Cities (1859)* Dickens referred to "husky chips of potatoes, fried with some reluctant drops of oil." Mayhew records fried fish with a slice of bread as being a regular offering in public houses and estimated in 1851 that there were some 300 street-sellers of fried fish as opposed to 150 selling whelks and another 300 selling pea-soup and hot eels.

Itinerant sellers offered lumps of fried fish from a tray, without bread but strewn with parsley and with the option of a box of salt to dip the fish in. Itinerants were often allowed to ply their trade inside pubs because the salty fish encouraged sales of beer.

Watts Phillips' *The Wild Tribes of London* (1855) describes a fried fish-shop, whose proprietors are Jewish, catering to a predominantly Jewish clientele. The fish, sliced, was cooked in oil in a frying-pan and no mention is made of any accompaniments, The honour of being the first ever chippie is contested between Joseph Main of Cleveland Street London, claimed to have been in business in 1860, and a Mr Lees of Mossley, near Oldham who sold fish and chips from a wooden hut in the market around 1863. This chronology fits with the evidence of Col. Newnham-Davis *(see p. 163)* who referred to chips as a novelty of his youth. In his novel *Workers in the Dawn* (1880) George Gissing described a fried fish shop in Whitecross Street:

> "behind the long counter stands a man and a woman, the former busy in frying flat fish over a huge fire, the latter engaged in dipping a ladle into a large vessel which steams profusely; and in front of the counter stands a row of hungry-looking people, eagerly devouring the flakes of fish and greasy potatoes as they come from the pan, while others are served by the woman to little basins of stewed eels from the steaming tureen."

In 1968 the Ministry of Health decreed that newspaper was an unhygienic wrapping for fish and chips and banned its use. Henceforth fish friers used unprinted newspaper stock. The National Union of Journalists nevertheless continued to send its cheery annual greeting to the Federation of Fish Friers "Your trade is wrapped up in ours."

FOOD TO GO

Large numbers of Londoners were for centuries compelled by the circumstances of their lives or daily routines to rely on street traders for at least part of their diet. Labourers working on building sites or along the riverside constituted a ready market, as did the meat-porters at Smithfield who sustained the cookshops of nearby Pye Corner. The multiple occupancy of formerly grand houses condemned many to rooms without access to a proper kitchen. Tens of thousands more were lodgers with families who might not care, or be able, to feed them. Servants on their day off and visitors from out of town were a further source of custom, as were the patrons of such annual jamborees as Bartholomew Fair or Southwark Fair.

The earliest visual depiction of London street traders, by an unknown artist, dates from about 1600. The provisions offered include wheat, carrots, parsnips, radishes, 'cocumbers', 'whyt scalions', garlic, 'scurvygras', potatoes (perhaps surprising in view of the date), 'payres fyn', 'rype straberies', 'pomegranites', walnuts, 'hot codlings hot', 'hot podding pyes', 'hot eele pyes', 'fyne oate cakes', fresh cheese and cream, smelts, 'periwinckels', whiting, 'soales' and 'birds and hens'– the former depicted as small, dead and strung on a stick, the latter in a wicker cage. Of thirty-two trades depicted in this series twenty-three were items of food. Of the vendors depicted only the sellers of pears and 'birds and hens' are shown as male.

Street traders continued to provide a picturesque subject-matter for artists for the next three centuries. *The Cryes of the City of London* of c.1640 included a seller of 'Lilly White Mussels'. Marcellus Lauron's *Cries* of c.1687 showed purveyors of puff pastries and hot stewed pears. A painting of c.1730 depicts a blind Cheapside purveyor of curds and whey – a favourite summer refresher – patronised by soot-blackened chimney-sweeps. Paul Sandby's *Hot Pudding Seller* of 1759 pushes a wheelbarrow which is suspended from his shoulders on straps, leaving his hands free for

115. A shellfish stall in 1876. These were usually strategically positioned outside pubs.

business; the barrow also sports a tattered Union Jack and beside him a dog looks longingly up at a steaming pie as he shakes condiments on it. Francis Wheatley's 1796 painting of the seller of *Hot Spiced Gingerbread* likewise pushed a barrow. His wares, shaped like dogs or sheep or even the king on horseback, were a great favourite with children. How far such representations can be taken as hard evidence of social reality remains problematic. As Celina Fox has observed, "as an alternative to portraits and town prospects, picturesque depictions of street traders fitted admirably into the middle-class home, urban life being tamed and prettified for domestic consumption." Wheatley's series of *Cries,* first exhibited at the Royal Academy between 1792 and 1795, went through thirteen engraved editions by 1797 and were being reissued as late as 1927. Given the hygienic realities of some street-trading practices *(see p. 81)* the grotesque caricatures of the Wheatley genre as celebrated by Gillray and Rowlandson may have come nearer the mark. The increase in the number of shops in early nineteenth century London made the street-seller an increasingly marginal figure in the city's economic life. Whereas previous portrayals had shown them as usually well-fed and often well enough dressed in an unremarkable country style, Victorian sensibilities tended to lump the street-trader in with the casualty class of urban life, on the edge of vagabondage and semi-criminality, implying that many were less genuine entrepreneurs than beggars or

116. *An itinerant mackerel seller, one of F. Wheatly's popular 'Cries of London' series published in 1793.*

117. *A baked potato seller, depicted in Mayhew's London Labour and the London Poor (1861/2).*

prostitutes using their assumed trade to mask their true intent from the recently established police. Some who were genuine traders pursued their vocation by routine fraud and deception — boiling oranges or prunes to make them swell out, spreading a layer of best English cherries over a pile of indifferent imported Dutch ones or mixing in dead eels with live ones. The disposal of unsold surplus represented another opportunity for debasing the food chain. Eel pies were routinely made of dead eels and oysters were regularly turned into sausages.

Despite their vestigial significance in the economic life of the mid-Victorian metropolis, street-sellers continued to exercise a fascination for social investigators quite as much as for artists. In his *London Labour and the London Poor* (1861-2) Henry Mayhew estimated that street folk constituted only one-fortieth of the capital's working population, but he devoted no less than three of his four volume *magnum opus* to chronicling their activities. Reckoning the total number of "street-sellers of eatables and drinkables" at 6,347, he noted the largest contingents to be vendors of ginger beer, lemonade and sherbet (1,700) cat's and dog's meat (1,000), muffins and crumpets (500), and sheeps' trotters (300). He also attempted to estimate the amount of capital tied up in their enterprises in the form of stalls, cads, baskets, scales, trays. cutlery, kettles etc (£9,077 12s 5d) and the amounts of comestibles distributed annually — 1,000,000 pounds of hot eels, 5,000,000 whelks, 4,798,000 bottles of ginger-beer, 3,640,000 trotters, 747,000 lbs of butchers' meat, 486,800 ham sandwiches, 1,755 tons of baked potatoes etc. etc.

118. A pipe-smoking Irishwoman selling oranges, c.1860. Many Irish were forced into street-selling for lack of alternative employment.

119. A street oyster-stall c.1860. Oysters were still cheap enough to be a working-class favourite and were also used to enrich stews.

The most successful street sellers were also the largest contingent – those who had been born to the streets. The least successful were skilled workers who had lost their jobs and were forced onto the streets to survive, and Irish refugees from the famine; neither of these groups had the skills needed to buy well, in terms of price or quality, or to sell effectively to others.

The street-sellers of food themselves ate on the streets:

"They breakfast at a coffee stall. For a penny they can procure a small cup of coffee and two 'thin' (that is to say two thin slices of bread and butter). For dinner . . they buy... small dark coloured pieces of meat exposed on the cheap butchers' blocks. These they cook in a tap room ... If time be an object the coster buys a hot pie or two, preferring fruit pies when in season, and next to them, meat pies. Saveloys with a pint of beer or a glass of 'shod' (neat gin) is

with them another common weekday dinner. The costers make all possible purchases of the street dealers and pride themselves on thus 'sticking to their own'. On Sundays only might they have dinner at home – a joint and 'taters' if the week had gone well, a stew made of offal if it hadn't."

Mayhew's sketches included profiles of sellers of items which depended on their supposed freshness, such as fish, rabbits, oysters, bread, water-cress or milk, on their status as treats or indulgences, such as fruit tarts, buns, pancakes, rice-milk or hot elder wine, or on their value as sustaining fast food for the working man, such as baked potatoes, pigs' trotters, mutton-, kidney- or eel-pies, dumplings or hot green peas. Hot foods, such as baked potatoes or muffins, were naturally in demand in the winter, while ice cream and cooling drinks enjoyed a summer trade. The nature of the goods determined the nature of the

120. *A woman selling apples at 'an 'aypenny a lot'.*

A fourteen-year-old seller of muffins and crumpets alerted Mayhew to the flexible tactics needed to cope with the unpredictable factors which governed the varying level of each day's sales:

> "If there's any unsold, a coffee-shop gets them cheap and puts 'em up cheap again next morning ... I likes wet days best, 'cause there's werry respectable ladies what don't keep a servant, and they buys to save themselves going out. We're a great conwenience to the ladies, sir – a great conwenience to them as likes a slap-up tea. The shops don't love me – I puts their noses out."

Ever alert to record the stratagems evolved for the survival of trades under threat, Mayhew noted the decline in popularity of such traditional products as roast apples or gingerbread and their replacement by new foods, such as ham sandwiches, Brazil nuts and pineapple sold by the slice. He also recorded with fascination how street-sellers of pies resorted to exploiting the cockney's weakness for gambling to meet the challenge of the newly-emergent pie-shop:

> "the pieman makes a practice of 'looking in' at all the taverns on his way 'Here's all 'ot!', the pieman cries as he walks in – 'toss or buy!' ...If the pieman win the toss, he receives 1d without giving a pie; if he lose, he hands it over for nothing. The pieman himself never 'tosses' but always calls head or tail to his customer. At the week's end it comes to the same thing, they say whether they win or lose ...'Very few people buy without tossing. Gentlemen 'out on the spree' at the late public-houses will frequently toss when they don't want the pies and when they win they will amuse themselves by throwing the pies at one another or at me."

'round' pursued by their vendor. Sellers of treats would congregate around parks, theatres or other places of public amusement. Milk could be bought fresh from the cow in St James's Park while the Lodge in Hyde Park offered cheesecakes and syllabubs as well. Purveyors of more mundane goods had other strategies:

> "If they visit a respectable quarter, they confine themselves to the mews near the gentlemen's houses... They go down and through almost all the courts and alleys ... If they have anything inferior they visit the low Irish districts – for the Irish people, they say, want only quantity and care nothing about quality... But if they have anything they wish to make a price of, they seek out the mews, and try to get it off among the gentlemen's coachmen, for *they* will have what is good, or else they go among the residences of mechanics – for their wives, they say, like good living as well as the coachmen."

This bizarre mode of retailing could never do more than stave off the competition. By 1874 *Kelly's Trade Directory for London* was listing the existence of thirty-three eel and pie shops. The Italians, however, had by then developed yet another new street-trade – ice-cream *(see p. 107)*.

121. *Food on the go, modern style. A City catering firm loading up their van with boxes of packed lunches, for workers who eat 'at desks'.*

Thomas Wright, describing *Some Habits and Customs of the Working Classes* in 1867, asserted that the busiest time of all for the street-vendors of 'relishes' was Sunday morning, when working-men were lying abed and their wives were assembling a breakfast 'the Master' could enjoy at leisure and therefore expected to rise above the level of the routine – "for extra relishes are a so universal and well understood part of a working man's Sunday breakfast as on that day scarcely to be regarded as relishes." These might range from "fresh-gathered watercresses" to Gravesend shrimps "penny a pint" to Yarmouth bloaters or smoked haddock. These vendors would be followed by a later round of costers dealing in dinner vegetables

Writing a sketch of *'Kerbstone London'* in 1901 the experienced journalist George R Sims was still able to find scattered survivors of the street food trade in operation:

"In High Street, Marylebone there is a small boy who sells home-made crumpets on the kerb ... In the Whitechapel Road there is a kerbstone trade in hot peas. In the neighbourhood of Charing Cross you can buy gauffres at the kerb cooked 'while you wait'; and in Hoxton and Whitechapel a kerbstone delicacy largely patronised is 'eel jelly'."

KETTNER'S

Auguste Kettner, an Austrian, formerly chef to the French emperor Napoleon III, opened his restaurant at 29 Romilly Street in 1867. Soho was then regarded with disdain or distaste by respectable Londoners. Half a century later John Galsworthy could still refer to it in his Forsyte saga as the quarter of London "least suited to the Forsyte spirit. Untidy, full of Greeks, Ishmaelites, cats. Italians, tomatoes, restaurants, organs, coloured stuffs, queer names, people looking out of upper windows ...".

Soho's long ascent, if never towards respectability then at least towards a certain raffish chic, might be said to have begun in 1869 when an 'anonymous' letter appeared in *The Times* praising a dinner eaten at Kettner's as "better than could have been obtained at a West End club and which cost considerably less." The author of this appreciative missive was handsome, charming Eneas Sweetland Dallas (1828-79), a Jamaica-born journalist of Scottish parentage and education, whose literary skills were greatly admired by both Dickens and Sala.

In 1871 Kettner's was mentioned in a guidebook for American visitors to London. But while Kettner's star was in the ascendant, the career of E S Dallas seemed doomed to an eclipse as his marriage broke up and he fell into financial difficulties. That and the commercial failure of his critically acclaimed study of the principles of literary criticism (*The Gay Science*) may help to explain why Dallas authored *Kettner's Book of the Table,* which was published in 1877. Readers took its eponymous title as a crowning endorsement of a decade of success. Dallas explained it modestly by acknowledging that "he has undertaken the responsibility of the practical receipts – a point of some importance as affecting the sale of the work." In fact the 'receipts' form only a small part of a veritable encyclopaedia of gastronomy. Dallas himself proclaimed that "if a man or woman has not the soul of a cook, the most minute receipts will only end in failure."

Wit was a conspicuous feature of the Dallas style. Eating veal he described as being "as insipid as kissing one's sister." Describing the artichoke as the "best of thistles", he dismissed elaborate French recipes for their preparation as "frantic attempts to paint the lily and perfume the violet." Skate he recommended to be served not with a mustard or caper sauce but with a dressing of shallots and Gruyère cheese. Shoulder of mutton should not be roasted but grilled.

Dallas survived his composition by only two years. The restaurant, however, went from strength to strength and by 1880, when Kettner had handed over its management to his son-in-law, had expanded to occupy four former houses. On the upper floors were several private dining-rooms, much favoured by a fashionably Bohemian clientele which included J A M Whistler and Oscar Wilde. When Col. Newnham-Davis *(see p. 163)* was faced with the conundrum of where to take the vivacious young wife of a friend (and bore) from Indian Army days he chose to book a Kettner's *cabinet particulier* (Room A with paintings of the Italian countryside and gilt candelabra) and regale her with caviare, consommé, filet of sole, ox-tongue with mushrooms and spinach *followed by* chicken and salad, asparagus and an ice – quite a stomach-lining for an evening at the Palace Theatre, followed by a masked ball at Covent Garden.

THE HOLBORN

Located at 218 High Holborn on a site which formerly accommodated a casino, a swimming-baths and a dance hall, the Holborn Restaurant opened its doors in 1874, offering diners the choice of a Grand Salon, Duke's Salon, Ladies Salon, Grill Room, Lincoln's Inn Buffet, private dining-rooms and no less than three Masonic temples. In 1879 the Table D'Hôte menu, served from 5.30 until 8.30 p.m., presented a choice of Giblet Soup or Consommé with Rice, followed by Salmon with Lobster Sauce and Cucumber or Whitebait, either served with boiled potatoes. The entrées consisted of Croquettes, Sauté Potatoes, Pigeons and Peas or Lentil Sauté with Butter. The Removes were Mutton with Red Currant Jelly or Beef with Horseradish, served with Cabbage and Boiled Potatoes. Desserts included Victoria Pudding, Coffee Eclairs, Fruit Jelly, Vanilla or Strawberry Ices, Cheese, 'Trench Salad', Oranges, Pineapple, Cherries, Olives, Nuts or Grapes – all for 3/6d.

Described by Gandhi as 'palatial' in 1889, the Holborn was further extended and

122. The interior of the much-missed Holborn Restaurant, c.1954, on the eve of its demolition.

redecorated in 1896 by T E Collcutt. It was at the Holborn that in 1901 Liberal party leader Henry Campbell-Bannerman excoriated the concentration camp policy introduced by Kitchener to corral Boer civilians suspected of aiding Boer commandos, demanding in ringing tones, "When is a war not a war? When it is carried on by methods of barbarism ....."

The regular meeting place of the St Luke's Masonic Lodge from 1898 until 1954, the Holborn was also much favoured as a venue for reunion, club and celebration dining. Clients ranged from the Old Boys of Reading School to the Durham University Society and the Jersey Society in London. From 1911 it accommodated the monthly meetings of the Sales Managers' Association, the ancestor of the Chartered Institute of Marketing.

Routinely patronised by business regulars and visiting tourists alike, the Holborn also catered for special occasions. In 1891 the Jubilee of Uniform Inland Postage was celebrated by a dinner in the 'Venetian Chamber'. In 1926 the Directors of Leyland Motors gave a well-deserved congratulatory luncheon for three intrepid travellers who had driven 12,000 miles from Singapore to London in a solid-tyred Trojan Utility Car of Leyland manufacture. The Holborn survived World War Two but was demolished in 1955.

123. *Postcard advertising the Holborn Restaurant. Museum Station on the Central Line was closed in 1933 when the new interchange between Piccadilly and Central lines at Holborn was opened.*

LOST RESTAURANTS
London Tavern. 123 Bishopsgate
Rebuilt after a fire in 1765, the London Tavern had a massive wine cellar and another cellar just for live turtles. Cook John Farley, supposed author of The *London Art of Cookery (see p. 53)*, built a reputation for food of such excellence that it won the unqualified praise of socialite William Hickey, who declared that it "surpassed every other tavern we went to. The dinner excellent, served in a style of magnificence peculiar to that house, wines all of the best" The 1793 edition *of Roach's London*

Pocket Pilot assured readers that "at this house are to be met all the most delicate luxuries upon earth". The three-storey London Tavern had a dining-room which could seat over 350 and was therefore used by corporate clients such as the East India Company. The British and Foreign Bible Society was founded there in 1804. Dickens used the venue to satirical effect in *Nicholas Nickleby* (1838-9) as the gathering-place for petitioners to Parliament on behalf of the "United Metropolitan Improved Hot Muffin and Crumpet Baking and Punctual Delivery Company". In 1851 Dickens was himself to preside there over the annual dinner in aid of the General Theatrical Fund. The London Tavern closed in 1876 to make way for an office of the Bank of Scotland.

Verrey's
Charles Verrey, a resident of Regent Street, began his catering career with an ice cream shop at no. 218. By 1848 he and his daughter Fanny were running a restaurant at no. 229, later at 233. Cunningham's 1850 *Handbook of London* described Verrey's *'café et restaurant'* somewhat ambiguously as "the best of its kind in London" and recommended its coffee. Jane Welch Carlyle in 1852 was enthusiastic about her "beautiful little mutton chop and glass of bitter ale... " Other clients included Dickens, Disraeli and the Prince of Wales. Conan Doyle had Sherlock Holmes send out to Verrey's for a treat when he tired of Mrs Hudson's cooking.

The St James's Restaurant
Built at 24-26 Piccadilly by the owners of St James's Hall in 1875, the St James's was said to be London's first restaurant with a small kitchen for each dining-room – "an indispensable adjunct to hot and rapid service." The flamboyant Venetian Gothic facade was designed by Walter Emden, an architect who normally specialised in designing theatres. The restaurant, like the Hall, was demolished to make way for the building of the Piccadilly Hotel.

124. *A 'lost restaurant' in Beak Street, Soho. The Blanchard Restaurant c.1890. Established in 1862, Blanchard's passed out of family ownership in 1923 to become a night club. Dickens attended a birthday party for his mistress Ellen Ternan here shortly before his death.*

KEEPING CASTE

The high-caste son of the prime minister of the princely state of Porbandar in Gujarat in western India, Mohandas Karamchand Gandhi (1869-1948) had sworn to his ultra-orthodox mother that he would remain both celibate and a vegetarian while studying law in London. The latter pledge proved much harder to keep in the carnivorous metropolis than the former. Ironically, gastronomic salvation was to transform not only Gandhi's attitude to his own Hindu heritage but also to lead him for the first time to question the inevitability of British rule in India.

The vegetarian movement in which Gandhi finally found a legitimate means of satisfying his hunger exhibited a sectarian complexity which paralleled the intricacies of caste itself. The Dietetic Reform Society, whose members pledged themselves to vegetarianism and abstention from alcohol and smoking, had been founded in London in 1875. This body had been followed in 1877 by the London Food Reform Society, whose members included a young doctor, T R Allinson, later immortalised in the brand of wholemeal bread named after him. This latter organization soon dropped the word London to become the National Food Reform Society, then merged with the Manchester-based Vegetarian Society in 1885 to become its London branch, then broke away in 1888 to become the London Vegetarian Association, with its own magazine *The Vegetarian*. In 1889 this London organisation founded the Vegetarian Federal Union with a view to promoting contact between vegetarians worldwide.

The London Vegetarian Association was based in Farringdon Street, where there was also a vegetarian restaurant, presumably associated with it. It was there that the unhappy law student found not only food but food for thought as well. Gandhi was thrilled to discover in Henry Salt's *Plea for Vegetarianism* and in the writings of Dr Allinson moral and medical justifications for a practice he had followed as a matter of religious tradition. Gandhi became a member of the Executive Committee and started a short-lived vegetarian club in Bayswater, inviting the distinguished orientalist Sir Edwin Arnold, translator of the *Bhagavad Gita,* to become its Vice-President. Gandhi, however, soon resigned from the Committee following the expulsion of Dr Allinson for advocating birth control, a stance which offended the puritanical and self-promoting Dr Hills, the proprietor of the Thames Iron Works and the Association's main benefactor.

On the eve of his departure Gandhi managed to engineer a significant dietary milestone by organising a vegetarian farewell dinner for friends in the well-known but normally non-vegetarian Holborn Restaurant *(see pp. 158-9).* Nevertheless Gandhi's involvement with the LVA was to have profound and lasting effects. Not only did it confirm his own lifelong commitment to vegetarianism, it also brought him into contact with wider circles of avant-garde thinkers who openly criticised the continuation of British rule in India – an idea so incredible that it had never even occurred to him before. Gandhi had had to come to the capital of the worldwide British empire to experience an epiphany which revealed to him for the first time the possibility that it might be challenged – which was rather less likely to have occurred had he been content to dine in Middle Temple.

LADIES WHO LUNCH

In the Regency period respectable women might eat alone at confectioners' shops but there were few other alternatives until mid-century. In 1852 Jane Welch Carlyle, lunching at Verrey's *(see p. 60),* reassured herself that "I see single women beside myself ... not improper ...

governesses and the like". In 1858. however, the author of *London at Dinner* noted that:

> "it is true that, since our intercourse with the Continent, some coffee-houses have been opened where gentlemen may take their wives and daughters; but it is not yet become a recognised custom ... One evil of long standing still exists in London – and that is the difficulty of finding an Hotel or Restaurant where strangers of the gentler sex may be taken to dine ... in Greenwich, Hampton Court, Windsor, Slough and Richmond ladies are to be found as in the Parisian cafés and at 'Verrey's' in Regent Street; but to give a dinner with ladies it is necessary to take a private room at the 'Albion' or the 'London Tavern'"

By the 1880s polite society accepted that respectable women might dine out in hotels and restaurants. Frederick Gordon *(see pp. 31-2)* had pioneered the potential of the female market at his Crosby Hall restaurant by providing a ladies 'boudoir' and retiring rooms with female attendants. The Midland Grand hotel at St Pancras station, opened in 1873, had a separate ladies' dining room. By the 1890s there was even a restaurant which *only* served ladies, the Dorothy, at 448 Oxford Street. By 1900 there were tea-rooms at department stores such as Swan and Edgar, Derry and Toms, Owen's, Liberty's, Shoolbred's, Owen's and Whiteley's. Females with the time and income to indulge themselves also tended to favour continental-style cafes which specialised in patisserie. Working girls, employed in the expanding retail and clerical sectors, might, from pressures of time and cash, be more likely to patronise the chains of restaurants run by John Pearce or the tea-shops of Messrs Ridgway or the Aereated Bread Company or Mr Lockhart's coffee-rooms. As young girls Virginia Woolf and her sister Vanessa once even dared, on the way home from a dressmakers' appointment, to stop off at an ABC and ate "bath buns driving down Oxford Street on top of the bus."

Active discrimination against women survived in commercial establishments, as well as gentlemen's clubs for almost another century.

Stone's Chop House only admitted women in 1921 and Simpson's in the Strand maintained a 'men only' dining room until it fell foul of sex equality legislation in the 1970s.

THE AGONY AND THE ETIQUETTE

In the first decade of the twentieth century H G Wells' literary emphasis shifted from science fiction to social criticism, but often employing a sardonic humour to achieve his effect. His own lower middle-class background made him very aware of the perils to be faced by the *arriviste* in polite society. This awareness was shared by the author of *The Diners-Out Vade Mecum* who emphasised that rapidly-acquired wealth "often places small men in large positions, and thus opens the door of hospitality, without having first graduated in the art of entertainment."

Kipps, published in 1905, recounts the career of shop assistant Arthur Kipps who inherits an unexpected fortune and is propelled into social circles entirely unknown to him. To familarise himself with the lifestyle to which he wishes to become accustomed Kipps books into the mythical Royal Grand Hotel where he encounters his nemesis in the dining-room. The selection of a clear soup presents no challenge but he becomes confused over the correct knife and fork for the fish course and makes a disastrous assault on a vol-au-vent which splatters onto his shirt-front. Mutton arrives accompanied by peas. Knowing the catastrophic potential of the latter Kipps has them taken away. A further dish is turned away untasted while Kipps sates his remaining hunger with his bread roll. Presented with an iced green *bombe* he assaults it with spoon and fork only to have the summit fly off abruptly and land a yard away on the floor. Upon which Kipps retires with as much dignity as he can muster, leaving the melting ice as a potent symbol of his evaporating social ambitions. Wells' own memories of simple fare are implied in his description of a meal relished by another of his heroes, Mr Polly – cold pork left over from the

Sunday roast, "some nice cold potatoes" and Rashdall's Mixed Pickles, followed by cold suet pudding with treacle and pale, hard cheese, complemented by three thick slices of "greyish baker's bread" and washed down with a jugful of beer.

CAVALRY CRITIC

The prototype of the *Good Food Guide (see p. 199)* was composed by a professional soldier, Lieutenant-Colonel Nathaniel Newnham-Davis (1854-1917), and initially appeared as a series of articles for the *Pall Mall Gazette* before being reprinted in volume form as *Dinners and Diners: Where and How to Dine in London* (1899). Newnham-Davis hit on a simple but highly effective literary device to structure his survey of London's dining possibilities – selecting appropriate places for varying social types, from an actress ('Miss Dainty') to a debutante ('Miss Brighteyes'), an American ('Prima Donna'), a maiden aunt and a man-about-town to an old school friend down on his luck. He not only described the food but also the decor, the ambience and even the head waiter. Normally the Colonel was scrupulously un-partisan (though he did have a partiality for the Savoy) but occasionally he entered upon an evening in the spirit of a contestant, determined to prove a point, as with a rich uncle he dubbed 'the Nabob', who denied the possibility of getting a decent curry in London outside the portals of the East India Club. Newnham-Davis took him to the Hotel Cecil where they consumed *hors-d'oeuvres*, consommé, sole, ribs and a mousse of *foie gras* and ham in champagne *before* they got to the curry and Bombay duck – *followed by* asparagus and two desserts. Including champagne, liqueurs and cigarettes, the bill came to £2 8s.6d – which might be astounding value but must be set against the fact that well over a million Londoners were surviving on half that as a family income per week. Colonel Newnham-Davis's judgments and information were well received and led him on to a new career as a food critic. In 1903 he published *The Gourmet Guide to Europe* and in 1914 came *The Gourmet's Guide to London*. Newnham-Davis included in his reportage an account of the meal he ordered specially at the Carlton hotel, for the delectation of the Princess Lointaine, every course of which demanded elaborate preparation. The soup, for example, was enriched with eggs and chopped truffles, while the fillets of sole were served in a style which had become a speciality of the house − with vermicellli and crayfish tails, flavoured with champagne and parmesan. The bill for ten courses came to sixpence under three pounds. the most expensive items being a bottle of vintage champagne at a guinea and ortolans at ten shillings. Newnham-Davis was not, however, a man to restrict himself to simply ordering and praising the best. Five minutes walk away, at the Comedy Restaurant in Panton Street, he recorded a set meal with a choice of nine courses − including *filet mignon* and snipe − for half a crown. Another short stroll could take the cost-conscious diner to the Restaurant Lyonnais in Soho where soup, a meat course with two vegetables, dessert and a coffee, with as much bread as wanted, would set the customer back a princely eightpence. That excursion proved more successful than his dutiful foray into a vegetarian restaurant in St Martin's Lane, where the set meal consisted of soup, flageolet beans, duck's eggs, salad, cheese and fruit. It cost £1 1s 10d but the intrepid colonel "went forth feeling rather empty."

Not only capable of offering advice on food, decor and ambience Newnham-Davis was also *au fait* with the ultimate insider information − timing: "The man who loves his Cheshire Cheese pudding is in his place at table a few minutes before the pudding is brought in at 6.30 p.m., a surging billow of creamy white bulging out of a great brown bowl ...".

LITERARY LUNCHING

Now largely forgotten, Samuel Rogers (1763-1855) enjoyed great success in his prime as a poet but won even greater renown as the host of celebrated breakfasts held at his house in St James's Place for forty years. The son of a banker, he had an income of £5,000 a year, no family to support and the leisure to indulge his tastes for collecting and conversation. Simultaneously noted for his withering sarcasm and kind-hearted generosity, Rogers was admired by Byron and befriended Fox, Sheridan and Wordsworth. His breakfasts were genuine breakfasts, not "luncheon in disguise", though he did offer his guests delicacies, such as plover's eggs, which might not have routinely graced the breakfast table even in such up-market areas as St James's. Rogers features in no less than seventeen portraits in the National Portrait Gallery collection including a watercolour *Breakfast at Mr Rogers* depicting him with Tom Moore, the poet and biographer of Byron, and the artist of the picture, Jemima Blackburn. Rogers' eminence is attested by the fact that the other portraits include sketches by the architect George Dance, Sir Thomas Lawrence and Sir Edwin Landseer.

When the American writer Julia Ward Howe (1819-1910) visited London in 1843 she was treated to a hectic round of literary entertaining. Samuel Rogers gave her breakfast, Dickens hosted a dinner and Carlyle provided tea in his usual grumpy style − "Mrs. was out and I poured tea for him and he handed me the preserves with 'I do not know what thae little things are, perhaps you can eat them, I never touch them mysel'. Lord Morpeth gave a very grand dinner − thirteen servants ... strawberries ... green peas, pines, peaches, apricots, grapes, all very expensive."

Versatile Abraham Hayward (1801-84), a barrister and translator of Goethe, became celebrated for the dinners he gave in his chambers at the Temple, where his guests included such luminaries as Macaulay and Sydney Smith. Essays on gastronomy and

125. The Gay Hussar in Greek Street is renowned for its Hungarian cuisine and as a favoured venue of the political left.

gastronomers written in 1835-6 established him as the authority on the subject, although the author professed that they had been got ... up just as I would got up a speech from a brief." They were published as *The Art of Dining* in 1852.

The staff of *Punch* magazine, founded in 1841, decided to hold their main weekly meeting over a meal, initially in a pub on Ludgate Hill run by the publisher's brother-in-law. By the 1850s the meals were eaten at the office, around a table which became notorious for the carved initials inflicted on its surface by editors and proprietors. Apart from staff, selected guests have also been invited to carve. These have included Sir John Tenniel (famed illustrator of *Alice in Wonderland),* Sir John Betjeman,

Anthony Powell, James Thurber and A A Milne. The Duke of Edinburgh carved the Greek letter 'Phi' and Prince Charles the three feathers of his crest, surrounded by a C. In 1975 Mrs Thatcher became the first woman ever to attend a *Punch* lunch. The *Punch* tradition has been imitated by other London publications, such as *The Spectator* and *Private Eye,* whose staff meet above the Coach and Horses in Soho. In 1996 *The Oldie* magazine, with the support of Stannah Stairlifts, began holding monthly literary lunches at Simpson's-in-the-Strand. Featured speakers tended to come as much from the world of show business as from literature viz. Michael Palin, Terry Wogan, Maureen Lipman, Ned Sherrin, Joanna Lumley etc.

Workaholic bookseller William Foyle was content in his youth to live on bangers and mash cooked at the back of the shop and, as he prospered, tried to promote sales by sponsoring literary lectures. His daughter Christina (1911-99) had a great deal more success through organising literary lunches. She was just nineteen when she launched the first, in 1930. Usually held at the Dorchester or Grosvenor House, these occasions featured speakers ranging from Evelyn Waugh, H G Wells and Yehudi Menuhin to Margaret Thatcher and John Lennon, addressing audiences of up to two thousand. George Bernard Shaw is alleged to have turned down an invitation after looking at the proposed menu on the grounds that the sound of two thousand people eating raw celery simultaneously was too horrendous to contemplate. Christina Foyle herself famously never even tried to learn to cook but employed an excellent chef.

Asked what she would do if she lost him she retorted that her refrigerator always contained smoked salmon and champagne. Champagne was her only drink and she could afford it, leaving some £60,000,000 at her death. In September 2002 Foyle's held its first literary lunch for children, at London Zoo.

PART SIX

Eating In

PEPYS'S PLEASURES

The name of Samuel Pepys (1633-1703) has become synonymous with his diary, the most celebrated in the English-speaking world. But it was never written for publication and its very un-selfconsciousness is what makes it so invaluable as a reflection of the life of an ambitious, but increasingly affluent, man in Restoration London.

During the years covered by the diary, 1660-1669, Pepys rose rapidly in the service of the Navy Office, becoming wealthy in the process (his assets increased from £40 to £7,000) and enjoying spending his income quite as much as getting it. As an influential official employed in purchasing and awarding contracts Pepys routinely received bribes, often gifts of wine but also oysters, a jar of olives and on one occasion chocolate. Working long hours, he might eat hurriedly but when opportunity allowed he relished good food, good drink and good company. He often rose before dawn and breakfasted on a bewildering variety of mid-morning delights – cold turkey pie, herrings, 'bread and butter and sweetmeats', 'chocolatte' and on one occasion "a great deal of wine, a barrel of good oysters and anchovies." When the Great Fire of 1666 threatened to destroy his official residence in Seething Lane Pepys took care to bury for safe-keeping not only his financial records but also his wine and a great Parmesan cheese. As his work required him to move constantly between the court at Whitehall and the royal dockyards at Greenwich and Deptford, Pepys ate out

frequently. His wife also had recourse to the cookshop when the monthly washday made it impossible to cook at home.

Entertaining gave him great pleasure. At his first recorded dinner party the guests were offered "a dish of marrow bones; a leg of mutton; a loin of veal, three pullets and two dozen of larks all in a dish; a great tart, a neat's tongue, a dish of anchovies; a dish of prawns and cheese" – which seems plenty for eleven people. Pepys gave a special dinner party each year to celebrate his successful operation for the removal of a stone. In 1662 there were six diners, who shared stewed carp, salmon, ox tongues, cheese plus a roast chicken *each*. The following year's dinner was for twelve and comprised fricasee of rabbits and chicken, a leg of mutton, a side of lamb, three carp, four lobsters, three tarts, a lamprey pie, roast pigeons and a dish of anchovies. Pepys's wife. Elizabeth, liked to cook. He records her making pies and tarts to try her oven with when they moved into a new home. She would often prepare a dish at home, such as a venison pasty, but send it out to be cooked at a baker's, sometimes because the results were more reliable, the baker's oven giving a more durable, even heat; but sometimes, in mid-summer, because she wanted to avoid sweltering in her own kitchen.

As he prospered Pepys could afford for his wife to hire in a cook to assist her and her regular serving-girl with the preparations, although Elizabeth Pepys still had to get up at five to go to market to get the freshest

126. Samuel Pepys (1633-1703)

127. John Evelyn (1620-1706)

ingredients. This meal for eight, a late lunch by modern reckoning, consisted of oysters, 'a hash of rabbits', a lamb and a rare chine of beef. Next a great dish of roasted fowl, and a tart; and then fruit and cheese. Before his guests departed at ten they supped again on cold meats, washed down with a sack posset. Pepys reckoned the whole to have cost him nearly £5, compared with six shillings he would pay for a meal for two in a French 'ordinary'*(see p. 100).*

Evening excursions eastwards were a special delight for Pepys at the end of one of his long days: "after dinner by coach with my wife, only to take the air, it being very warm and pleasant, to Bow and Old Ford and thence to Hackney...played shuffleboard, eat cream and good cherries." The drive was usually accompanied by treats of some kind – pullets, eel pie, neat's tongue, "a noble Supper" at Lady Pooly's at Bow or dinner at the Queen's Head, Bow with Sir William Batten, Surveyor of the Navy and Pepys's boss. Batten himself had a fine place at Bethnal Green, whose garden had

"the greatest Quantity of Strawberrys I ever saw." At Lord Brooke's place in Hackney Pepys saw oranges growing some green, some half, some a quarter and some full ripe, on the same tree. Typically he confessed to having purloined and eaten a tiny green one.

DILETTANTE DELIGHTS

Courtier and diarist John Evelyn (1620-1706) lived at Sayes Court, Deptford, then a semi-rural riverside village well outside the capital, for forty years. Possessed of independent means, Evelyn was a prominent member of the Royal Society and could afford to indulge his many interests, which ranged from collecting antique medallions to garden design. In 1683 he noted how the fabulously rich East India merchant Sir Josiah Child had gone to prodigious expense in planting walnut trees about his seat at Wanstead, which Evelyn considered a barren spot, as well as making fishponds, many miles in circuit. In 1685 he was fascinated to see how "Mr. Watts, keeper of the Apothecaries' garden of simples at Chelsea" had introduced a pioneering system of artificial heating in a conservatory, making it possible to grow vines, peaches and citrus fruits.

Scholarly by inclination rather than from necessity, Evelyn liked to follow up any question that intrigued him and to publish his conclusions in pamphlet form. Placed in charge of the welfare of Dutch prisoners-of-war, he was taken aback by their complaint that the bread they were given was *too fine.* The result of his subsequent enquiries was the publication of *Panificium,* which described "the several manners of making bread in France, where by general consent the best bread is eaten."

Evelyn was a friend of Samuel Pepys, despite his own much less ebullient character. He proved himself a friend indeed when, in 1679, Pepys was incarcerated in the Tower on a trumped up charge of participating in treasonous intrigues. Evelyn sent Pepys a piece of venison and went to dine with him in person.

In 1699 Evelyn published *Acetaria, a Discourse of Sallets,* which proved very popular. Evelyn argued that a diet incorporating more vegetables and herbs would be far more wholesome than much of what was currently seen on the tables of the fashionable. His own recipes for salads included raw, cooked, blanched and candied varieties. Waxing poetic, he likened the mixing of a salad to a harmonious composition: "every Plant should come in to bear its part, without being over-powered ... but fall into their Places, like the Notes in Music." His list of standard ingredients included olive oil, wine vinegar, salt, pepper, mustard, orange and lemon peel and hard-boiled eggs. Lettuce he regarded as "the principal Foundation of the universal Tribe of Sallets" and ascribed to it an impressive range of beneficial properties, being able to extinguish thirst, stimulate the appetite, improve sleep and even reduce pain. Noting that only the Dutch ate cabbage raw, he nevertheless apppreciated the need not to overcook vegetables. Asparagus, he recommended, should be plunged into water already boiling, and then cooked speedily so as

not to lose the verdure and agreeable tenderness. When dealing with artichokes Evelyn recommended slicing the heads in quarters and either eating them raw with oil, vinegar, salt and pepper or, if still tender, fried in butter with parsley. The bottoms should be baked in pies with marrow, dates and other rich ingredients. Those with a taste for the exotic might care to try them Italian-style, eating the broiled leaves basted with oil and sauced with orange juice and sugar.

Evelyn was especially aware of salad ingredients newly introduced via Europe, such as celery, chard and 'Coss Lettuce' from Turkey. Normally keen to urge diners to accept the challenge of a novelty he absolutely forbade all but the slightest touch of one ingredient – garlic. "We absolutely forbid it entrance into our Salleting, by reason of its intolerable Rankness, and which made it so detested of old, that the eating of it was...part of the Punishment of such as had committed the horrid'st Crimes. To be sure, 'tis not for Ladies Palats, nor those who court them, farther than to permit a light touch on the Dish, with a Clove thereof."

TWO WAY TRAFFIC
One of the most striking characteristics of English, as opposed to French, society in the seventeenth and eighteenth centuries was the inter-penetration rather than separation of the life of the capital and the countryside. Whereas the French *noblesse* regarded the rural estates from which they drew their incomes as just that – a source of income – and regarded with horror the prospect of actually living there as a form of banishment or exile, many English aristocrats were actively involved in estate management and participated joyously in the life of 'county' society and its rustic amusements. But they also expected to spend some months, usually in the winter and spring, in the capital. The greatest made attendance at court, the next layer sat in the House of Commons. The rest had business to attend to with lawyers, doctors, or tailors and took the

opportunity to shop for items not readily found in country towns, such as books. In gastronomic terms this pattern of seasonal movement promoted a reciprocity between the urban and rural seats which most great families invariably maintained.

Bedford House on the Strand was the London home of the Russell family, Earls, and later Dukes, of Bedford. They were to develop the area to the rear of their property – Covent Garden – as London's first planned square. Surviving account books from the mid-seventeenth to the late eighteenth century afford much insight into the running of this aristocratic household, and especially its provisioning. The picture that emerges is of a two way traffic between the Russells' London base and their estates at Woburn in Bedfordshire and Thorney in the Cambridgeshire fens. Perhaps surprisingly rather more came *from* London than to it. From the country came occasional luxuries of the hunt, such as hares or swans. From London came not only imported luxuries, such as tea and coffee and seafood like soles, smelts, salmon, lobsters and barrels of oysters, but also fruit from Covent Garden and pork from Smithfield. Bacon from Essex, brought down by carrier's cart to Bedford House, was redirected from there to Woburn. The butter from Hackney is repeatedly mentioned and must have been something special because it was clearly distinguished from the butter obtained from local farmers and cost tenpence a pound against the usual sixpence.

London also made a particularly important contribution to the country estate's horticultural endeavours. The Strand was home to a number of specialist seedsmen. Commercial nurseries at Brompton, Brentford and Whitechapel supplied pear, plum, peach, apple, apricot and cherry trees in bulk. A Brompton order for 1685 included a hundred each of currant and gooseberry bushes, fifty pear trees and two hundred apple trees.

Over the period covered by the account books it is clear that the Russells came to live on a larger and more lavish scale. In the mid-seventeenth century the kitchen staff at Bedford House consisted entirely of men and boys. A hundred years later they had been joined by four, sometimes five, kitchen maids, paid a modest £8 a year each. They were answerable to the clerk to the kitchen who received a princely £60 a year plus his keep. This was equalled by the salary of the Duke's French chef, Monsieur l'Allemande who lived out in a nearby Russell property. The English chef by contrast received only £30. The other specialist, the Confectioner, was paid £52.10s.

In 1658 luxuries consisted of fairly basic commodities such as sugar and rice, raisins and currants, nutmeg, mace, ginger, cloves and cinnamon, almonds, figs and prunes. Around 1670 the Russells began to drink coffee on a regular basis. By 1756 Richard Robertson of New Bond Street was supplying aniseed, limes, pistachio nuts and 'prunellos' and could also provide ice on demand. Some luxuries were imported direct from overseas suppliers – fish from faraway Newfoundland, confectionery from France and hams from Westphalia.

Some provisions were bought from nearby Covent Garden. Tea, sugar and chocolate came from Tom's famed coffee-house (see p. 134). Tea and coffee were always procured from specialist dealers, never from general grocers. The latter, located in fashionable St James's, supplied special treats, often in substantial quantities. In 1769 a single order from Bartho Valle and Brother at the Sign of the Orange Tree and Two Jars in the Haymarket included six pounds each of capers and anchovies, seven of macaroni and three of 'French plums', plus four mangoes. Interestingly, the containers in which these products were delivered were charged for as extras.

SCHOOL DINNERS

Children in institutional settings, like the inmates of prisons and workhouses, have traditionally had little say in what they have been obliged to eat.

Christ's Hospital

Founded in 1553 by teenage Edward VI ten days before his death, Christ's Hospital was originally intended to serve as a refuge for London orphans and was located in the deserted buildings of the former headquarters of the Greyfriars (Franciscans). The survival of much of its domestic documentation over centuries provides valuable insights into the sort of diet deemed suitable for children at varying periods. The earliest accounts show regular purchases of mutton, beef, whiting, herring and plaice as well as gallons of milk. In the late seventeenth century imported rice entered the diet, partly as a substitute for cheese. The weekly allowance of beer per head was two and a half gallons. Three pints a day would have accounted for about 500 to 600 calories – a fifth of the essential daily intake. Other major dietary items were bread, cheese, butter, beef, oatmeal and dried pease – compared with Tudor times a major shift away from protein-rich foods towards carbohydrates. In 1721 the Governors, acknowledging that the "Dyett from Thursday Noon to Sunday Noon was only Bread Butter and Cheese Pease Porridge and Water gruell", approved the addition to the diet of "Leggs and Lynns of Mutton Boyled". By contrast the

128. Supper at Christ's Hospital, c.1870.

129. The kitchen at Charterhouse School, 1867. Despite the imposing surroundings in which it was prepared the childhood diet of Britain's future ruling elite was invariably Spartan.

indigent children cared for by the Grey Coat Hospital, Westminster were set to spinning, sewing and knitting to offset the costs of their keep and received an even more miserable diet which allowed of butter with the morning bread on only four days a week and provided only bread and cheese for supper every night. As far as the main mid-day meal went Sunday was their high spot: beef broth and peas. On Monday there was only bread and butter, on Tuesday and Thursday broth, on Wednesday frumenty (hulled wheat boiled in milk, with sugar), on Friday peas porridge and on Saturday milk porridge. The essayist Charles Lamb, a pupil at Christ's Hospital from 1782 to 1789. endured three meatless days a week, "milk porritch, blue and tasteless, pease soup ... coarse and choking'... detestable mangolds ... to poison the broth ... scanty mutton scrags ... rotten-roasted or rare". Not surprisingly there had been outbreaks of scurvy, counteracted from 1770 onwards by the addition of potatoes to the diet on the advice of the school's Physician-Apothecary. When potatoes became scarce later in the century scurvy reappeared and, in mild form, was still apparent in 1816, well after it had been eliminated in the navy. The reason appears to have been that fruit was regarded as a superfluous luxury and bread (admittedly by then the best and a lot of it) was thought to be an adequate substitute for vegetables in the diet. In 1834 the Christ's Hospital diet came in for severe criticism from the *Lancet (see p. 191)*. The Governors responded, with expected self-justification, that their care and attention, cannot be too much eulogised ... particularly as regards the diet, which has always been sufficiently wholesome and good, but did make some adjustments, doubling the weekly potato allowance to two pounds and adding vegetable soup twice a week, while reducing the ration of butter by two-thirds to an ounce and a half. By the end of the nineteenth century, however, the school diet had been immensely improved by the inclusion of fresh peas, greens and lettuce and even stewed fruit. It was presumably the younger boys who had suffered most over the centuries, as the older ones, with more pocket money and greater freedom of movement (whether authorised or otherwise) could gain access to the pie-shops of nearby Giltspur Street and the capital's ubiquitous street-vendors of fruit and fast food.

THE FOUNDLING HOSPITAL

London's first orphanage, the Foundling Hospital, was granted a royal charter in 1739 and eventually settled in Bloomsbury. The dietary regime established for the children in 1747 divided the year into the Pork Season and the Other Season. In the Pork Season the midday meals began with Roast Pork on Sundays, followed on successive days by Potatoes, Boiled

Mutton, Rice Milk, Boiled Pork, Dumplings and Hasty Puddings. In the Other Season the sequence was Roast Beef, Potatoes, Boiled Beef, Rice Puddings, Boiled Mutton, Suet Pudding and Hasty Pudding. Regardless of the season breakfast consisted of Broth, Gruel or Milk Porridge in rotation. Supper consisted of bread three nights a week, milk and bread two nights and bread and cheese two nights. There is no mention of vegetables, fish or eggs. This reflected the contemporary belief that vegetables and fruit were dangerous for children, being indigestible or liable to cause diarrhoea. In 1750, however, the Hospital's General Committee was offered contrary advice by the eminent physician William Cadogan who recommended that small children should progress as soon as possible from bread and butter to a little meat and then to fruit – raw, baked or stewed – and all the produce of the kitchen garden. In 1762 vegetables were added

130. Cold comfort – the dining room at the Foundling Hospital, early 20th century.

to the children's diet – greens three times a week, broth with herbs and roots twice, potatoes or parsnips mashed with milk once and rice pudding once.

To commemorate the granting of the charter there was an annual holiday and dinner for the children on 17 October, consisting of Roast Beef and 'Plumb Pudding'. The staff of the Foundling Hospital, by contrast, enjoyed a hot meat dish every day, consisting of pork and veal as well as beef and mutton, complemented with carrots, turnips, greens, roots and pease pudding.

DR SAMUEL JOHNSON

"A man seldom thinks with more earnestness of anything than he does of his dinner."

A chronic depressive, afflicted with nervous tics, asthma and dropsy, impaired in sight and hearing, Samuel Johnson (1709-84), thanks to his devoted biographer James Boswell, is, of all inhabitants of eighteenth-century London the one we know most about. Boswell, a trained lawyer, recorded his mentor's preferences with as much accuracy as his pronouncements. The author of the first true dictionary of the English language achieved fame with the completion of his great enterprise in 1755 but Johnson never forgot the truly severe poverty in which he had lived when he first came to London and had had to survive as a Grub Street hack. As a consequence Johnson, despite his almost morbid concern with his conscience, was much tempted to indulgence at the table. As Boswell noted acutely:

"when at table ... his looks seemed riveted to his plate; nor would he, unless when in very high company, say one word ... till he had satisfied his appetite; which was so fierce, and indulged with such intenseness, that while in the act of eating, the veins of his forehead swelled ... it must be owned that Johnson, though he could be rigidly abstemious, was not a temperate man either in eating or drinking. He could refrain but he could not use moderately."

Despite a manner which could be gruff,

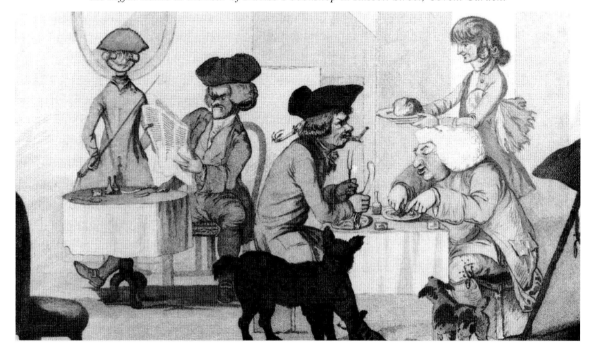

131. Boswell and Johnson in a chop house, by H. Bunbury. Johnson first encountered his future biographer in the coffee-house at the rear of Davies's bookshop in Russell Street, Covent Garden.

aggressive or pompous, Johnson won friends through his wit, learning and kindness. None were more generous than the Southwark brewer Henry Thrale and his wife Hester, who dined Johnson at their home or their villa in Streatham for weeks at a time for over twenty years. Johnson himself noted of an informal supper served to him in 1782 that it consisted of "a roast leg of lamb with spinach chopped fine, the stuffing of flour with raisins, a sirloin of beef and a turkey poult; and after the first course, figs, grapes not very ripe owing to the bad season, with peaches – hard ones." In 1778, when dining with the Dilly brothers, noted publishers, Dr Johnson announced expansively that he "could write a better book of cookery than has ever yet been written", proclaiming that "it should be a book upon philosophical (i.e. scientific) principles". Arguing that "pharmacy is now made much more simple, Cookery may be made so too", Johnson declared that whereas a prescription which once had fifty ingredients in it had now been reduced to five, "so in cookery, if the nature of the ingredients be well known, much fewer will do." Johnson promised, moreover, to provide guidance on choosing the best meat and poultry, "the proper seasons of different vegetables" as well as "how to roast and boil and compound." Dilly, speaking on behalf of the book trade, referred to Mrs Glasse's *Art of Cookery (see p. 53)* as the best existing work but alleged that "half the trade" knew that it had really been written by Dr John Hill. Hill (?1716-1775), a botanist of some eminence, had also been an actor before descending to the roles of quack and hack and styling himself 'Sir John' on the strength of a Swedish honour. He was a man of whom almost anything might be believed, Johnson judging him "an ingenious man, but had no veracity". On this occasion Johnson strongly denied that Hill could be the author of Mrs Glasse's book on the grounds that she thought saltpetre and sal-prunella were different substances whereas they were the same in different states, which Hill would have known. He did concede, however, that "as the

greatest part of such a book is made by transcription, this mistake may have been carelessly adopted". When Johnson concluded his peroration by promising Dilly the copyright of the projected masterpiece a female guest drily observed that it would be "Hercules with a distaff indeed". Johnson was characteristically unmoved. "No, Madam. Women can spin very well; but they cannot make a good book of Cookery." Nor did Johnson.

PRINCE OF PLEASURE

"Not a fatter fish than he
Flounders round the polar sea.
See his blubbers – at his gills
What a world of drink he swills...
By his bulk and by his size
By his oily qualities,
This (or else my eyesight fails)
This should be the Prince of Whales ."
Anon. (Actually Charles Lamb) 1812

George IV (1762-1830) was a man of exquisite taste and gross appetites. He spent far beyond his means and indulged himself unstintingly as the poor of his country were pressed into ever deeper misery. Time worked out its revenges inexorably. Ambitious to be considered 'the first gentleman of Europe', by the time he actually achieved the throne his physical grossness made him a figure of ridicule and severely curtailed his daily existence, though not his intake of food and drink. Briefly the employer of the incomparable Careme *(see p. 55)*, as Prince of Wales, he complained that his chef's creations were simply impossible to resist. Careme responded with an appropriate hauteur, "Your Highness, my duty is to tempt your appetite; yours, to control it".

When the death of his youngest daughter Princess Amelia in 1810 tipped George III into final and irretrievable insanity, the Prince of Wales was accordingly recognised by Parliament as Prince Regent in his father's stead. To mark his *de facto* accession to power on 19 June 1811 the Prince Regent gave a supper party for over two thousand guests in the conservatory of his London residence, Carlton House. At this "costly entertainment of the most tasteless and extravagant kind" – to quote a Victorian obituarist of the 1880s – the Prince sat on a raised throne, flanked by tables piled with gold plate. Behind him a three tier buffet, piled with more plate, was surmounted by an urn allegedly seized by Drake from the Spanish Armada. In front of him, running the entire length of a table two hundred feet long, was a raised table plateau. At its head a silver fountain cascaded water into a miniature lake, bordered by a colonnade between whose arches perfumieres burned fragrantly. From the lake the water flowed into a stream, alive with tiny silver and golden fish, which meandered the length of the plateau between flower-lined banks. The prodigality of this occasion was lampooned in a gross caricature – *Regency Fête or John Bull in the Conservatory* – which appeared within ten days of the event.

As might have been anticipated the coronation banquet was similarly unstinted as members of the House of Lords were treated to 160 tureens of soup and the same number of dishes of fish, of vegetables, of lobster and crayfish, of cold roast fowl and hotjoints, eighty each of savoury pies, of dishes of savoury drakes, of goose, of braised beef, of braised capons and of cold lamb, complemented by 1190 side dishes and 480 boats of lobster, mint and butter sauce, and topped off with 320 dishes of 'mounted pastry' and 320 more of 'small pastry' and 400 of jellies and creams. The wives of the members of the House of Lords were, meanwhile, confined to galleries as onlookers. Despite inflammation of the bladder, gout and dropsy, and despite being obliged to swathe his voluminous bulk in dressing gowns – he who had once run up £10,000 a year in tailor's bills – as a recluse the king continued to gorge himself to the end. On his deathbed he consumed two pigeons, three beefsteaks, three-quarters of a bottle of Moselle, a glass of champagne, a glass of brandy and two glasses of port – for breakfast.

BELOW STAIRS

At the age of thirty London footman William Tayler (1807-92) decided to keep a journal with a view to improving his hand "as I am a wretched bad writer". His daily jottings afford a rare insight into the catering routines of an affluent household as seen from below stairs. Tayler was employed by a wealthy widow living at Great Cumberland Street, Marylebone, then one of London's most fashionable residential districts. Apart from Tayler, the widow and her spinster daughter employed a cook and three maidservants to wait on them. While their personal requirements were modest, routine and relatively undemanding, they did like to entertain. In the normal course of a day Tayler got up at 7.30, served, cleared away and washed up after four meals and went to bad at eleven. A special occasion, such as a dinner party, involved getting up at seven and not getting to bed until he was "very tired". Tayler himself ate sparingly, having cocoa and a roll mid-morning, skipping lunch, taking tea with bread and butter at four, a hot meal in the early evening and a cold supper at nine. Normally his was traditional plain fare – roasts, suet pudding, Irish stew, dumplings, rice and bread puddings, damson or gooseberry pie – but this was frequently supplemented by "many nice little things that come down from the parlour", such as left-over 'egg hot', a winter warmer of beer, eggs, sugar and nutmeg. According to season they might also have veal or duck and, of course, turkey at Christmas.

The widow and her daughter usually ate a simple breakfast of hot rolls, dry toast, a fancy loaf and a plain loaf, with tea or chocolate. Lunch was equally unfussy – cold meat and vegetables or whatever the servants themselves were having. Dinner, served at six, was by far the most elaborate meal of the day. One meal consisted of sole with a sauce, a leg of mutton with vegetables, a rhubarb tart, a tapioca pudding and cheese and butter, followed at eight by bread and butter and dry toast; but "never any supper – it's not fashionable".

132. 'Servants helping themselves behind the screen in the dining room', by William Tayler, 1837 – a candid confession from below stairs?

Very occasionally the widow threw a party for as many as fifty or more people. On such occasions Tayler was assisted by two extra footmen, hired for the occasion, to show in and announce guests and serve refreshments, which consisted of sweet cakes, biscuits, lemonade, orangeade and negus (port or sherry with spices, lemon and hot water), the highlight being ices "made of ice pounded, mixed with cream, and juice of strawberry, some of apricot or oranges", eaten out of glass saucers with a spoon.

PRISONS

The inmates of London's eighteenth-century prisons received a daily allowance of bread, usually about half a pound. Prison reformer John Howard (1726-90) asserted that prisoners needed three times as much, plus a quart of warm vegetable soup twice a day. Even this compassionate man, however, accepted that the provision or denial of food should be used to control behaviour:

"If once a week (suppose on Sunday) some coarser pieces of beef were boiled and half a pound of the meat ... given to each prisoner, with a third of the broth, this Sunday dinner might be made an encouragement to peaceable or orderly behaviour: the turbulent and refractory should not have it."

For anything more tasty or nutritious than bread prisoners had to rely on what they could afford to pay for, or what the generosity of family, friends or the compassionate might bring their way, or what he could seize or beg from fellow-prisoners. A diet entirely restricted to bread and water would soon see the prisoner subject to scurvy. Naval prisoners in the hulks at Woolwich, divided into messes of six, shared a daily ration of half a bullock's head and four pounds of biscuit and an oat-meal broth. "Most of them complain of diarrhoea; few are free from scorbutic blotches."

At Whitecross Street, a 'model' debtors' prison built in 1813-15 by the Corporation of London, inmates were still locked up for sixteen

133. The Millbank Penitentiary. It was built in 1816 to principles suggested by Jeremy Bentham. The Tate Britain gallery is on the site today. Londoners condemned to transportation to Australia were assembled here before transfer to naval hulks at Gravesend.

hours out of every twenty-four. Prisoners too poor to pay for their own food were allowed a daily diet of one and a half pounds of bread and two pints of oatmeal gruel, supplemented by a weekly ration of three pints of soup, two pounds of potatoes and twenty-one ounces of meat. Fortunately for most, the average stay was about ten days, thanks to the existence of charities established for the express purpose of freeing otherwise respectable persons incarcerated for relatively trivial debts.

Before 1822 the prisoners in Millbank penitentiary received a breakfast and supper of bread and gruel. On four days of the week they were given six ounces of beef and a pound of potatoes for dinner, on the other three, vegetable soup. It was then decided that this regime was too generous and the diet was restricted to bread, gruel and soup, cutting its calorific value by almost half to *c.*2,000 calories daily. The soup was thin stuff indeed, made from one ox-head per hundred prisoners, bulked out with

pease, barley or vegetables. Within less than six months more than half of all prisoners were showing symptoms of scurvy and over one-sixth had dysentery. Emergency rations of meat, rice and oranges soon curbed the scurvy epidemic. In 1824 a new dietary was established, providing six ounces of meat daily, substituting potatoes for gruel and adding in a quarter of a pint of milk.

In 1842 the Home Secretary decreed that in prisons "that quantity of food should be given … which is sufficient and not more than sufficient, to maintain health and strength at the least possible cost". Two further principles were enunciated, that at least two of the day's three meals should be hot and that "the diet ought not to be made an instrument of punishment". Even so, prisoners serving for twenty-one days or less were restricted to a diet of bread and gruel. Inmates serving longer terms qualified for meat, soup and potatoes. Prisoners at hard labour received larger allowances of meat and potatoes, plus cocoa. Even so, they would have been seriously under-nourished, receiving only about two-thirds of the calories nowadays deemed necessary for the performance of even light work. Loss of weight, lethargy and weakness were the inevitable outcomes. Contemporary authorities blamed these symptoms on the effects of confinement rather than inadequacies of diet.

At the House of Detention in Clerkenwell in the 1840s diets were regarded as generous, the inmates consisting not of hardened criminals but of delinquent cabmen, remand prisoners, bail defaulters and army deserters. Although they were required to make their own bed and clean their cell, they were not required to do any work involving heavy exertion. The daily allowance for their sustenance consisted of twenty ounces of bread, a pint of gruel and a pint of cocoa plus either a pint and a half of soup or six ounces of cooked meat and eight ounces of potatoes. They were also allowed to receive food from outside though they were barred from selling or even sharing any they did get.

THE WORKHOUSE

Although seldom to be preferred to living in one's own home on out-relief (i.e. weekly payments in cash or kind) the workhouse was not in the eigtheenth century the dreaded institution that it came to be. For old, single men, infirm, childless widows and the seriously disabled there was likely to be no better alternative. In the eighteenth century, when the 'deserving poor' were still recognized as such, provision for their sustenance was not ungenerous. In the 1750s the parish of St. John's, Hackney allowed each adult daily seven ounces of meat (without bones), four of cheese and two of butter plus a pound of bread and three pints of beer. Hackney was then, of course, a distinct rural community and well known as a centre of dairy production. As late as 1823 the parish of St Anne's, Westminster – effectively now Soho – allowed its workhouse inmates a daily ration of thirteen ounces of

bread and two pints of beer. On Sundays, Tuesdays and Thursdays this was supplemented by a seven-ounce serving of boiled beef or mutton, with vegetables and a pint of broth. On Mondays the supplement was a pint of milk pottage, three ounces of butter and three ounces of cheese. On Wednesdays it was a pint of pease soup. On Fridays the same portions of butter and cheese, with a pint of rice milk and on Saturdays the milk pottage with twelve ounces of suet pudding. Britain's rapid rise in population in the century after 1750 was made unambiguously clear by the results of the national censuses held every decade from 1801 onwards. In rapidly industrializing areas this expanding labour force was absorbed into the factories but elsewhere it meant unemployment and increasing dependency on the public purse. As rate-bills rose inexorably the propertied classes represented in Parliament endorsed a policy of brutal retrenchment in costs of relieving poverty. Under the terms of the New Poor Law of 1834 workhouses would henceforth be conducted on the principle of 'less eligibility' – i.e. in such a way that any person with any other feasible alternative would seek it in preference to entering what the poor were quick to dub 'bastilles'. Henceforth bread, gruel and thin soups formed the staple fare. The standard gruel recipe specified that each pint should contain two ounces of oatmeal and a half ounce of treacle, flavoured with salt or allspice. Broth was usually the water left over from boiling the dinner meat, with a few onions, leeks, carrots or turnips added and possibly barley, rice or oatmeal to thicken it. In 1841 the typical workhouse regimen was denounced as being inferior even to what was provided for transported convicts. Children suffered particularly as it was not understood that their dietary needs were different from those of adults, that under-nourishment in their formative years could have permanently debilitating effects and that their needs were not directly proportionate to their small size.

Local dietary patterns seem to have ensured

134. Supping in silence – the men's dining hall at St Marylebone Workhouse in 1902.

that in the north of England vegetables, especially potatoes, and milk seem to have continued to figure in workhouse provision. Inmates in the 'soft South' were less fortunate. When vagrancy peaked in London in the 1840s as a result of the influx of refugees from the Irish famine the workhouse in St Marylebone considered abolishing the inmates' Christmas pudding in the interests of economy but compromised by retaining it but limiting portions to eight ounces and substituting raisins for currants. In the 1840s inmates staying overnight only were given eight ounces of bread and a pint of gruel or soup for supper and breakfast. Twenty years later the ration had been cut to six ounces.

Frugal as the workhouse diet was it could still serve as an instrument of control. Neglect of work might be punished by withholding the day's main meal, noise and swearing by twenty-four hours on bread and water, fighting in school by denial of cheese for a week. The normal arrangements for dining had, in any case, a punitive air about them. Men and women ate separately, in silence, seated in rows all facing the same way, rather than opposite each other. A complete revision of workhouse diets was not achieved until 1897 and new scales implemented in 1901. In terms of calorific intake they were far more adequate. They also recognised children's special need for plenty of milk. On the other hand three ounces of boiled bacon three times a week was the only meat element in the entire provision and a heavy reliance on white bread and margarine could scarcely be regarded as an advance.

135. Dining at the Lambeth Asylum, c.1810, by Pugin and Rowlandson. The Asylum was founded in 1758 by Sir John Fielding, The building shown above was at the corner of Westminster Bridge Road and Kennington Road on the site of Morley College and Christchurch and Upton Chapel. It moved to Beddington Park in 1866.

DICKENS' DELIGHTS

Dickens knew real poverty in his childhood and as an adult enjoyed a lavish income which enabled him to keep a good table and to entertain generously. Paradoxically he was himself abstemious to the point of it being remarked on, one of his guests noting that he "seemed to participate in other people's enjoyment of what was laid before them rather than to have any pleasure in the good things himself". At the Athenaeum he was observed to lunch on a solitary sandwich, eaten standing up. Dickens' own office boy confirmed that "he wasn't but a light eater himself". The author's writings are, nevertheless, replete with descriptions of meals. In *Pickwick* alone there are ten luncheons, thirty-two dinners and thirty-five breakfasts. Dickens frequently invoked the presence of plentiful food as an indicator of domestic contentment, as with the Cratchits in *A Christmas Carol*. Scrooge's moral reformation is signified by the purchase of a magnificent turkey. The absence of hot food at Paul's christening in *Dombey and Son* is, by contrast, a symbolic indictment of the family's frigidity. In *Great Expectations* Miss Havisham's abandoned wedding-feast represents the wreckage of all her dreams. David Copperfield's marriage to the pretty but feckless Dora is clearly doomed by her inability to manage even a simple dinner party which turns into a catalogue of disasters. The peculiarities of individual appetites enrich the definition of many of his characters. Sam Weller, for example, is provoked to the philosophical observation that "poverty and oysters always seem to go together ... Blessed if I don't think that ven a man's wery poor he rushes out of his lodgings and eats oysters in reg'lar desperation". Sarah Gamp favours "a little bit of pickled salmon, with a

136. Oliver Twist asking for more, drawing by George Cruikshank. This famous plea for food no doubt reflects the hungry childhood of Charles Dickens.

nice little sprig of fennel and a sprinkling of white pepper" complemented by a "cowcumber" and washed down with "Brighton Old Tipper". In *David Copperfield* the extensive meal recommended by Mrs Crupp, "a pair of hot roast fowls ... a dish of stewed beef, with vegetables ... a raised pie and a dish of kidneys... a tart and ... a shape of jelly" are all to be ordered in from a pastry-cook's, thus leaving her "at full liberty to concentrate her mind on the potatoes and to serve up the cheese and celery as she could wish to see it done". Although Dickens might have been making particular fun of Mrs Crupp, the characters in his novels bring cooked food to eat in their lodgings with sufficient regularity to confirm this custom as still being a regular feature of London life well into the middle years of the nineteenth century. Dickens also incorporated real London eating-houses into his scenarios – the George and Vulture off Cornhill in *Pickwick Papers* and the George in Borough High Street in *Little Dorrit*. He is also known to have patronised the Olde Cheshire Cheese off Fleet Street but when working as editor of *All the Year Round*, which had its

offices in Bow Street, he habitually dined at Carr's in the Strand, an establishment which survived until 1903.

Dinners were a central feature of Victorian social life and could be occasioned by a great variety of events, in Dickens' case often to celebrate an anniversary or a publication or to raise money for a charity. In 1851, for example, himself a frustrated actor and keen producer of amateur theatricals, he presided at the annual dinner in aid of the General Theatrical Fund held at the London Tavern, Bishopsgate. An accomplished after-dinner speaker, Dickens, on another occasion, orated so powerfully on behalf of the Great Ormond Street Hospital that he raised a staggering three thousand pounds on the spot.

In 1865 Dickens' wife, Kate, masquerading under the pseudonym of Lady Maria Clutterbuck, published a volume of menus under the disarmingly straightforward title *What shall we have for Dinner?* Quite a lot of mutton, macaroni and mashed potatoes apparently, plus some real oddities like curried lobster or raspberry jam sandwiches for dessert at a dinner-party.

A LA RUSSE

Mid-Victorian London witnessed a minor revolution in dining habits with the adoption of service *à la Russe*, which gradually superseded service *à la Française*, a mode of dining perfected in France on the very eve of its revolution. This was slightly paradoxical in that the transition between the two styles began around the time of the Crimean War (1854-6) when the Russians were the hated enemy and the French were Britain's gallant allies. Fancy name cards to mark the *placement* came in at around the same time. Guests were conventionally expected to arrive about half an hour before the appointed hour of dining – lateness was a grave discourtesy – and the interval was whiled away by looking at photograph albums. (Had London Society gone wholly over to Russsian ways it would have taken up the custom of filling this void with the consumption of astringent appetizers such as salt herring, anchovies or caviare. washed down with brandy or kummel). By the time the announcement came that 'Dinner is served', the preliminary soup course already had been. After this was removed the 'first service' was completed by the presentation of a selection of light fish and meat dishes, such as turbot, salmon, hare or veal, to which diners helped themselves as they pleased. Although these might actually include such quite substantial 'made dishes' such as croquettes, patties or vol-au-vents, they were still regarded as what Careme would have classified as entrées and served as but a preparation for the main course which consisted of a choice of three or four roasts, again offered simultaneously, with respectively appropriate accompaniments in the form of gravies, sauces, vegetables or salads. Custom decreed that the host, aided by servants, should personally carve for his guests – which made skilful carving an important social accomplishment. The third course consisted of a like profusion of hot and cold desserts – pies, puddings, ices, flans, tarts, custards or syllabubs – flanked by fresh fruit, cheeses and bon-bons. Covering the table with such a cornucopia left little room for floral decorations, so usually there was only a large candelabra or silver epergne as a centrepiece. In more modest establishments the second and third courses might be merged.

The London socialite Count Gronow, a member of the Prince of Wales's 'set', described a typical grand dinner served in this manner, or at least the English approximation to it:

> "Mulligatawny and turtle soups were the first dishes placed before you: a little lower the eye met with the familiar salmon at one end of the table and the turbot surrounded by smelts at the other. The first course was sure to be followed by a saddle of mutton or a piece of roast beef; and then you could take your oath that fowls, tongue and ham would as assuredly succeed... what were called French dishes were, for custom's sake, added to the solid abundance. The French, or side dishes, consisted of very mild but abortive attempts at Continental cooking: and ... met with the neglect and contempt that they merited. The dessert ... if for a dozen people, would cost at least as many pounds. The wines were chiefly port, sherry and hock; claret and even Burgundy being then designated poor, thin, washy stuff."

Service *à la Russe*, by contrast, required that each dish was offered individually to each diner by a servant, who brought it from the sideboard. This offered some manifest advantages – adequate hospitality was no longer equated with covering the table with dishes, much of which might be wasted; dishes could be served direct from the kitchen and therefore hotter – giving chefs more chance to show their skills in preparing dishes which had to be eaten as soon as cooked; the service *should* be faster; and, lastly, the arrangement left more scope for the decoration of the table itself. The lawyer Frederick Pollock introduced the custom in his Montagu Square home in 1858 and wondered that he had not done so before. "It is the greatest comfort to get rid of the carving on the table for a large party". Pollock's friend, the novelist Anthony Trollope, by contrast, heartily deplored 'handing round' as an alien innovation and "a vulgar and intolerable nuisance". Burdened with a large family, he could not as a self-styled member of the "second-class gentry", afford to keep an army of servants and in practice found that he seldom received his vegetables before his mutton had been eaten or gone cold – and the wine rarely came round often enough. In *The Last Chronicle of Barset*, Trollope has Mr Toogood warn fashion-conscious diners that if they accepted his hospitality at No 75 Russell Square they would not be "regaled *à la Russe*". Only by the 1890s would such resistance to the newly established mode have seemed eccentric. A 'Foreign Resident' surveying 'Society in London' in 1886 noted the difference between generations: ".... among the newer generation the strict observance of modern society's rules gains ground. The evening meal is dinner *à la Russe* – evening dress *de rigeur*, champagne the favourite wine, and cigarettes are smoked as unfailingly as at Marlborough House" (the home of the future Edward VII).

SUBURBAN SNOBBERIES

George and Weedon Grossmith's *Diary of a Nobody*, published in 1892, is a spoof diary attributed to Charles Pooter, a City bank clerk and proudly preening owner of The Laurels, Brickfield Terrace, Holloway. Supremely unaware of the absurdity of his petty pretensions, Pooter perpetually teeters on the edge of social disaster. Doorstep transactions with the initially obsequious butcher and 'butterman' (who also supplies eggs and salt) swiftly deteriorate through mutual sniping to straightforward abuse. When Pooter accuses his cook of making away with an undue amount of left-overs she rejoins bitterly that in the Pooter household there never are any left-overs. In his attempts to assert himself as a gracious host Pooter constantly invites his acquaintance to join his family in a "meat tea" – this designation implying a meal of some substance. When such an invitation is accepted, however, Pooter's resourceful wife, Carrie, is obliged to conjure up "a little extemporized supper, consisting of the remainder of the cold joint, a small piece of salmon (which I was to refuse in case there was not enough to go round) and a blanc-mange and custards. There was also a decanter of port and some jam-puffs on the sideboard". For the Pooters' first proper party Carrie makes "little cakes and open jam puffs and jellies ... sandwiches, cold chicken, ham ... cold beef and a ... tongue for the more hungry ones to peg into if they liked". They even go to the expense of hiring a waiter and ordering in half a dozen bottles of champagne. Pooter tremulously invites his boss from the bank, Mr Perkupp, to join the gathering but is graciously informed that he is already engaged to dine at Peckham that evening – but *might* drop in for half an hour. When Mr Perkupp

137. Not far from the Pooters' fictional home in Holloway was Beale's Restaurant, a landmark on the Holloway Road, when that thoroughfare was a prime shopping street for north London.
Beale's was well known for its tea shop and banqueting halls. It was demolished in 1970 to make way for a Sainsbury store.

actually does trek halfway across London to do just that, Pooter is mortified to find that not only has all the champagne and food been demolished by his feckless son, Lupin, and his crowd of hangers-on, but there isn't even a glass of seltzer left, which is all the (actually very kindly) Mr Perkupp asks for. Undeterred, Pooter continues to issue invitations, provoking a further petty crisis, to which Carrie responds with habitual loyalty, "I can turn over the cold leg of mutton, dress it with a little parsley and no one will know it has been cut ..."

PRINCE OF PLEASURE

As a young man the future Edward VII was an enthusiastic sportsman but self-indulgence rapidly overwhelmed his athletic frame and made him fully deserving of the nickname 'Tum-Tum'. As king-in-waiting until the age of fifty-nine, Edward had, indeed, little to do except indulge himself, which he did with evident satisfaction. Annual visits of a month to a Continental spa, such as Bad Homburg, enabled him to shed a couple of stone and allow his liver to undertake much-needed self-repair so that he could return refreshed to the task of pleasing his palate.

Unlike his mother, Queen Victoria, Edward VII revelled in public pomp and was enthusiastic to put on a good show. The banquet prepared for his coronation in the spring of 1902 was a case in point – fourteen courses, conspicuously featuring such expensive ingredients as caviare, *foie gras*, quail and sturgeon, not to mention a strawberry dessert which took three days to prepare. Oversight of the preparations was entrusted to the celebrated hotelier M. Cèsar Ritz. Just days before the great event the king was convulsed with acute abdominal pain. Pleading for pain-killers so that the coronation might proceed on schedule, the ailing monarch was informed by the eminent surgeon, Sir Frederick Treves, that either he had his appendix taken out immediately or the next royal event would be a funeral, not a coronation. The coronation was accordingly postponed until August. The food prepared for the banquet was distributed by the Sisters of the Poor among the needy of the East End. The king recovered well from his operation. Treves got a knighthood, but Cèsar Ritz had a nervous breakdown from which he never really recovered.

The postponed Coronation banquet, when it did at last take place, enabled the two hundred and fifty guests to regale themselves with sole poached in Chablis, garnished with oysters and prawns, asparagus with Hollandaise sauce, one quail and a third of 'a very plump' chicken per person, roast beef, snipe cutlets, soufflé Parmesan and strawberry dessert, plus a handmade sugar crown to take home as a souvenir of a great gastronomic occasion. The king also paid for (actually towards) a dinner for an estimated 456,000 of the poorest Londoners, who enjoyed roast beef, followed by plum

138. *Edward VII – superb tailoring disguised the impact of a lifetime of self-indulgence on a formerly athletic frame.*

pudding, cheese, chocolate and tobacco, sluiced down with ale or 'temperance cordials' according to choice. Over 700 venues were involved. The king actually chipped in some £30,000 of his own money. He was also very good at getting his rich friends to sponsor worthy causes and did not fail on this occasion, the big brewers being especially obliging.

In the normal course of events the king began his day with a substantial breakfast of haddock with poached eggs, followed by bacon or kidneys and perhaps a serving of woodcock. Lunch could run to ten or twelve courses. During weekends at country houses afternoons were usually punctuated by tea with sandwiches, scones, muffins and cake. The king liked parties and hostesses competed to lure him to their tables, most successfully with the assistance of the redoubtable Rosa Lewis *(see p. 69)*. His personal contribution to simplifying the art of dining was to have champagne served throughout the meal but he personally preferred the complex dishes associated with French grande cuisine; one of his favourite dishes was a pheasant stuffed with snipe which had themselves been stuffed with truffles. As Prince of Wales Edward had also favoured the new fashion for dining out in restaurants and hotels such as the Carlton. Both Rule's *(see p. 145)* and the Northumberland Hotel made private rooms available so that the prince could combine the pleasures of the table with a post-prandial assignation with one of his mistresses.

A typical dinner menu at Buckingham Palace might include turtle soup or consommé, served with an 1816 Madeira, followed by cold trout with a Johannesburg 1868, then a chicken dish with an 1884 champagne, followed by venison with a Chambertin 1875, then ortolans and asparagus with a Chateau Latour of the same vintage, rounded off with ices and a choice of ports, sherry or brandy.

A night at the opera, by contrast, would involve a one hour supper interval during which His Majesty would retire to a prepared room behind the royal box to work his way through nine cold courses, such as lobster mayonnaise, lamb cutlets, duck, trout, a jelly of chicken, tongue and ham, plovers' eggs and trays of sandwiches, desserts and French patisserie. A cold chicken was placed beside the royal bed at night in case the sovereign should be afflicted with hunger pangs before breakfast appeared to assuage them.

Edward's nine-year reign was followed by that of his far less flamboyant heir, George V. A career naval officer of fundamentally simple tastes, he, too, nevertheless presided over a coronation banquet of fourteen courses. During the Great War, however, he insisted that the royal household accept the same privations as the general public *(see p. 35)*, though he was doubtless privately mortified when his patriotic gesture of swearing to abstain from strong drink until he could toast victory was followed by virtually none of his court, let alone his subjects. After the war the great traditions of Edwardian

extravagance were not resumed – President Woodrow Wilson of the United States was feted with a mere ten courses.

THE BLOOMSBERRIES

The Bloomsbury group believed in hedonism. Its members managed quite well for themselves when it came to sex and alcohol but, when it came to food, they usually needed a helping hand. Virginia Woolf eventually became adept at making both bread and jam but when she and Leonard were first married and living in a flat at 13 Clifford's Inn they habitually dined out on steak and kidney pudding at the Cock in Fleet Street. Three years after her wedding Virginia was still baffled by the mystery of making scrambled eggs. Leonard came to believe that domestic work would help her relax from the strain of writing and persuaded her to go to cookery classes. *Mrs. Dalloway* and *To the Lighthouse* both contain elaborate descriptions of meals. E M Forster was to note:

> "real food is necessary and this, in fiction as in her home, she knew how to provide ... Food with her was not a literary device put in to make the book *(To the Lighthouse)* seem real. She put it in because she tasted it, because her senses were both exquisite and catholic...".

By the 1930s, when the Woolfs were living in Tavistock Square, Virginia had become a sufficiently accomplished cook to impress rising young literary stars such as Stephen Spender and William Plomer and to experiment with "adventurous strange dishes with dashes of wine in them". She still kept a cook, however, paying her £50 a year, which she herself could make by writing 2,000 words for *Vogue*. Ironically in Bloomsbury the memory of Virginia Woolf is perpetuated in the name of a burger bar in the Hotel Russell. The ground floor of her home at 46 Gordon Square is now a student snack bar.

The ability of Bloomsbury residents also to afford country homes made them aware of the desirability of fresh ingredients and their

Continental travels gave them a taste for foreign, especially French, cuisine. (When they were abroad for protracted periods, however, they were quite capable of sending to England for potted meat, jam and Quaker oats.)

Bloomsbury residents became enthusiastic patrons of Boulestin and indeed may be said to have started his career *(see pp. 103-4)*. L'Etoile in Charlotte Street was another favourite. Occasionally they would stray to a Russian establishment in Piccadilly, "a dreadful place with sham Cossacks", where artist Dora Carrington passed out on vodka. The opening of the Omega workshops at 33 Fitzroy Square in 1913 was marked by a celebratory dinner at Pagani's *(see p. 107)*. Visitors who came to view the avant-garde furniture and homewares produced at the Workshops were routinely offered tea, coffee, lemonade and sandwiches filled with Gentleman's Relish. When Lytton Strachey's writings brought him fame and fortune he enjoyed lunching with friends at his favourite eating-place, the surprisingly conventional Simpson's in the Strand *(see pp. 145-6)*. Larger than life, the Russian mosaicist Boris Anrep was an exuberant and expert cook, shopping for his ingredients at Schmidt's *(see p. 116)* and capable of producing his own delicious brawns and first class mayonnaise.

Lady Ottoline Morrell, flamboyant heiress to an Oxford brewing fortune, dispensed lavish hospitality at 44 Bedford Square and then at 10 Gower Street, where she threw a tea party in honour of Charlie Chaplin. Despite their self-conscious Bohemianism the leading 'Bloomsberries' employed full-time cooks, though they habitually rejected the conventional ritual of dressing for dinner. Dining out in style became something of a rarity, especially during the pinched war years when the Woolfs had to settle for chicken rather than turkey for Christmas. In July 1919 after dining at the Savoy Grill with Clive Bell, Virginia recorded that night in her diary:

> "it is long since I had taken part in the great ceremony of dinner with others believing in it, assisting at it and dressing for it. Fish and meat and melon and ices have come to their own again. Clive parted with a good deal of paper money. He pointed out to me Picasso and Mme Picasso making off for the ballet".

Clive Bell was also an enthusiastic patron of Fortnum's and when he retired to the country would bring down saddles of mutton, pheasants and boars' heads. When entertaining in London he would hire a butler from Fortnum's.

Thursday evenings, when the Bloomsbury group habitually gathered for high-toned conversation, was the servants' night off and refreshments were limited to buns, coffee and whisky. When professional helpers were on hand it was different. Clive Bell and Maynard Keynes once hosted a sit-down supper party for forty-plus members of Diaghilev's *Ballet Russe* including Picasso and Derain, the hosts themselves acting as waiters. Perhaps this would prove good practice. Although the Bloomsberries' correspondence frequently contained complaints about their servants they were loth to contemplate doing without them and found the post-war 'servant crisis' particularly threatening to the ordered disorder of their lives. In 1929 Dora Carrington bemoaned the departure of her cook: "I dread starting all over again teaching someone to cook and our habits. My mind wavers between getting a Swede or Finn, two sisters, a Chinese boy, an elderly housekeeper, a country girl. But whatever nationality they are, or sex, or age, they are bound to be terrible."

PART SEVEN

Quantity and Quality

LIQUID CHARITY

It was the inventive and socially responsible Huguenots who introduced Londoners to the concept of the soup-kitchen as a remedy for the sort of acute but short-term distress occasioned by a run of bad harvests or a trade depression. One was established in Soho, the other in Spitalfields. Given the dependence of Spitalfields' silk weavers on a luxury market and an imported raw material 'La Soupe' was, in fact, destined to become a semi-permanent feature of that district. Applicants for charity received "a pan of good broth mixed with six ounces of bread and half a pound of meat; and the same weight of good bread". After 1741 the charity, which had no endowment and was permanently dependent on outside contributions, could no longer afford meat. For the rest of the century it only issued bread with its soup, and even that on a gradually reducing scale. In 1776 the 'Soupe' was still distributing bread to 127 families.

Despite the unprecedented expansion of the metropolitan economy which accompanied Britain's industrialization, London's poorest inhabitants faced the risk of actual starvation well into the nineteenth century. Soup kitchens were one of the subsidiary charities to which the Quaker prison reformer, Elizabeth Fry, also devoted her efforts. Two years after the implementation of the vengeful New Poor Law in 1834, 'S.W.', author of *The New London Cookery, adapted to the use of Private Families*, was urging readers to recycle ruthlessly to enable them to feed the less fortunate.

> "Nothing should be thrown away. The boiling of meat, however salt, might, with the addition of vegetables, bones and bits of meat collected from the plates, with rice, barley, oatmeal or grits that have been boiled etc. stewed for a length of time, be the means of affording nourishment for the poor families who have neither the fuel nor the time to dress it for themselves. Fish bones, heads and fins all afford great nourishment. After the fish is served, let part of the liquor be put by; the bones, heads etc. bits collected from the plates, as likewise any gravy that may be left. Boiled together it makes a very nice broth, with the addition of a little rice flour rubbed smooth, and seasoned with pepper, salt and an onion. When strained it is a great improvement to meat soups, especially for the sick. The fat should never be taken from anything, as it affords nourishment, and the poor prefer it."

During the 'Hungry Forties' (*see p. 193*) the great Alexis Soyer (*see p. 59*) organised soup kitchens in both Dublin and London. The North-West Public Soup Kitchen, set up in 1846 at 295 Euston Road, served up to 140 gallons of soup to over five hundred people a day. The standard fare included pea soup, rice milk and beef soup made from ox heads. There was a charge of twopence ha'penny for a quart – but the administrators of the enterprise sold tickets which philanthropic members of the bourgeoisie could distribute to

139. The North West London Soup Kitchen in Euston Road, 'instituted to assist in preserving the health of the labouring classes' a philanthropic response to the crisis of the 'Hungry Forties'.

the poor of their choice so that they could eat free. In 1854 a soup kitchen for the Jewish poor was opened on Leman Street. Eventually there would be four. The Ragged Schools patronised by Lord Shaftesbury and William Booth's Salvation Army would also organise soup kitchens as part of their strategies of reaching out to the capital's human casualties. Writing in the 1890s one of Charles Booth's investigators described the clientele of the St Agnes' soup kitchen at Bangor Road, Notting Dale,

> "a tail of school children along the pavement, girls one side and boys the other, about 30 boys and girls waiting to get in, inside was full, inside they get bread, a thick vegetable soup, some bring it away, these have to pay a trifle ... Children all waiting patiently ...Tickets are given out in school. All the missions and churches here have a soup kitchen in winter."

Apart from local schoolchildren there were also casual workers who "come back to Notting Dale in the winter for the soup season".

STARVATION, SCIENCE AND SELF-SACRIFICE

The terrible weather that afflicted Europe in the years 1315-17 blighted successive harvests and was accompanied by disease which devastated livestock. At such times villages in marginal farming areas were obviously most vulnerable, major cities, with stores of grain, and ports, with possible access to imported supplies, were less so. But this visitation was so severe that even in mighty London itself substantial numbers perished of starvation. The last time significant numbers died of famine in England was in 1625, a year of major plague outbreak in the capital. Thereafter individual deaths from sheer hunger continued to occur but were normally recorded by coroner's juries or noted in parish registers as unusual and regrettable incidents. Nevertheless, as late as 1890 the death of a man in St James's Park was attributed to lack of food, the deceased having just walked from Liverpool in five days in search of work and entirely without sustenance. Other individual deaths from starvation have been recorded which were – how might one put it? – less involuntary.

A MARTYR TO SCIENCE

William Stark came to London to study medicine at St George's Hospital and anatomy under the eminent John Hunter. He then graduated MD at Leyden. A chance conversation with Benjamin Franklin, still preaching, if no longer practising, the virtues of the simple life, aroused in Stark a desire to investigate, by experimenting upon himself the nutritional value of different dietary regimes. He was encouraged in this notion by Sir John Pringle, physician to the army and a future President of the Royal Society. In June 1769 Stark set himself to live on bread and water with occasional allowances of sugar. His daily self-prescribed allowance of twenty ounces of bread would have yielded only 1,400 calories and it is unsurprising that he rapidly lost weight from his initial 12 stone 3 pounds. Increasing his intake to thirty ounces, he continued to lose weight, though less rapidly. After ten weeks he was suffering from swollen and bleeding gums and sore nostrils, but did not recognise these symptoms as the onset of scurvy. A month later, in early September, illness compelled him to revert to "animal food, milk and wine" and he swiftly recovered. Stark next tried bread and cooked meats and then in November switched to home-made puddings. After a month the symptoms of scurvy reappeared. Pringle, an acknowledged expert on scurvy, advised Stark to omit salt from his diet, which he did but to no effect on his condition. On Boxing Day Stark obtained some relief by devouring half a pint of blackcurrants. According to his notes Stark next planned to test the relative value of fat and lean meat and after that a vegetarian diet. Had he done so his by then chronic scurvy might well have abated but instead he decided to opt for honey puddings and Cheshire cheese. This provoked an intestinal disorder which, combined with the scurvy, led to his death on 23 February 1770 – not yet thirty.

A MARTYR TO LITERATURE

Born the posthumous son of a Bristol schoolmaster, Thomas Chatterton (1752-70) was writing poetry by the age of eleven. Apprenticed to an attorney at 14, he used his new-found familiarity with legal documents to concoct a fake geneaology and a medieval travel narrative, complete with false pedigrees and deeds to 'authenticate' it. He also began to compose poems which he attributed to a fifteenth-century monk (also fictitious) Thomas Rowley, supported by a forged correspondence between the author and a real historical personage, William Canynge. Encouraged by the publication of one of his poems in the *Town and Country Magazine* and by the dilettante Horace Walpole's initial acceptance of a fake treatise on painting 'bie T.Rowleie', Chatterton, desperate for fame, set out in April 1770 to conquer literary London. His letters home to his mother and sister contained encouraging accounts of his progress and ripening friendship with influential publishers and writers. He meanwhile maintained and diversified his literary output by completing a play, a satire and a further Rowley ballad. Chatterton also contributed items to no less than eleven publications and wangled himself an interview with Lord Mayor Beckford. Further encouraging letters home were acccompanied by gifts as proof of his success – fans, tobacco and a china tea-service. Such bravado was to cost him dearly. Chatterton did, indeed, make some slight acquaintance with the London literary establishment but had gravely under-estimated the time required to put a play into performance or the amount he would receive from Grub Street publishers. One batch of sixteen songs brought him just 10/6d and 250 lines of poetry the same amount. Meanwhile, as his slender capital dwindled, so did he. Indifferent to food from childhood, he preferred tea and cakes to hot meat. The kindly landlady of his lodgings in Brooke Street, Holborn, appropriately named Mrs Angel, constantly invited him to sup with her family but he resolutely declined, preferring to scribble alone through the night, subsisting, quite literally, on bread and water. A single lapse of pride tempted him to share some oysters, which he ate voraciously. Then followed, to Mrs Angel's certain knowledge, three days without any food whatsoever. She begged him once again to dine with her. He assured her he was not hungry, retired to his garret, tore up every scrap of writing still in his possession and took arsenic to forestall the inevitable. He was not yet eighteen, quite penniless – and was owed eleven guineas by publishers or editors who had accepted work from his pen. After his death, Chatterton was hailed as a huge lost talent. Dr Johnson called him 'the most extraordinary young man' he had ever met. A generation later Keats dedicated *Endymion* to his memory. Not until 1871 was it finally proved to the entire satisfaction of the scholarly world that Chatterton's medieval 'discoveries' were not to be considered as forgeries but triumphs of youthful genius, blighted by hope and literally starved by indifference.

ABUSES EXPOSED

Friedrich Accum (1769-1803) was born in Westphalia of a Jewish father and Huguenot mother, trained as an apothecary and came to London in 1793. His knowledge of languages made him useful to the chemist William Nicholson, who was to further Accum's career and encourage him to write. In 1798 Accum began to compile a series of articles on the adulteration of drugs and medical preparations. By 1800 he had his own business at 11 Old Compton Street, Soho where he sold scientific apparatus and materials and offered his services as an analyst of the purity of commercial products. By 1803 he was lecturing on science at the Surrey Institute to fashionable audiences who were as much interested in amusement as self-improvement. Undeterred, Accum compiled textbooks on chemistry and mineralogy before joining forces with a fellow German, the entrepreneur and publisher of prints, Rudolf Ackermann, to promote the novel technology of

lighting by gas. Accum's *Practical Treatise on Gas Light* (1815) reached a third edition within a year and was swiftly translated into German, French and Italian. Accum's eminence then obtained him the post of librarian at the Royal Institution in Albemarle Street, where he turned his attention to alimentary affairs, producing treatises on the manufacture of beer, wine and bread. Far more controversial, however, was his pioneering work on food adulteration, published in 1820 – *A treatise on adulterations of food and culinary poisons, exhibiting the fraudulent sophistications of bread, beer, wine, spiritous liquors, tea, coffee, cream, confectionery, vinegar, mustard, pepper, cheese, olive oil, pickles and other articles employed in domestic economy And methods of detecting them.* The cover of the book was nothing if not dramatic – snakes writhing around a web, with a spider grabbing a fly, underneath a skull and crossbones and the admonitory quotation 'There is death in the pot' (2 Kings Ch. 4 Verse 40). In his text Accum named and shamed specific individuals and businesses, supporting his accusations with quotations from official court records. Routine frauds exposed by Accum included adding red lead to recolour faded cayenne pepper, extending ground pepper with floor sweepings of pepper dust, drying used tea-leaves on copper plates to turn them green again for resale and adding copper coins to pickles to produce "a lively green colour". The *Literary Gazette* declared that "we are almost angry with Mr. Accum for the great service he has done the community by opening our eyes, at the risk of shutting our mouths for ever". The first edition of a thousand copies sold out in a month, and produced a crop of threatening anonymous letters. A second and an American edition were nevertheless printed and a German version set in hand. Nemesis, however, was imminent. A complaint was made that Accum had been cutting colour-plates out of expensive books in the Royal Institution's library and selling them. A trial date was set but Accum, believing that he was the victim of a carefully constructed plot, failed to appear and forfeited his bail, returning to his native country after an absence of thirty years. The disgrace wounded him so deeply that his subsequent writings appeared either anonymously or under a pseudonym. New editions of his food adulteration treatise appeared in London, but minus his name. Food adulteration was to flourish virtually unchecked for another thirty years, thanks to the discrediting of the first crusader to confront malpractice with the weapons of science.

ADULTERATION OUTLAWED

In 1848 chemist John Mitchell published the results of a series of chemical analyses he had carried out under the title *Falsification of Food*. Although the scientific rigour of his work set new standards his findings failed to reach a wider public. A general awareness of the scale and depth of the problem of food adulteration had to find its champion elsewhere.

Britain's best-known medical journal, *The Lancet*, was initially founded not to publish learned articles but to expose, and, as its title metaphorically implied, thereby to cut away, the fraudulent and the abusive. In 1850 its crusading editor, Thomas Wakley (1795-1862), himself a doctor and the coroner for West Middlesex, turned his attention to the problem of food adulteration which, despite Accum's revelations a generation previously, continued unabated and unchecked by official intervention. Wakley appointed an 'Analytical Sanitary Commission' in the person of Dr. Arthur Hill Hassall (1817-94), a lecturer at the Royal Free Hospital, who was bidden to conduct a rigorous and systematic enquiry into the manner of production of more than thirty common articles of food and drink on sale in the capital. Henry Letheby, a future Medical Officer of Health for the City of London, was appointed as Hassall's assistant. Their findings, based on 2,400 laboratory analyses, were to be printed at length in the pages of *The Lancet* over a four year period, from 1851 to 1854, including the names of

offending traders and manufacturers. Only one offender dared to challenge the findings and he withdrew his complaint on learning that his product had been tampered with without his knowledge. Hassall demonstrated that of forty-nine randomly selected samples of bread every one had been doctored with alum, as had half of the samples of flour he tested – the latter practice ensuring that the consumer received a double dose. Tea was routinely bulked out with the leaves of common trees or shrubs such as the sloe, sycamore and horse-chestnut. Of twenty-nine samples of coffee, twenty-eight contained alien additions such as acorns, mangel-wurzel or dried horses' blood. Cocoa was 'extended' with brick dust, pepper with sand, mustard with flour and turmeric. The dilution of milk with water ranged from ten to fifty per cent. The latter was merely a fraud but the worst instances, such as using toxic chemicals to colour, preserve or flavour pickles, fruit or confectionery, were serious hazards to health. Hassall's findings were publicised by daily newspapers which printed extracts from *The Lancet* articles and were further confirmed by expert witnesses summoned to testify before a Commons Select Committee which sat through the 1855-56 session and by further scientific exposes such as Dr Marcet's *On the Composition of Food and How it is Adulterated* (1856) and Dr Postgate's *A Few Words on Adulteration* (1857). Exposure of the most gross frauds and malpractices did lead to their voluntary abandonment by many manufacturers and traders, who swiftly saw the commercial advantage in being able to promote their products as 'Pure and Unadulterated', often with the explicit endorsement of a medical man or a chemical analyst. In 1857 a Sanitary Commission Bread Company was established with Hassall as one of its directors. Thomas Blackwell of Crosse and Blackwell informed the Commons Committee that, as a direct result of *The Lancet's* crusade, his firm had entirely renounced the practice of adding copper to pickles and fruits as a colourant, though this had involved considerable advertising expenses to explain to the public why the firm's products now looked so markedly different. Mr Horniman, who had pioneered the idea of selling tea in sealed packets, rather than as loose leaves, benefited from a gratifying expansion in sales to become Britain's largest supplier by the 1870s, selling over five million packets a year. At the lower end of the market consumers benefited from the higher ethical business practices followed by the emerging Co-operative Movement, which had originated in the new industrial towns of northern England. Eschewing profit in favour of social purpose, 'cooperators' made the supply of pure goods a basic principle of their retailing. The first Adulteration of Foods Act was finally passed into law in 1860. As usual the legislation was permissive rather than pro-active. It empowered local authorities to appoint public analysts to examine samples of food and drink 'on complaint made' and on payment of a fee of 10s. 6d. For most of the capital the relevant bodies were District Boards or Vestries but in the City of London the Commissioners of Sewers were deemed the proper supervisory institution. No central authority was appointed to promote the application of the Act, nor were powers granted for analysts to act on their own initiative in collecting samples of suspect products. Over the course of a dozen years only seven public analysts were actually appointed under the terms of the 1860 Act and of those four never exercised their powers. As Public Analyst for the City of London Henry Letheby, Hassall's former colleague, examined only fifty-seven samples over the course of nine years. Of these twenty-six were found to be adulterated, but not one resulted in legal proceedings. Continued pressure from *The Lancet*, supported by the Royal Society of Arts, led to a significant upgrading of the 1860 legislation in the Adulteration of Food, Drink and Drugs Act of 1872, which incorporated many specific proposals put forward by Dr John Postgate. Henceforth it became a criminal offence to sell

goods containing ingredients adding weight or bulk unless specifically declared to the purchaser. Any borough with its own police force was empowered to appoint an analyst and Inspectors of Nuisances were empowered to collect samples of products on their own initiative. Within three years of the 225 districts empowered to appoint analysts, 150 had done so and 1,500 convictions of adulteration had been secured. Nevertheless the operation of the 1872 Act revealed numerous weaknesses, especially in relation to just what did constitute adulteration. In 1874 a Select Committee Report on the working of the law concluded reassuringly that people were "now cheated rather than poisoned". Tightening up the provisions of previous legislation resulted in the 1875 Sale of Food and Drugs Act which remained the basis of subsequent regulation. Adulterations injurious to health became punishable with a heavy fine, and imprisonment for a second offence. More effective in practice, however, was the catch-all proviso that an offence could be constituted by the sale of any article not "of the nature, substance and quality of the article demanded", which freed the prosecution from the burden of proving either intent or knowledge on the part of the seller or injury to health on the part of the buyer.

Thanks largely to the energy of the members of the Society of Public Analysts, founded in 1874, huge improvements in food safety were achieved in the course of little more than a decade. Whereas a *Lancet* sampling of bread in 1872 had revealed that half was still adulterated, by 1884 the figure was down to 2%. By 1892 the Local Government Board could record with satisfaction that "It is now certain that the bread supplied to the people of England is practically pure".

Of course, human greed and ingenuity evolved new deceptions, particularly in relation to exotic or luxury items. As *Law's Grocer's Manual* noted in 1901, "Gourmets have for years been eating eggs never laid by plovers and paying fancy prices for them. A large section of the gull family... lay eggs precisely similar to those of the plover. These are collected in hundreds on the small islands in the inland lochs of north Scotland and sent to London. They are ridiculously cheap (to the collectors) ...".

BUDGETING FOR SURVIVAL – THE HUNGRY FORTIES

The propagandist purpose of the author of *The Rights of the Poor and Christian Almsgiving Vindicated* (1841), S R Bosanquet, is manifest in his chosen title but the weekly budgets he collected from London working families have all been authenticated. Here are three, descending from reasonable comfort to the edge of desperation.

The first, a man, his wife and five children spent £1. 9s.1½d. Their largest single item of expenditure, a dozen eightpenny four-pound loaves, represented over a quarter of their weekly outgoings and twice what they had to spend on rent The third largest item was butcher's meat (3/6d), followed by bacon (2/6d). Next came fuel (2/3d), sugar (1/9d) and butter (1/6d). Interestingly more was spent on coffee (10½d) than tea (3d) but the latter mounted to only two ounces as opposed to seven of the former. Bulk was supplied by eighteen pounds of potatoes (9d) and an unspecified quantity of greens, turnips and onions (6d), savour by herrings (9d) and pepper, salt and mustard (3d). The only other expenditures were soap, soda, blue and starch (9d), candles (7d) and a single luxury – snuff (6d).

The second, a man, his wife and three children lived on only half as much as the first family – just fifteen shillings. Again the largest item was bread (3s 6½d), but this bought only five loaves instead of twelve, followed by rent (2/6d). The rest of the food budget consisted of five pounds of meat (2/1d) a pound of butter (9d), three ounces of tea and a pound of sugar and a staggering forty pounds of potatoes (1/4d) – which accounted for just a little more than the father's daily pint of porter (1/2d). The other items of expenditure were coal (9½d), soap and

candles (6½d) sundries (5½d) and, remarkably, schooling (4d). Nothing was left for other vegetables, milk, medicine or clothing.

Finally there was a widow with four children. Depending for her income on charing and brushmaking, her weekly earnings could vary from 5/8d to nothing. She was consequently £1 13s in debt and in the week when interviewed by Bosanquet had received five four-pound loaves from the parish. Her own spending – 2/5d – had bought another loaf, seven pounds of potatoes, four pennyworth of tea and sugar, two pennyworth of bacon and three-halfpence worth of butter, the rest going on coals and candles, it being December.

In the bitter winter of 1854-5 ice on the river threw 50,000 dock-workers onto parish relief. There were bread riots in Whitechapel. Over the river in Tooley Street, Southwark, "men, dressed in the garb of labourers ... in gangs of twenty to thirty" took to "levying a species of blackmail on ... the bakers' and chandlers' shops" until their search for sustenance induced the shopkeepers to hide behind their shutters. A month of heavy frost in 1861 brought another crisis of desperation as ravenous riverside workers milled around Whitechapel and Mile End and "attacked bakers' shops and eating houses and every morsel of food was carried away". Mounted police were mobilised to break up the mob but "it was impossible for them to act against so large a number of people". The sudden collapse of Thames shipbuilding in 1866-7 led 30,000 men to claim relief in Poplar alone. Bread riots followed for the third time in a dozen years.

In the late-1860s the diet of young Spitalfields weavers could still be described in the following terms:

"Stale bread and butter or dripping – penn'orths of that unctuous and pasty pudding that may be seen in all the cookshops of this neighbourhood and an occasional (very occasional) basin of leg-of-beef soup. a saveloy or a plate of pieces, such as the trimmings and coarse fat of ham and brisket of beef are their ordinary articles of diet. Their luxuries are baked potatoes, stewed eels dispensed by teacupfuls at street stalls, fried fish and whelks ...".

When work was available pressure of long hours ensured that weavers were dependent on cookshops selling "great slabs of pease-pudding, long rolls of 'spotted' or 'plain'....ha-porths of pie crust, flat, damp, hot, flabby slabs of greasy dough, four inches square...'faggots' and dense, peppery, saveloys ...".

(STEP-) FATHER OF THE LOW CARBO-HYDRATE DIET

William Banting (1797-1878) ranks alongside Captain Boycott and Louis Pasteur as one of the few men whose surname has entered the English language as a verb – though of the millions nowadays following a diet few might be aware that they are 'banting', unless they are Swedish, where the verb survives. Had Banting himself not become increasingly overweight from his mid-thirties onwards it is likely that he would remain unremembered by posterity, except as the maker of the Duke of Wellington's coffin. An undertaker by profession, with premises in up-market St James's Street, Banting was short – five feet five inches – but not inactive. Over the course of thirty years, however, he expanded to reach 202 pounds so that by his mid-sixties he could no longer stoop to tie his own shoes and had to go downstairs backwards to avoid jarring his knees and ankle-joints. Acting upon medical advice he tried walking prodigious distances, swimming, riding and rowing for hours at a time, only to find that these exertions simply stimulated his appetite. Turkish baths, spa waters and 'gallons of physic' proved similarly useless. Worried by the onset of deafness, in August 1862 Banting consulted an ear specialist, Dr William Harvey, of Soho Square, who diagnosed obesity as the cause of his patient's defective hearing and many other afflictions. Harvey advised him to cut out most of the staples of Victorian 'plain food' – bread, butter, milk, sugar, pork, potatoes, beans and beer – and substitute meat, fish, fruit, non-root vegetables and dry toast. Following this regime

Banting lost weight steadily. By Christmas he was down to 184 lbs, by the following August to 156. As well as losing weight Banting also began to sleep longer and better and lost twelve inches off his waistline. The process had, moreover, been almost miraculously painless. Feeling hugely reinvigorated, Banting sought to spead the gospel according to Harvey by publishing a short pamphlet written in simple, non-technical language, *A Letter on Corpulence Addressed to the Public*, which first appeared in 1863. The novelist Anthony Trollope was one of the first to try the Banting regime and did indeed succeed in losing some weight, which George Eliot observed to improve him in soul as well as body. In his late novel *The Fixed Period,* Trollope has Mr Neverbend praise "that great Banting who has preserved us all so completely from the horrors of obesity". This was written tongue in cheek as Trollope had singularly failed to maintain his weight loss.

Banting gave away the first edition of a thousand copies of his pamphlet and the second of 1,500. Over 60,000 of a third edition were sold in the UK alone at a shilling each and it was soon translated into French and German and published in the USA. In his Preface to a fourth edition in 1869 Banting recorded, more in sorrow than in anger, that his altruistic campaign to offer information to relieve the sufferings of others had made him a target for ridicule and abuse, particularly from members of the medical profession who dismissed his regimen with contempt as 'unscientific'. Harvey, as a professional medic, was also defamed, even to the point of damaging his practice, because he could offer no scientific rationale for his regime, effective though it had proved to be. The fourth edition of Banting's *Letter* also included warm testimony from a selection of over 1,800 people who had written to thank and congratulate the author for his advice. Undaunted by his critics Banting was to maintain his weight loss and die in his Kensington home at the very creditable age of eighty-one.

As a footnote, as it were, it is interesting to

140. *A Punch cartoon of 1865 entitled
'Banting in the Yeomanry'.
Sergeant Major: "It comes to this, Captain, 'A mun e'ther
hev' a new jacket or knock off one o'my meals'"*

141. *Charles Booth – the entire Booth poverty survey
is available online at www.booth.lse.ac.uk*

note that data from a St James's Street institution which Banting would have known well contributed to a growing debate on obesity among London's scientific community. Berry Brothers, the celebrated grocers and wine-merchants, had long used their giant scales to weigh their aristocratic clientele. In 1884 the eminent Sir Francis Galton published an article in *Nature* which analysed the weights of three generations of English noblemen. This suggested that the social elite were no longer putting on weight as *rapidly* in their youth as their fathers and grandfathers had, although they did reach the same weight in the end.

A SCEPTIC INVESTIGATES
Charles Booth (1840-1916), a wealthy Liverpool shipowner, was totally unconvinced by the claim of H M Hyndman. leader of the radical Social Democratic Federation that, in the capital of the world's mightiest empire, a quarter of its inhabitants were living in such abject poverty that they were, in effect, slowly starving to death. Sensationalist journalism raised the spectre of major social unrest. As large-scale demonstrations alarmed London's West End in the mid-1880s Booth gathered together a team of investigators to penetrate the mysteries of London's East End. Having the fortune and making the time to undertake a detailed investigation to prove the socialists and the scaremongers wrong, Booth ended up proving them not only right, but right to an even greater extent than had been claimed. Under Booth's guidance his team surveyed London's neighbourhoods systematically, combining the accumulation of statistical data with the reports of London School Board attendance officers and their own street-by-street investigations,

usually in the reassuring company of the local beat copper. The results of their labours between the years 1886 and 1903 issued in the massive seventeen volumes of *Life and Labour of the People of London*, accompanied by detailed maps colour-coding each street according to its level of affluence or misery. Booth's overall conclusion was that 30.1% of Londoners were living in extreme poverty, which he defined as not earning enough to maintain physical working efficiency. A decade later he revised the figure upwards to 35%. Writing of London's East End – "the most destitute population in England" – Booth sub-divided those below the poverty line into four classes. The lowest, A, were loafers and criminals, estimated at 1.25% of the local population, or around 11,000, living "the life of savages, with vicissitudes of extreme hardship and occasional excess. Their food is of the coarsest description and their only luxury is drink." Class B, almost ten times larger – 11.25% or 100,000 – subsisted on casual earnings, mostly from dock work. Class C, dependent on intermittent earnings, accounted for a further 8% of the population, some 75,000. Class D, who overall might earn little more or, indeed, only the same as those in Class C, benefited hugely from the fact that their earnings were regular and reliable. This made orderly budgeting much easier and indebtedness to money-lenders much less likely:

"there is never the consciousness of spare cash; the effect of any unwonted expenditure is felt at once in short commons at the week end. The result is that such extravagances are avoided and the wife spends the regular sum she receives in much the same manner week after week. A good deal of bread is eaten and tea drunk, especially by the women and children, but the meals have a more attractive character ... Bacon, eggs and fish appear regularly in the budgets. A piece of meat cooked on Sunday serves also for dinner on Monday and Tuesday, and puddings, rarely seen in Class B, are in Class D a regular institution, not every day, but sometimes in the week. On the whole these people have enough, and very seldom too much, to eat: and healthy, though rather restricted lives are led."

Booth's large-scale investigation was complemented by a micro-study of the lives of thirty working-class families in Lambeth conducted over a four year period by Mrs Maud Pember Reeves and other members of the Fabian Women's Group. The results were published in 1913 as *Round about a Pound a Week*, which is what the investigators reckoned some eight million Britons were surviving on. The following was recorded as the expenditure of 'Mrs. X, a 'good manager' with a husband and four children under five:

Sunday. Breakfast: One loaf, 1 ounce butter, half ounce tea, a farthing's worth of tinned milk, a half pennyworth of sugar. Kippers extra for Mr. X. Dinner: Hashed beef, batter pudding, greens and potatoes. Tea: Same as breakfast, but Mr. X has shrimps instead of kippers.

Monday. Breakfast: Same as Sunday. Mr. X has a little cold meat. Dinner: Sunday's dinner cold, with pickles, or warmed up with greens and potatoes. Tea: One loaf, marmalade and tea. Mr. X has two eggs.

Tuesday. Breakfast: One loaf 1 oz. butter, 2d worth of cocoa. Bloaters for Mr. X. Dinner: Bread and dripping, with cheese and tomatoes. Tea: One loaf, marmalade and tea. Fish and fried potatoes for Mr. X".

SUFFRAGETTE SUFFERINGS

By the time the Women's Social and Political Union was founded by Mrs Emmeline Pankhurst in 1903 it had been half a lifetime since John Stuart Mill had introduced the first bill to grant the vote to women. Peaceful protest and petitioning had won some gains – the right to serve as school governors or Poor Law guardians and, for some women, to vote in local elections. But Mrs. Pankhurst and her disciples were prepared to challenge the law to hasten the achievement of their goal. The WSPU slogan was 'Deeds Not Words'. 'Militants' positively invited arrest to publicise the cause. In 1908 they began a campaign of window-smashing. Conviction for this offence normally resulted in a month in Holloway prison. In July 1909 sculptor Marjorie Wallace Dunlop. sentenced for daubing a slogan on the walls of Parliament, demanded to be treated as a political prisoner and announced her determination to go on hunger strike until this concession was made. When dainty food failed to tempt her the prison doctor asked her what she proposed to have for dinner. She allegedly replied "My determination" – and was released after ninety-one hours. Hundreds of women followed her example and were fed by force, either by nasal or stomach tubes. It was each woman's individual decision rather than a matter of strategic policy. Some militants went on hunger-strike every time they were imprisoned. The actress and music-hall artiste Kitty Marion was fed by force over two hundred times in a single year. Appropriately prisoners on their release were received at breakfast parties which served the purpose of a modern press conference. In May 1912 Frederick and Emmeline Pethick-Lawrence, business managers of the WSPU and co-editors of *Votes for Women*, were sentenced to nine months for incitement to violence. Both went on hunger-strike, were force-fed and released early after prison doctors decided they were so debilitated that they were endangering their lives. In February 1913 Sylvia Pankhurst, Emmeline's daughter and leader of the East End branch of the movement, refused water as well as food to get free the sooner. In April 1913 the Liberal government, frustrated by the continuing defiance of the militants, passed the Prisoners' Temporary Discharge for Ill-Health Act. This provided the authorities with the power to release a hunger-striking prisoner on licence until she had recovered sufficiently to serve out the rest of her sentence. Known as the Cat and Mouse Act, it failed because many of the released prisoners evaded rearrest and others committed further offences while out on licence. In June suffragettes began singling out Holloway prison doctors for physical attack. In

1914 the WSPU accused the prison authorities of drugging suffragettes to reduce their resistance to force-feeding. Only the outbreak of the war and the suspension of the suffragette campaign brought the confrontation to an end.

THE BOFFINS
V H Mottram (1882-1976)

After a double first in science in Cambridge Vernon Mottram gained international experience at universities in the USA, Germany and Canada before being being appointed professor of physiology at King's College, London, where he pioneered a degree course which combined science, economics and dietetics with a view to improving family and community health. In 1936 he inaugurated a postgraduate diploma in dietetics. Mottram was also concerned to reach a much wider audience and did so through articles for the press, talks on the BBC and books aimed at non-specialist readers. In *Food and the Family* (1925) he showed the practical value of nutrition research, and then, with co-author Jenny Lindsay, produced a *Manual of Modern Cookery* (1927) which applied scientific principles to the preparation of food and designing of meals. Unlike some pioneer nutritionists Mottram was aware that the enjoyment of food mattered as much as its value as the body's building material and fuel.

Sir Jack Drummond (1891-1952)

Appointed professor of biochemistry at University College, London at the early age of thirty-one, Drummond not only had a research interest in nutrition but was something of a gastronome and a pioneering scholar in the history of food. In 1939 he published *The Englishman's Food,* a ground-breaking study of five centuries of dietary habits, co-authored with his secretary and second wife, Anne Wilbraham. In 1940 Drummond was appointed scientific adviser to the Ministry of Food and with the active support of the Ministry's political head. Lord Woolton *(see p. 37)*, used his position not merely to maintain but to improve popular dietary standards by actively combating nutritional ignorance. His achievement was hailed by the American Public Health Association as: 'one of the greatest demonstrations in public health administration that the world has ever seen." In 1944 Drummond was knighted and became nutrition adviser to the Supreme Headquarters of the Allied Expeditionary Force. In 1945 he became adviser to the British contingent of the Control Commission for Germany and Austria and was elected FRS. He also received the US Medal of Freedom, the Order of Orange Nassau and an honorary doctorate of the University of Paris. In 1952 Drummond, Anne Wilbraham and their ten year old daughter, were all murdered while camping in the French Alps. Before identification of the victims was confirmed Drummond, aged sixty-one, was described by the French press as being about forty years of age. A 77-year-old farmer was convicted of the crime two years later. £30,000 subscribed in Drummond's memory was used to found a research fellowship in nutrition.

John Yudkin (1910-1995)

Trained as a bacteriologist, Yudkin succeeded to Mottram's chair of physiology in 1945 and within eight years pioneered the teaching of nutrition at undergraduate level. In 1954 he was appointed to Britain's first ever chair in nutrition, at Queen Elizabeth College, London.

An unrepentant populariser, Yudkin used his widely-read books to challenge the assumption that coronary heart disease was directly related to excessive intakes of fat. Blaming the combination of over-eating and inadequate physical exercise, he recommended cutting back on carbohydrates and sugar –

> "In order to gain an insight into the diet best suited to the human species, we have to look at how pre-neolithic man ate over the millions of years of evolution, before the development of agriculture, and certainly before the very recent developments in food technology. We shall then find that the nearer we get

to eating foods that are not man-made, the better our diets will be, not only in vitamin content but in all other respects."

The son of Jewish refugees from Russian pogroms, Yudkin also advised the infant state of Israel on nutrition at a time when food was particularly scarce. He bequeathed important collections of books on the history of food and nutrition to the University of Huddersfield and to the Hebrew University of Jerusalem, of which he was a governor.

Yudkin's non-technical publications included *This Slimming Business (1958), The Slimmer's Cookbook* (1961), *Our Changing Fare: two hundred years of British food habits* (1966), and *The Penguin Encyclopaedia of Nutrition* (1985).

CULINARY CRUSADERS
André L. Simon (1877-1968)

André Simon formed the International Wine and Food Society in London in 1933. Proclaiming itself as "the world's oldest and more renowned gastronomic society", it now claims 7,500 members in 140 branches in forty countries. Simon's articles of faith were summarised in his statement of the society's objectives:

> "to bring together and serve all who believe that a right understanding of good food and wine is an essential part of personal contentment and health and that an intelligent appproach to the pleasures and problems of the table offers far greater rewards than the mere satisfaction of appetite."

An accomplished writer on food and wine and a sparkling champagne salesman, Simon was honoured with a CBE and the Legion d'Honneur but was also complimented as "still essentially a French peasant, a man of the soil who had a knack for giving great parties." These included a bibulous annual Beer *vs* Wine Drinkers cricket match, hosted at his country home. Simon's *Concise Encyclopaedia of Gastronomy* was more encyclopedic than concise, running to nine volumes. In 1953 the Wine and Food

Society published Simon's modestly titled *Bibliotheca gastronomica. A Catalogue of Books and Documents on Gastronomy … The Production, Taxation, Distribution and Consumption of Food and Drink; their Use and Abuse in all Times and Among all Peoples*. His other publications included handbooks on the care and sale of wine and on making wines and cordials, a book of mushroom recipes and a history of champagne. Simon's own collection of books about food and wine is now held at Guildhall Library, London. The Guild of Food Writers now makes annual André Simon Awards to the authors of the year's outstanding food books. Elizabeth David won the first award, in 1973.

Raymond Postgate (1896-1971)

Postgate was the grandson of a distinguished Victorian campaigner *(see pp. 191-2)* against food adulteration but his own first interests were political. Rejected by his own father for refusing military service in World War One and having failed to complete his Oxford classics degree, he drifted into journalism. became a founder-member of the Communist Party of Great Britain and found more secure employment on the staff of *Encyclopaedia Britannica*. In the course of a varied career he also wrote detective stories and biographies of John Wilkes and George Lansbury, edited *Tribune*, co-authored with his brother-in-law, the Oxford economics don G D H Cole, a fat social history *The Common People* and worked as a temporary civil servant with the Board of Trade. In 1951, supported by a band of volunteer informants, Postgate published the first *Good Food Guide*. To this task he brought a mordant wit, observing of 'convenience foods', for example, that "the adjective, with its lavatorial connotations, is well-chosen." For the next decade each annual edition of the *Good Food Guide* was published from his home, until in 1962 he handed the venture over to the Consumers' Association, although he continued to serve as editor until 1968. Postgate also wrote *The Plain Man's Guide to Wine* (1951) and *The Home Wine Cellar* (1960), which brought him honours from the vintners of St Emilion. An OBE followed in 1966.

Egon Ronay

Born in Budapest to a restaurant-owning family, Egon Ronay received a triple training in law, commerce and catering. Migrating to London in 1946, he opened his own restaurant, the Marquee in Kensington in 1952, then began writing on food, wine, tourism and eating-out for the *Daily Telegraph*. From 1956 onwards he began publishing his own critical – often very critical – guides to eating out in restaurants, hotels and pubs. These were eventually taken over by the Automobile Association in 1985. It is perhaps fitting that in this book, as in so many other circumstances, he should be given the last word. In 1983 he founded the British Academy of Gastronomes. Elegant, exacting and combative, Ronay not only lambasted the shortcomings of establishments allegedly catering for the discriminating elite but also courted publicity in campaigns to raise standards for the general public, especially where consumers constituted a captive market, as in airports and motorway service areas.

Chronology

927   Tolls levied on eggs brought in by boat
1155   First mention of a Bakers' Company
1272   Fishmongers' Company chartered
1311   Fraternity of Cooks formed
1315-17 Major European famine
1320   First reference to salt-water fishing from Barking
1364   Vintners' Company chartered
1428   Grocers' Company chartered
1437   Brewers' Company chartered
1482   Cooks' Company charered
1486   Royal charter for London bakers of white bread
1500   Thomas Pynson publishes a *Boke of Cokery*
1508   Wynkyn de Worde publishes *A Boke of Kervyng*
1511   Innholders' Company chartered
1545(?) *A Proper Newe Book of Cokerye*
1548   Saturday reintroduced as a fish day
1550   Arrival of first Huguenot refugees
1553   Christ's Hospital founded
1559   Salters' Company chartered
1562   Alessandro Magno visits London
1563   Wednesday reintroduced as a fish day
1569   Sale of fruit banned during an outbreak of pestilence
       Royal charter for London bakers of brown bread
1585   Thomas Dawson, *The Good Houswife's Jewell*
1598   Giovanni de Rosselli *Epulario, or The Italian Banquet*
1599   East India Company founded
1602   Sir Hugh Platt, *Delights for Ladies*
1605   Worshipful Companies of Gardeners, Fruiterers and Butchers receive royal charters
1615   Gervase Markham, *The English Hus-Wjfe*

1625   John Murrell, *A Delightful Daily Exercise for Ladies and Gentlewomen*
1636   *A Closet for Ladies and Gentlewomen*
1639   *The Widowe's Treasure The Ladies Cabinet opened*
1651   La Varenne, *Le Cuisinier Francais* (English translation 1653)
1652   Pasqua Rosee opens London's first coffee house in St Michael's Alley
1653   *A True Gentlewoman's Delight*
1657   Clare Market opened
1660   Robert May, *The Accomplish't Cook or the Art and Mystery of Cookery*
1661   William Rabisha, *The Whole Body of Cookery Dissected*
1665   Poulters' Company chartered
       The Great Plague
1666   Pontack's opened
       The Great Fire of London
1669   Garraway's established in Exchange Alley
       The Closet of the Most Eminently Learned Sir Kenelme Digbie Opened
1670   Covent Garden market receives its royal charter
1671   Will's coffee-house opened
1672   Hannah Woolley, *The Gentlewoman's Companion*
1675   Charles II attempts suppression of coffee-houses
1682   Spitalfields Market and Hungerford Market opened
1685   Revocation of Edict of Nantes provokes Huguenot influx
1686   Newport Market established
1692   Slaughter's coffee-house opened
1693   White's founded
1699   John Evelyn, *Acetaria: a Discourse of Sallets*
1703   Kit Cat Club founded
1706   Twinings tea shop opened in the Strand

1707   Fortnum & Mason founded

1710   Patrick Lamb, *Royal Cookery: or, the Complete Court Cook*

1723   John Nott, *The Cook's and Confectioner's Dictionary*

       Robert Smith, *Court Cookery*

1730   Charles Carter, *The Complete Practical Cook*

1733   Vincent La Chapelle, *The Modern Cook*

1734   John Middleton, *Five Hundred New Recipes*

1735   Beef Steak Society founded

1737   Stocks Market closed

1739   Foundling Hospital founded

1742   Keen's mustard factory opened

1747   Hannah Glasse, *The Art of Cookery*

1757   Gunter's established

       Jonas Hanway, *Essay on Tea*

1764   Short Blue fleet established

       Almack's splits into Boodles and Brooks's

1768   London Tavern, Bishopsgate opened

1770   Death of William Stark from self-starvation

1773   First reference to curry on sale in London

       John Townshend, *The Universal Cook*

1778   Jonathan's coffee-house consumed by fire

1788   Richard Briggs, *The English Art of Cookery*

1798   Rule's restaurant opened in Maiden Lane

1805   Ranelagh Gardens closed

1808   Coffee tax cut

1810   Dean Mahomed opens his Hindostanee Coffee House off Portman Square

       Canada Club founded

       Guards Club founded

1811   London's population passes 1 million

1813   Louis-Eustache Ude, *The French Cook*

1815   United Service Club founded

1817   Dr William Kitchiner *Apicius Redivivus, or, The Cook's Oracle*

1819   Traveller's Club founded

1820   Friedrich Accum, *A treatise on adulterations of food*

1821   Oxford and Cambridge Club founded

1824   Athenaeum and Oriental Club founded

1828   Louis-Eustache Ude appointed chef at Crockford's

       Grand Cigar Divan (Simpson's) opened in the Strand

1828-30 Covent Garden market buildings erected

1829   Fleet Market closed

1830   Charles Fowler's Covent Garden market buildings completed

       Crosse & Blackwell partnership established

1831   Garrick Club founded

1832   City of London and Carlton Club founded

1834   New Poor Law introduces workhouse system of poor relief

1836   London Bridge station opened

       Reform Club founded

1837   Alexis Soyer chef at the Reform Club

       Great Silver Pits fishing ground discovered

1838   Army and Navy Club founded

1839   Chelsea Bun House closed

1843   Gresham Club founded

1845   Charles Francatelli, *The Modern Cook*

       Eliza Acton, *Modern Cookery for Private Families*

1846   Alexis Soyer *Gastronomic Regenerator*

       North West Public Soup Kitchen opened in the Euston Road

1848   John Mitchell *Falsification of Food*

1849   White Conduit House, Islington closed

       Alexis Soyer, The *Modern Housewife*

1850   Randall's Market established in Poplar

1851   Soyer's Gastronomic Symposium opened to cater for the Great Exhibition

       George Peabody hosts Fourth of July dinner

1851-54 *The Lancet* campaigns against food adulteration

1852   Abraham Hayward, *The Art of Dining*

       Charles Francatelli, *Plain Cookery Book for the Working Classes*

1853   Alexis Soyer, *History of Food in All Ages*

1854   Soup kitchen for the Jewish poor opened in Leman Street

1855   Caledonian Market opened

       Alexis Soyer, *A Shilling Cookery Book for the People*

1856   Charles Dodd, *The Food of London*

1857   Pratts and Savage Club founded

       Peek Freans founded

1859   Vauxhall Gardens closed

       St James's Club founded

1860   Adulteration of Foods Act

1861-5 Mrs Beeton's *Book of Household Management*

       Richard Terry, *Indian Cookery*

       Turf Club founded

1862   Short Blue fleet relocates from Barking to Gorleston

       Hungerford Market closed

       Charles Francatelli, *Royal English and Foreign Confectionery Book*

1863   William Banting's *Letter on Corpulence Addressed to the Public*

       Arts Club founded

City of London acquires Spitalfields Market
1921 J. Lyons factory opened at Greenford
1923 Marcel Boulestin, *Simple French Cooking for English Homes*
1924 Empire Exhibition held at Wembley
Good Housekeeping Institute opened
1925 H J Heinz factory opened at Harlesden
Veeraswamy's restaurant opened
Marcel Boulestin opens Restaurant Français
V H Mottram, *Food and the Family*
1926 Patisserie Valerie opens
1929 Wheeler's restaurant opened in Old Compton Street
Quaglino's opened
1930 First Foyle's literary lunch
1931 First Tesco shop opened on Becontree estate
1933 André L. Simon founds the Wine and Food Society
1934 Prunier's opened
1936 John Boyd Orr, *Food Health and Income*
Food (Defence Plans) Department established
1937 Marcel Boulestin gives the first ever TV cookery demonstration
1939 J A Drummond and Anne Wilbraham, *The Englishman's Food*
1940 Rationing introduced
1941 Points rationing introduced
1942 National Loaf introduced
5 shilling maximum on restaurant meals
1946 British Housewives' League founded
1947 Le Caprice opened
1950 First edition of the *Good Food Guide*
Sainsbury's opens first self-service store
Elizabeth David, *A Book of Mediterranean Food*
Fanny Craddock, *The Ambitious Cook*
1951 London's first supermarket opened in Earl's Court
Good Food Guide published
1953 André Simon *Bibliotheca Gastronomica*
1954 Rationing ended
John Yudkin appointed to Britain's first chair of nutrition at Queen Elizabeth College, London
1955 Gaston Berlemont founds Soho Waiters' Race
Holborn Restaurant and Oddenino's closed
Spaghetti House chain launched
1956 L G Pathak begins selling samosas

1958 John Yudkin, *This Slimming Business*
1959 Mario and Franco open La Terrazza in Romilly Street
1960 Prue Leith starts her outside catering service
1961 Cranks vegetarian restaurant opened
1962 Katharine Whitehorn, *Kitchen in a Corner*
Len Deighton, *The Action Cookbook*
1965 Trocadero closed
Peter Boizot founds Pizza Express
James Goldsmith founds Cavenham Foods
1966 Demolition of Columbia Market completed
1967 Jane Grigson, *Charcuterie and French Pork Cookery*
Roux brothers open Le Gavroche
1968 Ministry of Health bans sale of fish and chips in newspaper
1969 Cadbury's merges with Schweppes
1972 First branch of McDonald's opened in Woolwich
Magnus Pyke *Technological Eating*
1973 Covent Garden market relocates to Nine Elms
First André Simon Book Awards
1975 Prue Leith cookery school opened
1977 Last Days of the Raj opened
1979 Michelin restaurant guide to London published in English
1980 Kenneth Lo opens Memories of China
1982 Bombay Brasserie opened
Billingsgate Market relocates to Docklands
1983 Lyons' Cadby Hall headquarters demolished
1984 Guild of Food Writers established
1985 Alastair Little opens his restaurant in Frith Street, Soho
John Yudkin *The Penguin Encyclopaedia of Nutrition*
1987 The River Café opens
1989 Retirement of Gaston Berlement as proprietor of The French House
1992 First Tesco Metro opened in Covent Garden
1994 Bloom's kosher restaurant at Aldgate closes
1996 *The Oldie* launches literary lunches series
2001 Tesco profits surpass £1 billion
2002 Jamie Oliver opens 15 in Old Street
Cadbury-Schweppes acquires Apollinaris
Nestlé sell off Crosse & Blackwell
Foyle's first literary lunch for children

Further Reading and Reference

Joan Alcock: *Food in Roman Britain* (Tempus 2001)

Maggie Black: *A Taste of History: 10,000 Years of Food in Britain*
(English Heritage : British Museum Press 1997)

Tom Bridge and Colin Cooper English: *Dr. William Kitchiner: Regency Eccentric*
(Southover Press 1992)

John Burnett: *Plenty and Want: a social history of food in England from 1815 to the present day*
(Penguin/ Routledge 1989)

Lisa Chaney: *Elizabeth David : A Biography* (Macmillan 1998)

Christopher Driver: *The British at Table 1940-1980* (Hogarth Press 1983)

Christopher Driver and Michelle Berriedale-Johnson: *Pepys at Table*
(University of California Press 1984)

Sir John Drummond and Anne Wilbraham: *The Englishman's Food*
(Jonathan Cape 1957)

Edwina Ehrman, Hazel Forsyth, Lucy Peltz and Cathy Ross: *London Eats Out: 500 years of capital dining* (Museum of London, Philip Wilson Publishers 1999)

Christina Hardyment: *Slice of Life: The British Way of Eating Since 1945*
(BBC Books 1995)

Annette Hope: *Londoners' Larder: English Cuisine From Chaucer to the Present*
(Mainstream Publishing 1990)

Jenny Linford: *Food Lovers' London* (2nd ed. Trafalgar Square 2000)

Alastair Little: *Soho Cooking* (Ebury Press 1999)

Stephen Mennell: *All Manners of Food: Eating and Taste in England and France from the Middle Age*s
(University of Illinois Press 1995)

Sara Paston-Williams: *The Art of Dining! A History of Cooking and Eating* (National Trust 1993)

André Simon: *In the Twilight* (Michael Joseph 1969)

Colin Spencer: *British Food: An Extraordinary Thousand Years of History* (Grub Street 2002)

Margaret Visser: *The Rituals of Dinner: The Origins, Evolution, Eccentricities and Meaning of Table Manners* (Viking 1992)

C. Anne Wilson: *Food and Drink in Britain* (Penguin 1973)

Index

Asterisks denote illustrations or captions.